PARADOXES OF THE POPULAR

NUSRAT SABINA CHOWDHURY

PARADOXES
OF THE POPULAR

Crowd Politics in Bangladesh

STANFORD UNIVERSITY PRESS

STANFORD, CALIFORNIA

Stanford University Press
Stanford, California

Printed in the United States of America on acid-free, archival-quality paper

Library of Congress Cataloging-in-Publication Data

Names: Chowdhury, Nusrat Sabina, author.
Title: Paradoxes of the popular : crowd politics in Bangladesh /
    Nusrat Sabina Chowdhury.
Description: Stanford, California : Stanford University Press, 2019. |
    Series: South Asia in motion | Includes bibliographical references and index.
Identifiers: LCCN 2018057612 (print) | LCCN 2018059912 (ebook) |
    ISBN 9781503608863 (cloth ; alk. paper) | ISBN 9781503609471 (pbk. ; alk.
    paper) | ISBN 9781503609488 (ebook)
Subjects: LCSH: Protest movements—Bangladesh. | Crowds—Political aspects—
    Bangladesh. | Political culture—Bangladesh. | Bangladesh—Politics and
    government.
Classification: LCC HN690.6.A8 (ebook) | LCC HN690.6.A8 C4685 2019 (print) |
    DDC 303.6095492—dc23
LC record available at https://lccn.loc.gov/2018057612

Cover design: Rob Ehle

Cover photo: Tongi Railway Station, Dhaka, Bangladesh. Md. Akhlas Uddin |
Getty Images.

Typeset by Westchester Publishing Services in 10.75/15 Adobe Caslon

For my crowd
in Dhaka, Phulbari, and Chicago

CONTENTS

NOTES ON TRANSLATION AND TRANSLITERATION

Throughout the book, I have followed the standard spelling for Bangla words as they are written in Bangladesh. I have avoided the International Phonetic Alphabet for the ease in reading for both Bengali and non-Bengali readers.

All translations from Bangla, unless otherwise noted, are mine.

ACKNOWLEDGMENTS

This book exists because some very kind people in Phulbari shared their homes and lives with me. When the finish line seemed distant, their stories, only some of which have made it here, helped me to stay the course. My teachers at the University of Chicago—particularly William Mazzarella, Dipesh Chakrabarty, and Joseph Masco—played key roles in the process. At our first meeting, William asked me who my interlocutors were. I got flustered. I didn't think my work—and by extension, I—was important enough to have interlocutors. Fifteen years later, I am happy to realize that William is now one of my most cherished interlocutors. In the way only he can, he keeps on pushing me to think and write, always leading by example. Dipeshda had been my reason to go to Chicago. He remains so as I take every opportunity to land in Hyde Park for some solid *adda*. Still, it was in the classroom that he was the most thought-provoking. I thank him for his wisdom and friendship. Joe Masco opened up new intellectual horizons and urged me to write. Anne Ch'ien made sure that I got in and out of Haskell Hall in one piece. *Paradoxes of the Popular* owes everything to them.

Phulbari has given me a book, but more important, a host of friends without whom my life in Dhaka is now inconceivable. Anu Muhammad took me along on my first trip to Phulbari and many more since. Hopefully, the book somewhat makes up for those bumpy rides on Hanif Enterprise. Zonayed Saki made my fieldwork his personal mission and made sure I got it done. I thank him for his friendship. Zaeed Aziz has always gone out of his way to help my research and writing. He also introduced me to Mahmud Hasan Babu, who welcomed me to his home (thank you, Chacha and Chachi!) and kept me constant company in Phulbari. I thank Babu for prodding me to meet more people and to ask more uncomfortable questions. I hope he will be amused to occasionally find himself in the following pages.

I finished the manuscript in Amherst, which was enabled by the support and good cheer of the Department of Anthropology and Sociology at Amherst College. Chris Dole, Deborah Gewertz, Vanessa Fong, Amy Cox Hall, Alan Babb, Jerry Himmelstein, Hannah Holleman, Ron Lembo, Leah Schmalzbauer, Eunmi Mun, and Karen Graves have been the most wonderful friends and coworkers. Chris was the only person to read the manuscript in its entirely and convinced me that it was a book. It must be kismet that Hannah and I started teaching together. Her love, friendship, and food have sustained me these past years. Pinky Hota's house is my refuge in the valley. I thank Pinky for her friendship and intellectual sustenance, and for bringing Akila into our lives.

As my neighbor Emily Dickinson would say, "My friends are my estate. Forgive me then the avarice to hoard them." I have had an opulent life in that regard. Mandira Bhaduri, David Bleeden, Steve Burnett, Mark Geraghty, Shefali Jha, Jesse Knutson, Fatema Tanzia Hossain, Mona Mehta, Nazmul Sultan, and Rihan Yeh have been parts of the journey that led to this book. I hope Rihan knows how much I have learned from her as a scholar and a human being. Thanks to Mandira, I have a much-needed home in Hyde Park. I am grateful to Shefali for the laughter and the songs. I thank David for his continued friendship, and his kindness toward the cats. Nazmul and I met after I had left graduate school, but it's only fitting that he's now a part of my Chicago clan. Nazmul's brilliance is matched only by his wisdom beyond years. I hope this book, a result of our ongoing conversations, makes him happy, though I know at times my thinking won't meet his exacting standards.

My conversations with Taslima Akhtar, Aminul Islam Bablu, Akku Chowdhury, Omar Faruque, Saiful Islam Jewel, Ahmed Kamal, Naeem Mohaiemen, Seuty Sabur, and Faruk Wasif at various stages of this project have made it richer. Khaled Sarkar in Dhaka and Saiful Islam in Phulbari have graciously given me permission to use their amazing photographic and artistic work without any recompense. My conversations with the following people—some spread over many years and some brief—have deepened my thinking about the book and much beyond. I am grateful to Kamran Asdar Ali, Amrita Basu, Joshua Barker, Jessica Cattelino, Frank Cody, Lotte Hoek, Matthew Hull, Ritu Khanduri, Alejandra Leal,

Rosalind Morris, Thomas Newbold, Moishe Postone, Danilyn Rutherford, Austin Sarat, James Siegel, Pauline Strong, and Colleen Woods. I also thank Thomas Blom Hansen, Marcela Cristina Maxfield, Sunna Juhn, and two anonymous reviewers at Stanford University Press for their editorial guidance. An Overseas Research Travel Grant from the Division of the Social Sciences at the University of Chicago, a Charlotte W. Newcombe Doctoral Dissertation Fellowship from the Woodrow Wilson National Fellowship Foundation, and faculty travel funds from Amherst College provided indispensable material support for research and writing. It is because of the generosity of the Dean of the Faculty's office at Amherst College, frequently mediated by Austin Sarat, that this book looks and reads the way it does. So, thank you!

My parents, despite their uncharacteristically busy lives, have successfully instilled the love of reading in their daughters. I see this book as a little thank-you note to them for opening up the wondrous world of words. Whatever work I have managed to do is directly correlated with what my sisters have done to keep our family happy and sane. Both have made sure that Shantinagar remains my permanent address. As I put finishing touches to the manuscript, between the two of them they are taking care of two elderly parents, three kids, a hospital, two households, and about a dozen pets. I simply don't have the words to say what this has meant for my survival—both professionally and personally. In the past decade, Totinee, Zafir, and Zubin have been my reasons to hop on the plane to Dhaka as often as I could. Shantinagar is home also through the labor and love of many other people, especially Saleha Bua, Kaderer Ma Bua, Rina, Belal, and Aziz Bhai. Ayaji would have been all too happy to hold this book even if she couldn't read it. She taught me how family had not much to do with blood. For this, and so much more, I am infinitely in debt.

Just as I was getting done with the book, Yogi waltzed back into our lives after two years. I hope that her prodigal return promises more magic. Sufi hung around and made sure that I would finish the PhD, get a job, write a book, and set aside time to play, preferably with him. All this he did without knowing, thereby giving me a true gift. I have promised him these last lines in a failed attempt at reciprocity.

PARADOXES OF THE POPULAR

IN AUGUST 2006, a small township in northwestern Bangladesh became an unlikely focus of national attention. Tens of thousands of residents of nearby villages gathered at the center of Phulbari, about 180 miles from Dhaka, to protest possible open-pit coal mining. Most of them were there to expel a multinational energy company, then called Asia Energy Corporation, that was planning the country's largest development project. Three men were shot to death on August 26 in the confrontations between the paramilitary guards and the angry protesters.

"We are not discussing politics; we are discussing energy. One burns and the other creates," a local organizer joked loudly—deliberately, it seemed, in order to be overheard. We were walking out of an activist meeting in Phulbari a few months after the agitations against potential mining became violent. The activist's comment, at first, sounded like a neat allegory of the heightened crises around energy and democracy marking Bangladesh's entry into the twenty-first century. The young man's words, however, were more than a clever summary of the urgencies on the ground. They revealed a curious and counterintuitive valuation of energy (*jwalani*) and politics (*rajneeti*). Said with more than a touch of irony and loud enough for others to hear, the activist's words were especially telling within the stifling political climate of a nationwide emergency that was declared in early 2007. Protests in Phulbari that were interfering with a glib rhetoric of foreign direct investment and development were under strict state surveillance. "Spies," or low-ranking agents of the state security apparatus, followed around a renowned public intellectual with whom I had tagged along on my first trip. As we were paying visits to the families of those who were wounded or killed in the 2006 shootings, the organizers' mobile phones kept ringing. I counted at least ten phone calls asking for my name and other coordinates of identification. A meeting at the local press club was abruptly adjourned because of a warning issued by a security agent who was hovering at the doorway to see us out. The freshly minted Emergency Power Ordinance and Emergency Power Rules banned any activity deemed political and allowed for arrests without warrants.

The same day I had started on my second daylong bus ride to Phulbari, the leader of the opposition in the parliament and the president of the Awami League, Sheikh Hasina, was arrested. The caretaker government imprisoned first Hasina and then, within three months, her political nemesis, Khaleda Zia, the most recently incumbent prime minister and the head of the Bangladesh Nationalist Party. The two leaders, who have alternatively represented a two-party, clannish political culture since the fall of military dictatorship in 1990, had never before been sent to prison.[1] It was no surprise that for the activists and regular folks in Phulbari, a lot was at stake in this collective performance of nonpolitics.

Energy fit into a patently toothless rhetoric of sustainable development, but politics became suspect. Its seeming abjection had invited the military-backed, technocratic government. By late 2006, more than sixty political party workers were killed in street fights that started with a disagreement on the terms of national elections. The impasse between the two main parties eventually led to the army takeover. *One burns and the other creates.* In everyday use, however, energy is what is supposed to burn, producing power as a valuable by-product. The etymological intimacy between the Bangla words for "energy" (*jwalani*) and "to burn" (*jwala*) highlights the paradox at the heart of the comment, namely, politics taking on the role of energy. The former's once-creative potential was now relegated to a natural resource like coal that was widely believed to forestall an energy catastrophe. Politics burned, though producing nothing but ruin. Talking about energy in the bazaars and tea stalls was acceptable, but political organizing around it was subject to state scrutiny and at times tough intervention.

Despite the celebration of nonpolitics during this two-year period that brought into sharp relief the cultural logics of everyday democracy, it is rather the inexhaustible energy of politics that has marked the decade since. Within a few months of the emergency, a confrontation between the students and army *jawans* (soldiers) at the University of Dhaka campus led to one of the most powerful oppositions to the caretaker government. Thousands of students and a number of their professors at public universities were jailed for instigating what appeared to be contagious violence. Despite the ruthless treatment by the state, the student protests revealed the first cracks in the façade of the military government supposedly without political ambition, and therefore, without corruption.

In 2013, a much larger crowd gathered at the heart of the capital city hardly a mile from the University of Dhaka campus. With an elected government firmly ensconced and another national election on the horizon, the country was in the throes of an urban and admittedly middle-class uprising in Dhaka. At Shahbag, a busy crossroads near the national public library, the national museum, and two renowned hospitals, a group of young activists—some with party affiliations and many without—came together to challenge an early verdict of the International Crimes Tribunal (ICT). The Awami League government that had assumed power in the wake of the emergency set up the ICT. As part of its campaign promises, it had vowed to try the alleged collaborators of the 1971 war of independence. A long time in the making, the legal body had been at the receiving end of both warm praise and trenchant criticism. Many rights advocates and family members of the victims of war crimes had been demanding fair trials for the individuals responsible for siding with the Pakistani state and committing or abetting in war crimes. They saw in the founding of the ICT justice long delayed. The actual workings of the tribunal, with its various procedural loopholes and allegations of political appointments, made it one of the most controversial governmental steps in recent memory (Bergman 2016; D'Costa 2015; Sadique 2015).

The sudden outburst at Shahbag surprised political commentators, party bigwigs, and the general public. It questioned the seeming laxity in the ICT's judgment of war criminals, which to many reeked of strategic negotiations between the government and Jamaat-e-Islami, the largest religion-based political party. It stood to lose the most from being sympathetic to the idea of an undivided Muslim Pakistan at the time of the war. Some of its senior members were accused of collaborative activities. Protesters took to the streets demanding capital punishment. What was once a fight for justice within weeks came to be seen as a struggle between secularists and Islamists vying to be the voice of the nation. A powerful backlash against Shahbag and its blatant secularism came from an ad hoc religious right that read into the message of Shahbag a threat to religious identity. As in Phulbari and during the army rule that followed, the crowds in Shahbag initially challenged the legitimacy of the trial and by extension the state, and while doing so, also gradually began to stretch the boundaries of the political cause for which they had originally come together.

These uprisings mostly took shape outside of party political structures. This is unusual for Bangladesh, known for the centrality of party politics, which, though not divided along caste or ethnic lines as in India, is deeply polarizing (Suykens 2017). The scope of the protests was not delimited by organizations or institutions. Nor did they primarily use infrastructure—as both object and medium—to lay claims on the state, as seen elsewhere in the global south where technopolitics is often the language of the poor (Larkin 2013; Schnitzler 2016). The protests have been public in the sense that they took over public spaces for their articulation. In this they have been formally akin to some of the spontaneous assemblies that dotted different parts of the world this past decade (Hamdy 2012; Mittermaier 2015; Navaro-Yashin 2013). The protests in Bangladesh—whether against corporate capital, land grabs, military rule, or war crimes trials—defied easy labeling, their form and content veering between progressive, secular, patriotic, religious, reformist, violent, radical, and reactionary. As bookends to the Phulbari movement, the student dissent during the emergency and the protests that came years later in Shahbag highlight the scope, and the constitutive paradoxes, of popular sovereignty in Bangladesh.

The following ethnography attends to the minutiae of these protests by locating in the crowd the energy, agency, and indeterminacy of mass politics. It tacks between multiple sites of public political gatherings and pays attention to the ephemeral and at times accidental configurations of the crowd. It starts with a movement against open-pit coal mining and ends with the agitations against a war crimes tribunal. The events span both rural and urban Bangladesh, specifically between the years 2007, when the state of emergency was declared, and 2013, when the self-consciously secular demands of justice for war crimes and the backlash against them reached their peaks.

THE BANGLADESH PARADOX

Few places are as politically precarious as Bangladesh, even fewer as crowded. Its 57,000 or so square miles are some of the world's most densely inhabited. Here, population is a hoary governmental problem, but unruly urban traffic has become the most obstinate affliction. Native speakers use the term *bhir* along with and as often as the English "jam." The first refers to crowds of people; the second, an immobility caused by too many vehicles and too few roads. A growing number of Bangladeshis waste personal time and exhaust public resources being stuck in traffic in an ever-more atomized capital city (Hobbes 2014; Rosen 2016). They "fall into" or "get trapped" in a jam, as the Bangla expression *jam e pora* makes clear. "Jammed-up roads are the indelible image of Dhaka's agony. They may also be its single greatest cause," Jody Rosen (2016) wrote in the *New York Times* about a city that would be ranked "the world's second least livable" two years later (Chaity 2018). But a *jam* is also the effect and the condition of possibility of needs and desires that coalesce and turn the streets into sites of work, politics, fun, and survival. Rosen describes the chaos as pervasive and permanent: "Bangladesh is the 12th most densely settled nation on earth, but with an estimated 160 million citizens it is by far the most populous, and the poorest, of the countries at the top of the list. To put the matter in different terms: The landmass of Bangladesh is one-118th the size of Russia, but its population exceeds Russia's by more than 25 million" (Rosen 2016).

Comparisons of scale are strategies to put an out-of-the-way place on a familiar map. They make the global south legible to the Euro-American reader. They also point out how comparisons can be hopelessly misleading.

Rosen finds herself in Dhaka on a day of *hartal*, a tried-and-true model of public protest (Suykens and Islam 2013). As a political tool, it aims to halt the regular movement of people and things. Depending on who is calling the strike, the traffic during *hartal* can be relatively thin. But surely "relatively thin" is relative, Rosen discovers quickly, as she ranks Dhaka crowds above those of Mumbai and Cairo. This density is exaggerated when the cities and townships accommodate a different kind of traffic: the flow of a *michhil*, a procession powered by the movement of people, or *janata*, the other Bangla equivalent of the crowd but with a difference.

Many South Asian languages share some variance of *janata* (*janta* in Hindi, for example). In Bangla, *janata* is different in its political potentiality from the cognate term, *janogon* or "the people." The former is a close approximation of the crowd, the multitude, or the masses of social and political theory. The latter is more normative and is mostly at the service of official language, as in "We, the people," which begins the constitution of the People's Republic of Bangladesh.[2] To speak of *janata* is to note the historical and regional specificities of mass politics. More than a mere vernacular iteration of the crowd, it is a repository of the nuances of postcolonial sovereignty, where the popular and the uncivil come together (for more on civility and popular politics, see Mitchell 2018).[3] The crowd as *janata* is the ethnographic and analytical focus of my book.

Bangladesh, one often hears, has been a definitive case of the bankruptcy of postcolonial governance. Its fate seems to be lodged within a global despair around the collapse of the social and political hopes that had forged anticolonial imaginations and national sovereignties (Scott 2004). The resultant anxiety of exhaustion, as David Scott (2004) describes it, is manifest in the paralysis of will and vacancy of imagination, corruption, authoritarianism, showy self-congratulation, and instrumental self-interest. In spite of the rampant feelings of despair familiar to those who think and write about Bangladesh and many more who live here, the narrative of crisis comes with a few significant caveats. This may be why paradox often recurs as a motif when discussing Bangladeshi politics, economy, and history.

There are at least a couple of ways in which the Bangladesh paradox has become a way of thinking about the nation's becoming as well as its feats and failures in the first five decades. The first relates to progress in the economic sector simultaneous with the political instability, environmental disasters, and poverty. At least since 1991, the year that marked the end of roughly fifteen years of authoritarian rule of different stripes, the advances in social and human development indicators in Bangladesh have surpassed those of the neighboring countries. Regime changes, even when relatively frequent, have had little effect on the microeconomic policies and political commitments to social development (Mahmud 2017; Riaz 2016; Sen 2013). Per a September 2017 report in the *Economist*, Bangladesh edged past Pakistan with a slightly higher gross domestic product (GDP). The irony of the erstwhile eastern wing taking over the richer, western part from which it had broken away decades ago was not lost on the writer of the *Economist* article: "A country that once lacked cloth for shrouds now exports more ready-made garments than India and Pakistan combined." Bangladesh has transformed itself from being a dawdler to a leader in many indices—from gender to GDP—making some experts wonder at the so-called Bangladesh surprise (Mahmud 2017). Once the proverbial basket case, Amartya Sen writes, the country has surprised the naysayers by jumping out of the basket and starting to sprint ahead (Sen 2013).

Bangladeshi nationalism itself has been known to host a series of contradictions (Samaddar 2002). While history (beginning exclusively in or around 1971) remains a fecund site of scholarly and cultural production, it is profoundly out of step with postcolonial miseries. Some of the crucial silences in recounting the rise of nationalism—the repression and criminalization of progressive radicalism within the struggle for freedom, for instance—have yet to be redressed (Umar 2004). The weary tensions between ethnic, religious, and national identities—*Bangali* or Bangladeshi—inform rhetoric and policies, though mostly opportunistically by political leaders or a politically ambitious intelligentsia. The eclipse of the left within the first few years of independence has been partly ascribed to a regime of power set up with the help of bureaucrats, the coteries within the established political party, the politics of international aid, and the armed forces. The problems with the nationalist idea that Ranabir Samaddar identifies include, among others, an autonomy movement that overnight catapulted into a freedom movement, the ongoing suffering of ordinary citizens, and the leading role of a party that was at best a movement, more often a crowd, but never a party capable of waging a war of liberation with a social agenda of its own (Samaddar 2002; see also Lewis 2011; Umar 2004). Even *Bangali Musalmaner mon*—the Bengali Muslim mind—has presented itself as somewhat of a paradox (Sofa 2006). At the start of the new millennium, much of this had prompted at least one eminent literary figure to ask, *"Amra ki ei Bangladesh cheyechhilam?"* ("Is this the Bangladesh we had wanted?") The rhetorical question—and surely the pathos in it—has found many iterations in local commentaries since the book of the same title was first published (Azad 2003).

In this book, I foreground "paradox," at one level, to account for these historical and sociological contingencies that have generated a curious mix of optimism and despair, a distinctively postcolonial combination where the early zeal of anticolonial nationalism has been routinely banished to the "waiting room of history" (Chakrabarty 2000; Scott 2004). At another level, I do so in order to attend to the foundational contradictions within popular sovereignty, of which the crowd is an exemplar. The paradox of peoplehood begins with the very act of representing "the people," which has always been a fiction. Its very existence requires a suspension of disbelief, as Edmund Morgan has shown in the seminal *Inventing the People*: "Before we ascribe sovereignty to the people, we have to imagine that there is such a thing, something we personify as though it were a single body, . . . a collective entity more powerful and less fallible than a king or than any individual within it or than any group of individuals it singles out to govern it" (Morgan 1989: 153). The shift in cosmologies that made possible a transfer of power from the king's two bodies to the people's two bodies sustains a number of contradictions, such as the fact that the people are actual subjects as well as fictional sovereigns, and that not just anybody—or "mere" people, as Morgan would say—can constitute "the people" (Frank 2015; Kantorowicz 2016; Santner 2011; Wolin 1981). Its sovereignty must not be confused with the unauthorized actions of individuals or of crowds.

Still, protesting crowds have been the media of meaningful change in the democratic culture of Bangladesh as in many other places. The effects of these political collectivities spill over the boundaries of well-defined political projects. Established power and its opponents harness crowd potential even as it frequently betrays both. As an agent of politics, the crowd has been the much-touted nemesis of the people and the public in scholarly treatises on democracy and public life. Theories of popular sovereignty in the Marxist or liberal-normative tradition, as well as their critiques, are dotted with a figure whose energy surpasses the demands of democratic politics (Canetti 1984 [1962]; Dean 2016; Freud 1975 [1921]; Hardt and Negri 2005; Jonsson 2013; Laclau 2007; Le Bon 2002 [1896]; Tarde 2014 [1903]). It is at once a force to exploit, an entity to denigrate, and more often than not a symptom of shifting social and political conditions. Jodi Dean voices a familiar leftist lament when she says that by reducing autonomy to individual decision, we destroyed the freedom of action we had as a crowd (Dean 2016). And yet, Dean admits to the crowd's constitutive volatility and its limited freedom in becoming a possible unit of politics. Even when the "crowd's breach of the predictable and given creates the possibility that a political subject *might* appear," the crowd, instead of having politics, can only be an opportunity *for* politics (Dean 2016). In the *longue durée* of writings on the political, the crowd is a permanent fixture against which the acts and utterances of the people are defined.

In urban South Asia, giant political crowds and pedestrian rallies are the most spectacular political statements. In Dhaka, political groups aim to take over historically meaningful spaces of public gathering, like the Paltan Maidan, Bangabandhu Avenue, the roundabout called Shapla Chattar, the footpath in front of the National Museum in Shahbag, or that narrow stretch of concrete—a sidewalk more or less—named Muktangon. The word means "free space," and despite its gradual downsizing, it is still dedicated to offering a safe place for venting political and social grievances. But even these dense hubs of urbanity serving as spaces of dissent are now under threat as traffic becomes more unruly and space more rigorously managed (*Dhaka Tribune* 2013). Whichever political side one is on, the goal is to take over the street—not the agora or the arena, but "the asphalt in-between" (Morris 2013). This is why urban roads are blockaded and the highways that connect the cities to each other are obstructed as a first step toward making an effective political statement. These are not spontaneous crowds of angry citizens, though those too happen with relative frequency, as I show in the book, but are more or less rehearsed spectacles of presence. They are a visible gauge of popularity for a cause, an institution, or a leader. The political ritual of blocking streets has deep roots in mass democratic consciousness in Bengal (Chakrabarty 2011). Despite its longer lineage, the political uses of the street—what Dipesh Chakrabarty in a Bangla essay calls *"rajneetir rasta,"* or the streets of politics—became more frequent in the twentieth-century nationalist and communist movements in West Bengal. More recently, everyday demands as disparate as road safety, medical malpractice, or irregular supply of water or electricity bring people to the streets—similar acts that in the vernacular political languages of South Asia are known as *path aborodh, gherao, bandh/banda, hartal,* or *chakka-jam* (Lakier 2007).

The street is a public thing as are parks, prisons, schools, transportation systems, pipelines, libraries, airport security, and public phones (Honig 2017); they are aspects of modern life that are hidden in plain sight. Public things, according to Bonnie Honig, "provide a basis around which to organize, contest, mobilize, defend, or reimagine various modes of collective being together in democracy" (Honig 2017). The street is a public thing in that it gathers people together materially and symbolically, even when they are divisive. Genevieve Lakier, however, has shown in her ethnography of urban Nepal that the South Asian versions of "politics of the street" impede the individual autonomy of other citizens and transform the neutral space of the public into a politicized domain (Lakier 2007). Although it is imperative that we question the so-called neutrality of the idea of the public (or for that matter, the "private") (Kaviraj 1997), or the normative underpinnings of citizenship (Cody 2009), what is obvious is that the cooptation of the development infrastructure is at the center of everyday and spectacular performances of protest (Lakier 2007). In this, the relationship between public things and democracy is different from "democracy's infrastructure," where pipes, meters, and grids are becoming central to the strategies that members of political societies use in order to negotiate with the state (Chatterjee 2006; Schnitzler 2016). Although this book is about the subjects and not the objects of democracy, so to speak, it bears repeating that the latter are the condition of democratic sovereignty. To write about public things, then, is not simply to write about infrastructure but to make a case for embracing publicness in democratic life, for the sake of democratic life.

THE ORIGINARY CROWD

Popular politics in South Asia—be it revolutionary or nationalist—has long relied on the power of the crowd as have counterrevolutionary forces from the colonial to the contemporary (Amin 1995; Chakrabarty 2007; Guha 1983). From vibrant rallies that rouse mass affect (Chakrabarty 2011) to oppositional tactics of hurling homemade bombs to kill as many ordinary commuters as possible (Sultan 2015), the crowd is both a solution and a scapegoat, and in that sense, a true political *pharmakon*.

Indeed, in Bangladesh, *michhil* and meetings have played formative roles in the origin story of the nation. The crowd at Sheikh Mujibur Rahman's speech at the Ramna Race Course (now Suhrawardy Udyan) in 1971 is a significant part of national folklore.[4] Nearly a million people had assembled on the afternoon of March 7 to hear the leader. They chanted *"Joy Bangla"* (Victory to Bengal) and waived lathis to signal their readiness to fight (Ludden 2011). The event that was led by the future first president of Bangladesh was a grand moment of declaration where the boundaries between popular demands for independence and constitutionalism were blurred to produce one of the most iconic moments—and sound bites— of East Pakistan's struggle for nationhood:

> He directed people to make every home a fortress and to fight with whatever they had ready in hand. He ended his speech by declaring: "This struggle is for emancipation! This struggle is for independence!" His rousing speech had a double meaning. It evoked two meanings of independence [*mukti* and *swadhinata*, respectively] by promoting constitutionalism and a freedom struggle. Despite its ambiguity, however, this landmark speech inspired a popular revolution, whose force and organisation came from outside the halls of constitutional politics and quickly commandeered East Pakistani state institutions. (Ludden 2011)

Mahmudul Huq's 1976 novel *Jiban Amar Bon* (Life is my sister) starts a few days before Mujib's landmark speech.[5] The war begins and ends within the Bangla novel, which is narrated in the third person. *Jiban Amar Bon* is largely about its central character Khoka's struggle to make sense of the events that are sweeping away the region and with it a whole generation. It is a tale of the main character coming face to face with what he likens to a force of nature. Khoka calls this unreflexive, uncouth, and hysterical entity by the name *janata*. "To Khoka what was until then a skinny word wrapped in the wispy feathers of three letters, like *dayita* (beloved), *jamini* (night) or *madira* (wine), is suddenly spreading across the city in thunderous explosions—*janata!*" (Huq 1976: 44).

At the outset, *Jiban Amar Bon* is a story of a twenty-two-year-old college graduate casually ignoring the political urgency of his time. His family's bougainvillea-covered house in the East Pakistan capital and collection of books bespeak (upper) middle-class comfort. His friends are young men with whom he studies, smokes and drinks, and argues passionately. There are also a few women, specifically a married lover but others too whose advances he lusts after and loathes. Khoka tries his best to keep them away from his younger sister, Ronju, the space of innocence in his life.

Khoka does not recognize the power of history amidst which he finds himself. His deep disgust for any sign of its strength makes Huq's novel an unusual document of Bangladesh's birth. It is, however, an ode to *janata* as a political actor in the event of national independence (Sultan 2016). *Janata*, not Khoka, is the motor of history. When Khoka ignores the rumors of a military attack on civilians, or when he mocks the spark of nationalism in his friends, he denies the *janata* sovereignty. He fails to see reason in those who are occupying the streets, demanding political rights, or fleeing the city en masse. Khoka himself is fleeing the *janata* throughout the novel. Its dialectical movement forward ends in tragic synthesis. The crowd stampedes an ailing Ronju, Khoka's only surviving kin, whose adolescent innocence kept him sheltered from the riffraff of the outside world. The charging crowd was the same *janata* whose power Khoka had denied all along. At the end, it also sweeps him away—literally—when running from an advancing army.

We see glimpses of the paradoxical nature of popular sovereignty in the long internal soliloquies of Huq's protagonist. It is not easy for Khoka to go with the flow like the others. The whole business of politics (*rajneeti*) to him is "utterly, gorgeously slutty" (Huq 1976: 14). With equal (chauvinistic) disdain Khoka notices naïve schoolboys who still wipe their noses on the backs of their hands while taking political lessons at street corners. He calls the on-strike tannery workers guinea pigs and questions their newfound political consciousness. And yet, a deafening noise interrupts his thinking:

> A roar—yes, a roar—is getting louder and louder, crashing in the air. Khoka places his ear against it. The noise is fast becoming a grumble. Like an angry python a procession gets onto the main road from *Rayer Bajar* and moves towards the EPR [East Pakistan Rifles] barracks. How quickly Dhaka is changing; how fast the people are changing. Some with sticks, some iron rods, others with black flags, arrows, swords, oars, shovels, axes, and whatever else they could find on their shoulders. How swiftly the faces are changing. Shifting also are the shapes of those faces. Fast, fast, fast. It is approaching like a glacier; a glacier that is the onslaught of an impending death. People! People! People and people! [*manush*] . . . What Noah's flood is this? Khoka stumbles a little inside. His head starts to throb. (Huq 1976: 16)

Janata is an active, affective and political configuration of *manush*, which is the word Khoka uses for "the people." The Sanskrit-derived gloss for the human can be either singular or plural. *Manush howa* is the process of growing up; it is a progression toward becoming a fully functioning, humane adult. It is at once developmental and social as in the expression *manush kora*—to bring up a child. But the word does not pack a political punch in the same way *janata* or *janogon* does. *Manush* speaks to an innate humanity that need not include political maturation or participation. *Janata* is a higher level of collectivity than the more passive *manush* or the mundane *bhir* (literally, crowdedness).

Khoka highlights this disjuncture by comparing people to its abject other, animal (*janowar*). "We, half-animals, are only ever eager to become full animals. . . . At every opportunity we want to avow that animality with a roar," he says to his politically inclined friend (Huq 1976: 97). The becoming political of the people is also their becoming fully bestial. The beast as *janata* perplexes Khoka. His disgust is palpable as is his denial of its power to come together and multiply. His hatred for either *rajneeti* or *janata* is not familiar middle-class apathy toward mass politics. No doubt, South and Southeast Asian political cultures mirror the hierarchies of a deep-rooted class society. When Sudipta Kaviraj coins the hybrid term *pablik* to denote the creative uses of public space in Calcutta (Kaviraj 1997), or Vicente Rafael observes the cell-phone-toting prodemocracy crowds in Manila (Rafael 2003), or Lotte Hoek notes the coming together of the *mufassal* (peripheral towns) and the metropolis in Dhaka (Hoek 2012), they show in vivid detail how public life is riven by socioeconomic distinctions. If anything, Khoka's discomfort echoes the recurring ambivalences around the crowd in scholarly work. Those who have written on and during political upheavals in the West in the last couple of centuries, especially in interwar Europe, have taken a keen interest in the category. The crowd and the *janata*, as tokens of mass political entities, overlap and diverge in revealing ways.

At the center of Khoka's universe is Ronju, his younger sibling. At its edges are other characters, like Khoka's lover, who is the wife of an older friend; a cousin who tries and fails to romance him; and an independent professional woman whose character, or lack thereof, is the talk of the town. Khoka verbally abuses the women as well as the crowds and considers them mad. Ronju, the asexual, infantile girl-child, is the exception. "Between Ronju and the world, Khoka wants to stand guard," Nazmul Sultan writes in an engaging commentary on the novel (Sultan 2016). In Khoka's imagination, the boundaries of women, licentious men, and a boisterous *janata* start to blur. By the end of March 1971, Dhaka goes under the control of the army. Khoka gives in. He leaves the city with Ronju, but only to sacrifice her to an onslaught of people. As Ronju dies under the feet of the *janata*, Khoka is forced to become a part of it. "All he wanted was for Ronju to live. But [Khoka] doesn't know that that's where he is wrong. This desolate country would never give Ronju the sole right to live, he soon learns" (Huq 1976: 158).

The *michhil* has a catalytic role in another piece of fiction from the mid-1970s. Ahmed Sofa's well-known 1975 novella *Omkar* (The Om) reaches its climax in 1969 and, like *Jiban Amar Bon*, unsettles a rehearsed story of Bangladeshi nationalism (Sofa 2007). Here too the march of an insurrectionary crowd coincides with death. The relationship between the two is less direct though equally poignant as in Huq's novel. *Omkar* begins a couple of decades earlier with the reminiscences of its unnamed narrator. Unlike Khoka, this young man is of modest means. He owes his livelihood to a rich and hawkish father-in-law who is as good at defrauding others as in being all too familiar with the military regime. It is his mute daughter whom the main character marries in exchange for a job and a comfortable life in the capital.

In 1969, the protests against the military dictator, Ayub Khan, had spread across East Pakistan, leading to deadly violence. In the political trajectory of Bangladesh, 1969 reflected the most congealed form of contentious politics. For the first time, Bengali nationalism became a primary motif in the mass agitations that were gaining steam in East Pakistan and successfully joined forces with insurrectionary left politics that led to the toppling of Ayub Khan. The People's Uprising (*Gono Obbhutthan*) became a precursor to the war that broke out two years later. Asad, a student leader who was killed at a rally in 1969, is now considered one of the first martyrs of independent Bangladesh.

These were restless times. Mujib was in jail. Processions were everywhere. The protagonist/narrator of *Omkar* embodies this restlessness as he shifts his gaze away from the political posters on the walls and toward the sky. He keeps to himself, though unlike Khoka, more in fear than disgust. Every little thing makes him nervous, yet he knows he has been deluded; someone as inconsequential as he could never be the target of the hatred and anger of the thousands.

> I cannot stand processions [michhil]. I lose my hearing as soon as I catch the noise of slogans. I lose all perception. It feels as if the procession-goers are hitting me with a thousand sharp arrows. As soon as there was an incoming michhil, I would shut the doors and windows by habit. I acted as though they were not in front of me but very far. Even when the sounds came through, I would put my hands over my ears. This was my way of keeping the storm of time at bay. Later I heard that this was something I had in common with the late Ayub Khan himself. (Sofa 2007: 32)

While he covered his ears, it was his wife who opened the doors and windows at the first hint of a marching crowd. She struggled to understand what was being said. The sound of a *michhil* was a magnet to her inner being. Noises burst out of her without provocation while an uncanny presence took over her body. One day when a *michhil* was approaching their house, her happiness was palpable. She moved to its beat as if possessed by a *jinn*. The pieces of words that she struggled to form, which used to come out as little cobblestones, now rang different. A realization hit him. She too was trying to utter "Bangladesh" that wafted in from the *michhil*. With a sudden jolt, his mute wife leapt up. No sooner had the first intelligible word—*Bangla*—come out, she started bleeding in the mouth and fell unconscious on the floor as if something inside her tore into pieces. "I stare at the stains of fresh blood on the floor and at my unconscious wife and only one question comes to my mind: Whose blood is redder? Is it Asad's or my mute wife's?"—Sofa writes in the last line of the novella (Sofa 2007: 36).

Huq's and Sofa's stories end in cathartic sacrifice. The sacrifice, albeit accidental, is of the self for the sake of the collectivity. The two female characters are tragic victims to what Sofa calls the "storm of time" (*kaler jhor*). While Khoka's sister is killed by the crowd, the mute wife manages to echo the crowd by uttering her first meaningful word, which is the proper name of a yet-to-be-born nation. The two male protagonists, their self-appointed guardians, realized the urgency of history too late and lost what to them was the most treasured. Their inability to see the power of the crowd cost them dearly.

The role of the feminine in the narrative resolution of the stories demands a closer look. An obvious place to start are the concerns over female hysteria and the beastly behavior of the crowd that hover over notable nineteenth- and twentieth-century writings on the masses. Sigmund Freud and Gustave Le Bon have famously taken a psychosocial approach to understanding the popular. In *Group Psychology and the Analysis of the Ego* (Freud 1975 [1921]), Freud engages with Le Bon's influential late nineteenth-century text that elaborates on the hysterics of the crowd (Le Bon 2002 [1896]). The crowd is compared to the so-called primitive, the infant, the barbarian, and the feminine; in other words, the quintessential markers of the Other of Western rationality. The masses, it would seem, have always been the eclipse of reason and enemy of a well-ordered polis (Jonsson 2013: 23).

There are still important differences between the two famous decoders of crowd psychology. The category in Le Bon and Freud's studies does not necessarily denote the same thing (Dean 2016; Jonsson 2013). Freud's crowd, compared to Le Bon's urban working classes, is a far more encompassing epithet. The opposition posited between the crowd and the individual—the former being the bearer primarily of passion and the latter of reason—is more complicated in *Group Psychology* than what first meets the eye. The crowd here is not the antithesis of individual rationality. Rather, individuality is an effect of repression, sublimation, and inhibition of psychic drives. As Jacqueline Rose would later say of Freud's work, "We are peopled by others" (Rose 2004: 143). The crowd and the individual, therefore, are one and the same; the former is a window onto a society not yet encumbered by power, where institutions or authorities have not stabilized human passion (Rose 2004).

On the feminine, Le Bon and Freud's voices are more in concert. Passions supposedly drive women. Passions are also the constitutive elements of crowd action. In losing oneself in the crowd, one indulges in feminine behavior that is out of control. Individuality is a masculine phenomenon and the masses a feminine one, Jonsson adds when commenting on what he calls the stock item of mass psychology and its fascination with the crowd. The question of gender and crowds offers an added challenge when posed from the vantage point of South Asian public political life. Within the sizeable expanse of South Asian studies, one finds a quintessentially masculine, if not male-dominated, crowd. Sociologically speaking, the South Asian crowd and its imagination do not easily line up with the gendered thinking that has informed classical European literature on the masses. Among the ethnic rioters across South Asia's cities (Tambiah 1997), the unruly peasants in colonial Uttar Pradesh (Amin 1988), or the mourning fans at the funeral of their favorite film star in Dhaka (Hoek 2012), we see crowds as men. They participate in protests or celebrations the styles of which are culturally tied to young men. Fun or *jouissance* marks the urban masses ever-present in rallies, communal showdowns, cinema halls, and religious functions (Hansen 2001; Hoek 2012; Prasad 2009; Verkaaik 2004). They enjoy certain comfort in and control over public space that is not available to many women. While this may seem applicable to Western crowds as well, I would argue that the South Asian crowd tends to be at once empirically male and, in an ideological sense, masculine-gendered. This in no way belies the reality that millions of women across the subcontinent routinely find themselves in and as urban crowds. This is as true of Mumbai, the South Asian city best known for having a veritable presence of women in public (Phadke and Ranade 2011), as it is for Dhaka, infamous for routine unequal treatment of and violence against women in the streets and in public transport (Uz Zaman 2018). The fact that women's marches or gatherings to "take back the night" still need to be qualified as such shows how everyday access to space is hardly democratic and, in its "unmarkedness," decidedly masculine.

The cinematic gaze is often thought to be a male one. The passionate masses of cinemagoers, whose immaturity has been a source of consternation for the colonial and the developmental state, are primarily imagined as men, though in their *jouissance* still passively permeable. The subaltern spectator is routinely described as illiterate, uneducated, rural, ignorant, uninformed, working-class, adolescent, youth, and so forth (Prasad 2009: 70). Postindependent conservative cultural policy continues to treat the masses as a kind of "cultural reserve" in need of protection from the alienating effects of modern popular culture (Prasad 2009: 74). "Male viewers are inherently public and, *qua* pissing men, crowd-edly so," writes William Mazzarella (2013a).[6] As "pissing men" who need to be told where to relieve themselves because of their inability to read public signs, as rowdy cinemagoers who stomp their feet, whistle, and make catcalls at the movies, or as protectors of the women in the family, shielding them from the sensuous provocations of the cinematic image, men as crowds have provoked state measures of regulation and ideological dreams of development (Hoek 2013; Mazzarella 2013a).

Khoka's escape is more than an avoidance of patriotic responsibilities. His disgust for collective sovereignty and the ultimate loss in its hands are results of his strenuous disavowal to recognize crowd potential. His suspicion is challenged in the most traumatic way. "This desolate country would never give Ronju the sole right to live," Khoka realizes in the final lines of the novel (Huq 1976: 158). The crowd here is both a promise and a cause for panic; it is also a message and a medium that gathers and transforms elements, objects, people, and things (Rafael 2003). In the crowd of the nationalist literature, the auratic and the aural also seem to be closely linked. In *Omkar*, in which the mute woman speaks up with the crowd—an act that coincides with her death—brings sound squarely at the center of the narrative. She finds clarity with the utterance of her first intelligible word, *Bangla*. "Omkar" (from Sanskrit, *Omkara*) is the sound of the sacred syllable, Om, which is a fecund icon within Hinduism. Along with its profound polysemy, which includes the soul, the truth, and the supreme spirit, the sound itself is auspicious and a tool for meditation. The last noise that Sofa's otherwise silent protagonist manages to blurt out takes on the sanctity of the divine syllable. It is she who opened the windows to let in the din of an approaching crowd. Her husband could not tolerate the noise. But it was also more than mere noise. The crowds were chanting the name of the unborn nation. In *Jiban Amar Bon*, too, Khoka *hears* the *janata* before he sees it. As the noise gets closer, it reminds him of an angry python that makes its serpentine journey around Dhaka, a city on the brink of a war in the early 1970s.

Does participatory democracy have a sound, then? Writing on the sonic motif of contemporary politics, Laura Kunreuther asks the same following her research in Nepal, where she has identified *awaj* ("voice" in Nepali, Bangla, and a few other North Indian languages) as a metaphor for political participation (Kunreuther 2018). From the pelting of stones at businesses that have not shut down on a quiet day of a *banda* to the stunning absence of traffic noise, what becomes powerful in and as protest is noise itself. Still, noise is often thought of as prepolitical and nonreflexive, an unintentional effect of urban life rather than a calculated disruption (Kunreuther 2018). One could say the same for crowds. Kunreuther makes a similar observation when she writes, "But noise is also associated with the intentional unruliness of a crowd that threatens to spin out of control, to go against law and order, and to challenge some of the foundations of liberal democracy" (Kunreuther 2018). At the same time, mass mediation makes visibility compete with audibility and legibility, Rosalind Morris notes of contemporary populisms, in which being seen to speak often appears to be more significant than what is being said (Morris 2013).

Consider this story that I had heard even before setting foot in the mining area. It concerned the physical assault of a young man who had traveled to Phulbari from Dhaka with a documentary film crew. He was the younger brother of a well-known filmmaker who had sent his team to gather footage of the protests that flared up in 2006. While shooting the film, he was unsuspectingly sporting a T-shirt with the logo of a film festival with the word "Asia" in it. "Asia," by then a name familiar due to the presence of Asia Energy, was enough to anger the crowds. They attacked the man on suspicions of working for the company. Influential activist leaders had to intervene to save him from public wrath. Later when I spoke to a woman who was a part of the crowd, she remembered vividly: "We would've killed him. The situation was such that we would've killed him. If each one of us had hit him, he would've been dead." I asked her if she had seen the *genji* [T-shirt], to which she replied with equal excitement: "Yes! They, like, they looked like they had no life left in them. . . . They just came with cameras. . . . They knew someone. . . . [Two other leaders] had to verify if he was someone from [Asia] *energy* or if he was only wearing the *genji*." The same sign that was found on an outsider's clothing was also familiar as the corporation's logo. The crowd that vandalized the company's office and attacked its employees had located on the body of an urban youth a dangerous icon, which was not read the same way by all, if "read" is at all the right verb in this context. The woman confirmed seeing the T-shirt but most likely did not know the meaning of either *Asia* or *energy*; she used "energy"—in English—as shorthand for the company's proper name.

To understand democracy in the age of deep mediation, then, we need to view crowds as political actors who are self-consciously shaped through mass publicity (Cody 2015; Gürsel 2017) while also recognizing that it is in the tangle of representations and practices that one must always come to the political (Rosanvallon 2006). In my description of crowd politics in the following pages, the reader will routinely find words, actions, and characters that were not often the most striking or even, at least seemingly, the most significant. Despite the spectacular nature of these political assemblies, the figures that appear in and out of view were frequently lost in crowds, stood at the sidelines, or came together by accident. Hearsay more often than direct communication formed the basis of their reminiscences. Together, their words and actions cohere as what I describe as *imperceptible politics*. This is the politics that arises from the emergence of the miscounted, "those who have no place within the normalising organisation of the social realm" (Papadopoulos, Stephenson, and Tsianos 2008). Attempts to harness and work with these imperceptible potentials are generally misrecognized and translated into the given terms of representation. In *Escape Routes*, Papadopoulos and his colleagues give a history of such escapes, those of vagabonds, wandering poor, uprising peasants, and mobs who have for centuries made up the rebellious forces. National and local authorities have sought to prevent these free movements whether as measures to rein in poverty or to direct labor to manufacturing. The concept also has significance, I believe, for understanding political crowds. It is no mere coincidence that "mobility" refers to movement but at the same time to the common people, the working classes, and the mob (Papadopoulos, Stephenson, and Tsianos 2008). The escape of which the authors write is surely about dissent and construction, but it is not, or not always, resistance. It comprises everyday, singular, unpretentious acts of subverting subjectification and betraying representation, a strategy that cannot be reduced to one successful and necessary form of politics. These everyday cultural and practical exercises of escape are what I document in the following pages as the politics of the crowd.

This conceptual and ethnographic background raises a few related questions: What relationship between politics and energy was articulated in the pointed remark of the cynical activist, or the angry woman who had found in the English equivalent of *energy* that which needed to be violently excised from the social? What ideas of the political informed the crowds that attacked the suspicious film crew, and under what circumstances were they a part of the same protesting collectivity, if at all? More broadly, how and to what effect did the state of emergency's facile equation of noncorruption with nonpolitics—a familiar technocratic fantasy—intersect with the issue-specific organizing in Phulbari and Shahbag? In the aftermath of Shahbag, in what ways were the self-consciously secular and religious crowds co-constituted? How did an emergent tech-nomediatic environment simultaneously challenge and aid official ef-forts at surveillance and disaggregation of crowd politics? Extrapolat-ing from these ethnographic particulars, this book explores the contours of Bangladeshi democracy in order to offer useful analytical pointers in understanding mass politics globally. By focusing on the mediations of popular protests and the competing visions of the political that fuel and sustain them, the book ultimately asks: What does an anthropological account of the crowd teach us about the simultaneously enduring and tenuous object of mass democracy—the people?

LANDSCAPES OF PROTEST

Paradoxes of the Popular weaves together my experiences and observations of living in the mining area and my interactions with protesters and political personalities in Dhaka. It makes use of a rich textual culture coproduced by print and digital media, political activists, and ordinary people. My notes from the processions, meetings, and informal conver-sations help sketch Bangladeshi public life in one of its most vibrant and violent phases. Phulbari is the book's main physical location, while the protests that challenged the technocratic governmental façade of the mil-itary regime and the crowds that gathered later in Shahbag and else-where act as necessary backdrop and explanatory context. Together they underline the intertextuality of the events in Bangladeshi public life where a much-talked-about energy deficit came face to face with the excess en-ergy of crowd politics.

A few months before emergency was declared, in August 2006, large numbers of anti-mining protesters participated in a sit-in at the office of Asia Energy in Phulbari. The demonstrators set out to resist the forced displacement, the method of extraction, and the alliance between the gov-ernment and Asia Energy Corporation (Bedi 2015; Faruque 2017; Luthfa 2011; Muhammad 2007). By that time, homegrown anti-mining sentiments were increasingly boasting extralocal and international support. The event in August was one in a series of awareness-raising programs organized by the National Committee to Protect Oil-Gas-Mineral Resources,

Power and Ports.[7] A nongovernmental group, the National Committee, was founded in 1998 to address and resist national resource extraction by multinational capital. In Phulbari in 2006, it was set to make a statement by hosting speeches by local and central leaders, cultural programs by performers from Phulbari, Dhaka, and elsewhere, and *michhil*s around the township. The event was planned as a *gherao* of the office of Asia Energy. Literally "a siege," a *gherao* is a symbolic act of cordoning off a site of power to address political grievances. Many people who had traveled from afar to join the procession that day were nevertheless ready to expel Asia Energy right then and there, they told me later. *Gherao* took on different meanings as the message *Asia Energy desh chharo* ("leave our land, Asia Energy") spread to remote villages.

People started coming in the early morning, and the approximate number, 40,000 to 50,000 in total (some would say many more; see Luthfa 2011) exceeded the expectations of those in charge. The atmosphere was both festive and anxious; some members of the local indigenous communities joined with bows and arrows, cultural groups sang protest songs, and troops of police and paramilitary guards took position around the township's main thoroughfare and the building rented by Asia Energy. At around 4:00 P.M., a substantial crowd gathered at the highway near the center of town, close to a bridge a mile or so from the company's office on the other side of the river. The leaders were wrapping up their speeches, delivered from the top of a truck with loudspeakers in hand. Paramilitary guards and the police had already barricaded the bridge to stop people from crossing the river to get to the company's office. In response to the speeches and the repeated slogans demanding the company to leave Bangladesh, a local magistrate made a public promise on behalf of the district commissioner to expel Asia Energy from Phulbari by September 13, 2006 (Bablu 2006).

Right when the leaders were moving away from the barricade, the police began shooting rubber bullets and tear gas shells at the crowd, heightening the tension on the street. People retaliated by hurling stones while scurrying away from the lathi-charging and gun-toting troops. In the ensuing chaos, when some people were already halfway across the bridge and others were crossing the river by wading through the water, the Bangladesh Rifles (BDR) started shooting, at first at the sky and then at the scattered crowd. Three men were instantly killed and many more were hurt by the bullets and the beatings by the BDR and the police, respectively. This went on until the late evening.[8]

The next few days were a mix of tense silence and collective effervescence. On August 27, when the border guards entered the neighborhoods still randomly harassing people, rural and working-class women came out of their homes to protest. Phulbari, in the meantime, was separated from the rest of the country. Activists felled trees on the highway to interrupt communication, buses, trucks, and rickshaws stopped running, businesses closed, the houses and property of the so-called collaborators and sympathizers of Asia Energy were attacked and looted, and the model homes built by the company were destroyed. On August 30, a six-point Memorandum of Understanding was signed between the mayor of Rajshahi City Corporation[9] and the member-secretary of the National Committee on behalf of the people of Phulbari. The movement continues to make three major demands on the government: to declare moratoriums on the involvement of foreign companies, the method of opencast mining, and the export of coal: *bideshi na, unmukto na, raptani na* (literally, no foreign, no open pit, no export). With the tensions mounting, Asia Energy Corporation abandoned its Phulbari office and temporarily shelved the project.

Despite its remoteness from the heart of political activities in the capital, Phulbari managed to tie together widely circulating concerns about energy crisis with uncertainties about the volatility of national politics. Things got particularly messy when a lack of consensus between the Awami League and the Bangladesh Nationalist Party in late 2006 led to fatalities in the streets of Dhaka. On October 23, 2006, low-scale tensions erupted into full-blown street battles between government forces, their supporters, and the opposition. General strikes, transport blockades, destruction of public property, and the death of political activists due to clashes with law enforcement officers brought regular life to a halt (Riaz 2016: 83). In an email sent to a closed group of activists and academics, a public intellectual and senior activist summed up the close ties between the unfolding political and energy crises:

For Asia Energy the embedded journalists who were taken to Germany have been continuing their services to the company. Recently added some legal consultants activities. Lawyers from the firm that has been working as legal adviser of Asia energy are now holding key posts in Law ministry and Attorney General's office. Their efforts became apparent when law ministry issued a sermon against Phulbari agreement between government and the people. At this point British high commission seems to be very active in this matter. We keep our voices heard till now. In Bangladesh emergency rule is being tightened. All Public Universities are declared closed *sine die*. Student halls are made vacant. Some teachers are also arrested. In this context international campaign should gain momentum. (Email sent to phulbari _action@googlegroups.com, September 3, 2007)

The mining project of Asia Energy, then, brought together contesting hopes, fears, desires, and despair that traveled along its global circuits clustered around people and events, policies, and institutions that remained hidden from most people in Phulbari. The promissory notes of a well-lit national future and popular struggle and sacrifice were often at odds with each other. What became prominent in the slippages between these claims were the repeated attempts at unmasking connections that hovered just beyond the ethnographic imagination. The efforts in part of the crowds at unveiling power did not always fit neatly into the official narrative about Phulbari's wealth or the formalized political discourse that opposed it, and in the process, highlighted the power and perils of crowd politics.

THE BOOK

In Bangladesh, neither the inequitable distribution of resources nor a biased and compromised judiciary is big news. They appear as instances of long-standing political malaise. Student riots that had sown the seeds of defiance against the military-backed regime also have precedence in Bangladesh's political history, most recently in 1989–90 but earlier too: in the 1950s and again in the late 1960s during the East Pakistan era. Together, these uprisings have summoned the crowd, or mobilized a certain image of it that has succeeded in affronting the sovereign power of the state. The specter of the crowd during the emergency, for example, haunted the regime, which later became the mouthpiece of the demands of democratically elected officials who were either imprisoned or were being forced to go into exile. Months later, the same political elite, now with the force of electoral power behind it, criminalized the *janata* in whose name they had voiced their grievances.

Shahbag had self-consciously invoked and in many cases reinstated the slogans and imagery of anti-British and nationalist struggles, both of which rode on the extraconstitutional power of the *janata*. Shahbag, as the ethnographic moments in the book show, threatened state power while also making itself available for selective cooptation, giving rise to anxiety, despair, and crisis for counterrevolutionary and progressive political projects. It is in the crowds that one locates a similar kind of energy and excess that is the necessary precondition of imperceptible politics. That is why crowds remain subversive figures of political agency whose actions are never fully recoverable but still only available through political representation.

Chapter 1 engages directly with the question of crowd politics by analyzing a set of disparate texts in circulation during the emergency—letters published in newspapers, a national identification card, and a censored photograph. A month after the emergency was declared, Muhammad Yunus of Grameen Bank fame and winner of the 2006 Nobel Peace Prize, wrote a letter which appeared on the front pages of major Bangla and English dailies. Within a short span of time, he wrote two more in which he expressed his enthusiasm for—and subsequently, his disenchantment with—the idea of running for office. These letters are symptomatic of a crucial political conjuncture in Bangladeshi national life, where technocratic governance—and its promise of transparency, immediacy, and honesty—seemed to have left behind a plebian political culture riven by corruption and violence.

This chapter looks closely into the public culture of the state of emergency with two ends. First, it expands on the familiar impasse that South Asian democracies often experience when confronting the relationship of sovereignty and citizenship. In this logic, a repressive, corrupt, and undemocratic governmental apparatus is blamed for the underdeveloped political rationality of its citizens. For the very same reason, sovereignty as domination is justified as a way to protect the masses from their own unruly nature—say, from acting as crowds rather than exercising their rights as citizens. Second, the chapter expounds more on the presumed distinctions between a reading public versus unruly crowds. Yunus's letters remind us how the distinction between the stranger/citizen and an embodied (albeit fictional) crowd was mobilized with an aim to usher in a novel era in politics.

A democratic future where corruption would be a thing of the past—promised, ironically, by a military-backed regime—looked different from the vantage point of Phulbari where I was doing fieldwork. Against the backdrop of the transparency-fetish of the emergency, the protest culture in Phulbari presents an alternative politics of seeing, or what I call "seeing like a crowd." Chapter 2 expands on this idea by identifying the significance of money in aesthetic productions and political acts that was different from the nationwide drive against corruption. In the first half of the chapter, I focus on a painting by an artist in Phulbari. Its message, I argue, contrasts with the viciously apolitical and individualized desire for efficiency and good governance in a globally recognized language of neoliberal transparency. Similarly, in the second half of this chapter, I present the recollections of Majeda, a socially marginalized woman who had become the face of the grassroots nature of the mobilizations. I situate the looting and burning of money by the crowds, of which Majeda was a part, within the larger context of the crisis in national politics that also gathered steam around money. While still privileging visuality, these popular strategies were a form of a transparency-making enterprise, with different and potentially profound political effect than the anticorruption agenda of the state.

Chapter 3 is an ethnographic account of the accidental, the contingent, and the imperceptible nature of crowd politics. To understand the political possibilities of accidents and to assess their ethnographic significance, here I approach accidents both literally and conceptually. Can accidents be political? What kinds of politics take shape in the wake of an accident? And what are the ethico-political possibilities that are made available, or are foreclosed, within various discourses of the accidental?

Anthropological perspectives on accidents, I argue in this chapter, rescue the concept from its usual modernist and technicist moorings while opening up spaces of radical contingencies that are enframed in local logics of culture and politics.

Widely discussed and debated, collaboration—in the sense of working for the enemy and benefiting from it—has given rise to a particular kind of crowd politics, as I illustrate in chapter 4. From the vantage point of most protesters, a collaborator (*dalal*) was a figure that straddled the boundaries of the community and whatever stood beyond or against it. A *dalal* was by definition a local, though his (and at times, her) ties to the foreign were exposed within the community through suspicion, gossip, jokes, and assaults. Crowds were at arms against the collaborator, and the latter, for all intents and purposes, was a part of the crowd. Chapter 4 looks into this violent culture of accusation of collaboration in order to shed light on the entangled effects of aggressive resource extraction, collective sovereignty, and popular and state-initiated attempts at settling score with the nation's past. In Bangladesh, the individuals indicted for crimes against humanity and collaboration in 1971 are also called *dalal*, among other things.

Still, the phenomenon of collaboration in Phulbari exceeded the considerations of the state or the international economy. Following, respectively, Walter Benjamin's writing on the "intriguer" and scholarly interest in the category of the "neighbor" (Benjamin 2009; Thiranagama and Kelly 2010; Zizek, Santner, and Reinhard 2005), I submit that the *dalal* is a *third type* that disturbs the duality of friend and enemy. This ambivalence produces a culture of doubt and suspicion that demands certainty, which became a matter of particular urgency in Phulbari and was made abundantly clear in the national spectacle that has been the International Crimes Tribunal, the central focus of chapter 5.

This final chapter is located in post-emergency Bangladesh. Its primary sites are the physical and virtual spaces of politics and activism that are at once emergent and historically poignant. At one level, it explores a particular fascination with the body—of the collaborator, the blogger, and the militant—and its relationship to crowd politics under democratic rule. At another level, it comments on the proliferation of digital technologies that has deeply impacted social and political communication.

A rise in surveillance technologies in public spaces in Bangladesh also points to more rigorous efforts to control spaces and bodies as is illustrated by the two events I analyze in the second half of the chapter—a journalistic exposé of public harassment of women and a viral video of a public lynching. Both these examples from urban Bangladesh show, on the one hand, that the secular and religious crowds, in their desires to be seen and heard, often end up mirroring each other. On the other hand, individual online users of social media often act collectively, coming together and performing the excess and volatility associated with crowds. The call for adequate punishment demands a crowd for its execution. It also takes a crowd to protest the cruelty of collective violence against the disenfranchised or to make those in power accountable. The state, in turn, has made its allegiances known in an opportunistic fashion, either by indulging or repressing certain crowds over others.

And yet, the story of the crowd, its remediation through so-called new technologies, and its vexed relationship to institutions of power are not explained away as the vagaries of the state. What happens, then, when we start with the crowd—and the possibilities of politics that it opens up or forecloses—as constitutive of not only South Asian political modernity but understandings of publicness everywhere? What happens when we start rethinking the public sphere, as Francis Cody has urged us to do, from an illiberal perspective, which would entail taking the libidinal, corporeal, and poetic ties of kin and community, and not the empty stranger/citizen, as a starting point (Cody 2015; see also Yeh 2017)?

Doing so is not the same as rehashing some "hoary revolutionary myth" about the crowd (Frank 2015). This is not an attempt at finding in the crowd the direct expression of a unified and sacred popular voice but instead approaching it as a living image and a potent political representation. It is to ask when and how a numerical minority of individuals physically gathered in a public space can be understood to speak and act on behalf of a superior but forever disembodied entity called "the people" (Frank 2015: 2). It is also, ultimately, to interrogate what animates the popular that evokes hope and despair about the fate of democracy itself, particularly the postcolonial versions of it? Thinking beyond South Asia, how does the ephemeral ordinariness of the crowd contrast with the "populist resentment" that has become a prominent motif in understanding democratic politics globally? These are a few questions I take up again in the conclusion as I end the book with a political showdown around a Supreme Court verdict in Bangladesh that aimed, but spectacularly failed, to resurrect "the people" as a fundament of mass democracy.

CHAPTER 1

PICTURE-THINKING

A NOBEL LAUREATE'S LETTERS AND "NEW POLITICS FOR A NEW BANGLADESH"

In December 2008, the Awami League regained power in nationwide elections and effectively ended the two-year rule of the caretaker government. Sheikh Hasina became the prime minister with an overwhelming majority in Parliament. To coincide with this political transition, a parody of a mainstream film poster ridiculed Bangladesh's continued dynastic heritage in national politics (cf. Ruud and Islam 2016). The poster was from a fictional film, *Babar Kasam* (In the name of the father), a pointed reference to Hasina's father, Sheikh Mujibur Rahman, who is the indisputable *jatir pita*, or founding father of the nation. Hasina is Rahman's eldest daughter and had headed the ruling party for three terms since 1996.[1] In the poster, Hasina is in the guise of the protagonist, who is carrying a sack stuffed with familiar electoral promises, from lowering the prices of necessities and curbing violence and terrorism to increasing foreign investment, meeting energy demands, and reducing poverty (see figure 1). This filmic portrayal was partly a veiled reference to the high inflation rate that characterized both the emergency period and the Bangladesh Nationalist Party (BNP) era (2001–6) before it. A smiling Khaleda Zia, Hasina's real-life political nemesis and leader of the BNP, looms large in the background of the poster. In addition, *The Promise* is "presented" by Gopalganj Digital Films.

FIGURE 1 A film poster parody of Bangladeshi politics. *Source: Tushar's Weblog*,
https://tusharsblog.wordpress.com/bd-funny-image-alltimebd-com-jpg-18-2/.

Gopalganj is Sheikh Mujib's ancestral home in southwest Bangladesh, as
well as the Awami League's electoral stronghold. The filmic depiction of
the political saga, while comical, was also accurate, as it sought to portray
the state of national politics as a technicolor, mass-mediated family feud,
not unlike the run-of-the-mill blockbusters consumed by the crowds.

The captions that came with the image included cynical asides such
as the following:

Special Attraction: This film *highlights* [in English], the quarrel of
the co-wives, a heritage of traditional Bengal.

Starring: Sheikh Hasina and her innumerable followers.

Production: Indian *Dada Bhai* ["older brother"; a sarcastic comment on the AL's long-standing warm relations with India]

Special Acknowledgment: Bangladesh Army

While representing "the way things really are," the film poster cashes in on the truth-value of its subject, thereby turning the joke into a form of empiricism. After all, the promises carried on Hasina's back, literally burdening her, are the same that had made up her electoral mandate, and her archrival *was* the actual leader of the opposition in Parliament.

The animosity between Sheikh Hasina and Khaleda Zia, the two most powerful politicians in Bangladeshi history, is the stuff of legends. They had once shared a political agenda to end the authoritarian rule of H. M. Ershad in the late 1980s, but since then have never been seen in dialogue. In fact, they are almost never to be seen in the same room, not even in Parliament, a curious circumstance that has been the case for many years. A few days after the arrest of Khaleda Zia on September 3, 2007, the *Economist* pointed out the rare physical proximity that both leaders would come to share in prison: "Mrs. Zia . . . will be the next-door prisoner in Dhaka's idle parliament building to her nemesis, Sheikh Hasina Wajed, . . . This will be uncomfortable for both women, who loathe each other" (*Economist* 2007). The humor of the poster, then, lies not just in its creative take on the ironies of power among the Bangladeshi political elite but also in the fact that when matters are this close to truth, the unfolding saga of two leaders is capable of matching, if not surpassing, any "filmy" narrative with its conventional twists and turns.

A momentous exception to the melodrama that was national politics during this period was the persona of Muhammad Yunus, the Nobel Prize–winning "guru of micro credit." His failed attempt at joining national politics soon after winning the prestigious award made international news. Yunus's vision for politics and the manner with which he shared the desire with a national public are, however, revealing of a broader crisis of sovereignty and politics of citizenship that continues to shape democracy in Bangladesh. A month after emergency was declared, Yunus wrote a letter for a national audience, which appeared on the front pages of major Bangla and English dailies. In the letter, which was addressed to an individual yet generalized citizen (*prio nagorik*—dear citizen), Yunus expressed his desire to join politics. He requested his readers to send him their thoughts on his political aspirations via letters or text messages (as cited in bdnews24.com 2007). Within a short period of time, however, Yunus wrote two more letters in which he expressed his enthusiasm and subsequently his disenchantment with the idea of running for office. Yunus's correspondence with the nation was taking place at a time when the familiar modes of political communication, such as meetings, *michhil* (processions), and congregations were illegal as per the emergency provisions.

These letters, I argue, are symptomatic of a crucial political conjuncture in Bangladeshi national life, where technocratic governance—and its promise of transparency, immediacy, and honesty—seemed to have finally left behind a much-maligned plebian political culture of corruption and violence. They remind us how the distinction between the stranger/citizen and an embodied, albeit fictional crowd was mobilized with an aim to usher in a novel era in politics. In what follows, I aim, at one level, to expand on the familiar impasse that South Asian democracies often experience when confronting the dualities of sovereignty and citizenship. By "impasse" I mean the ideological loop that paternalistic authority, both in the colonial and nationalistic contexts, has historically resorted to in the name of governance. Be it in the case of Nehruvian developmental politics in India or in the withholding of democratic rights *for the sake of democracy* as in Bangladesh's emergency rule, or the censorship debates in colonial and postcolonial South Asia, governance has often taken on a familiar circular logic (Alamgir 2009; Chakrabarty 2007; Mazzarella 2013a). In this logic, a repressive, corrupt, and undemocratic governmental apparatus is blamed for the underdeveloped political rationality of its citizens (Chatterjee 1993; Cohn 1996). For the very same reason, sovereignty as domination is justified as a way to protect the masses from their own unruly nature—say, from acting as crowds rather than exercising their rights as citizens. Guarding the ideological borders between the citizen and the crowd became particularly untenable and therefore, all the more necessary for the purposes of governance.

At another level, I expound more on the presumed distinctions that lie between a reading public versus unruly crowds—a distinction that has had enduring implications for theories of popular sovereignty. In canonical scholarship, as discussed in the introduction, crowds are associated with face-to-face gatherings and embodied affect; publics, on the contrary, are forms of address or scenes of deliberate exchange (Gürsel 2017; Warner 2002; Yeh 2017). A reading public, more narrowly, is a relationship among strangers "that forges its own legitimacy through the medium of common discourse, without having to refer to a transcendent form of sovereignty from without" (Cody 2015: 52). This focus on "strangerhood" in modern political agency is what Francis Cody questions when he urges us to rethink the distinctions between publics and crowds, the latter supposedly more prone to passion and violence than reason (Cody 2015; see also Warner 2002). The element of agency that makes the concept of public so attractive to democratic politics also constantly comes up against its own limits in existing scenarios, such as postcolonial South Asia, where, in many ways, the public is often viewed as a potential crowd. However, the newspaper-reading public in whom Yunus had put so much faith, as we shall see, did not translate into the crowds that would help win elections.

A decade after the letters came out and more than a few years since an elected government has resumed business, it is tempting to summarily dismiss Muhammad Yunus's brief but torrid romance with politics. A few scholarly articles that offer detailed accounts of the legal and political ramifications of the emergency period either mention this topic in passing or overlook it altogether. In fact, how Yunus burst into the political scene and stoked unbridled hopes for some communities of interest, even if briefly, seems to have lost its appeal in academic retrospections. His distance from most matters political, and silence on many events of national significance since, has made his presence in public political life nearly nonexistent.[2] Exceptions are noted as he occasionally captures prestigious international awards, including the Medal of Freedom that he accepted from Barack Obama in 2009 on behalf of the U.S. government. A new dimension, however, was added to the Yunus phenomenon in 2011 when multiple events led to his (forced) resignation as the head of

Grameen Bank for fiscal irregularities. The acts and utterances of political vendetta that this fall from grace generated are symptoms of a wider culture of popular politics that go beyond Yunus, a point to which I return in the conclusion.

Much ink has been spilled on both sides of the Bangladesh-India border after Muhammad Yunus, the founder of Grameen Bank, won the prize for his role in poverty alleviation through microfinance. Yunus was effectively joining the illustrious ranks of Bengalis of Nobel fame, such as Rabindranath Tagore and Amartya Sen. He was readily assuming the role of a national guardian, while adding to his long-standing status as the poster child for NGO efficiency. As felicitations poured in from all quarters, including from influential friends abroad, such as the Clintons, a need to exploit the charged atmosphere of post-Nobel days was widely felt in Bangladesh.[3] Ironically, the news of the prize reached home at a time when the main political parties were taking their enmity to the streets. The violence was caught live on camera as shots were being fired in public by party members who tackled each other's occupation of public space and featured the public beating and eventual death of one political activist on the streets of Dhaka. Though random political violence was hardly news, this video image rapidly circulated, thanks to the ever-proliferating privately owned satellite TV channels. The gruesome turn of events shocked a national audience and stoked local anxieties over foreign censure. The Nobel Prize provided a welcome distraction and along with it an opportunity to up the national prestige quotient.

Amid the political upheaval, Yunus stood out as a figure of clean politics without the familiar burden of familial history. In the meantime, the technocratic façade of the military regime offered some semblance of stability from the dogfights on the streets. Interviewed a few weeks before his letters were featured in major dailies, Yunus was forthright on what he thought about national politics: "Bangladeshi politicians are all for money. It's about power, power to make money. There is no ideological thing, simply who gets the bigger booty" (Hashmi 2007). His comments evoked the wrath of veteran politicians and loud cheers from the members of civil society. A well-known emissary of the latter and an economist of national fame chimed in, "Can our politicians deny that most of them are not only inefficient, dishonest, timid and tame like the most obedient slave and thoroughly corrupt at the same time?" To this, he added: "If not they should shut their not-so-clean mouth for ever" (Hashmi 2007). This sentiment found official footing in the speeches of the army chief throughout the two years of the interim government. At an Independence Day event in March 2007, Moeen U. Ahmed more or less echoed the same when he pointed out that in the thirty-six years since independence, politicians have not given us anything good (Alamgir 2008: 145). In an essay titled "Context 1/11" (*Prekkhapot* 1/11), Ahmed further explained the army's rationale to take over on January 11, 2007: "1/11 was the commanding voice of the helpless people [*janagan*] for the sake of the existence of their country and nation" (M. Ahmed 2009: 319).

What interests me about Yunus of 2007 is not his Nobel Prize. I do not plan to unravel the politics behind the global recognition, a topic passionately debated in social and intellectual circles immediately following its declaration. Rather, my focus is on the letters, which are important documents for what they index in terms of the state of democracy in Bangladesh, the echoes of which carried far beyond the state of emergency. At one level, they were symptomatic of the reformist voice that tried to part ways with the old guards of national politics, thereby ingratiating itself with the military regime. This group was quickly punished or sidelined for their betrayal by both the major parties soon after the emergency rule was suspended and the elections were held. At another level, the language of the letters shows a desire for a reading (or, texting, as the case may be) public that would rise from the crowds and make the reasonable choice of finding their voice in Yunus. While the contents of the letters are predictably rife with tropes of change, their style and form revealed far more about the author's view of and vision for popular sovereignty. It is the individual citizen rather than a national collectivity that becomes Yunus's fellow witness to a political culture riven by destructive animosity. The communication that Yunus initiates in the public space of a newspaper betrays a sense of intimacy found only in private exchanges meant for specific people or closed groups. "Dear Citizen" (*Priyo Nagorik*), he starts his first letter: "I, like you, witnessed where our political culture has brought the country and how it attempted to destroy the country's future possibilities . . . It is now clear to all that it is not possible to reach the goal of maintaining the existing political culture; it is only possible by bringing a comprehensive change to the culture."

The *I* and *you*—Yunus and his addressee—aspire to constitute a national public. Both have observed with understandable horror the havoc wreaked by corrupt and inefficient political leadership. The *all* includes the individual citizen to whom he addresses the letter as well as to himself. Yunus and the citizen together have watched where the existing political culture had brought the country. Yet, the *all* is hardly everybody in the polity. The pronouns *I* and *You* exclude these others who were presumably responsible for the current situation but remain unnamed. Change is possible, he assures his ideal interlocutor, but as total transformation that could only be brought about by a new political force personified in Yunus. He explains that the politics of his party, *Nagorik Shakti* (Citizen's Power), would be to "move forward" toward a future by bringing his co-citizens under a unified goal.

Yunus was not the only one to volunteer plans for new democratic futures. "Advancing forward," "cleaning up," and "comprehensive change," made up the sound bites of the emergency at the time Yunus made his grand entry into politics.[4] Similar metaphors abounded in the obsessive preoccupation with democracy in the wider public sphere. Labeling Bangladesh as a "derailed train," the army chief, Moeen U. Ahmed, asserted that "the nation needed an efficient administrator to bring it to the right track for ensuring progress and prosperity" (Alamgir 2008: 146). The U.K. secretary of state for Commonwealth and Foreign Affairs, David Miliband, expressed similar sentiments. Miliband's checklist for Bangladesh echoed that of Yunus's and other voices of foreign concern: full, free, and fair elections; buttressing institutions to create a strong civil society; an independent judiciary that treats all cases on merit without fear or favor; a strong media that asks tough questions; and lastly, strong systems of education, health, and local government that support the formal institutions of democracy. Bangladeshi anthropologist Rahnuma Ahmed, in her analysis of Miliband's interview, writes: "As a recipient of this sudden surge of Western interest in Bangladesh, a poor, hapless nation, led often enough by wretched, self-serving leaders, as a recipient of endless lectures on democracy, often embellished by locomotive metaphors ('democracy derailed;' 'getting democracy back on track'), I have been at a total loss" (Ahmed 2008a). This particular interview parsed by Ahmed was hardly representative of the tough media Miliband was presumably encouraging. Self-evident questions were repeatedly asked to elicit self-evident answers, which were taken at face value. As is often the case with such prestigious encounters with foreign dignitaries, Ahmed comments, knowing English was a more important criterion than being an established journalist, which the interviewer was clearly not. A political scientist reaffirms some of Ahmed's observations: "The democratic West failed to come to the support of democratic institutions in Bangladesh. In fact, it had subscribed to the exact same storyline: all politicians in Bangladesh were corrupt and messy to deal with. They did not speak good English; their interests were complicated; they were not as presentable as polished military officers" (Alamgir 2008: 162).

The concerns voiced by foreign diplomats and powerful army personnel inside the country resonated with Yunus, both in his tenor and style. His strategy, however, was a little different, and curiously *not* premised on a national *we*, a familiar pronoun in assertions of nationalism. The first step that Yunus took toward articulating and confronting the concerns expressed by Miliband was to write a personal letter to seek the opinion of a citizen: "I want to know your opinion and seek your advice," he explains at the outset. *"Apnar uddeshye amar byaktigoto chithi"*—"My personal letter to you"—is the title of this letter, which starts with "I write this letter to you in the hope of receiving a personal letter in response" (*Apnar kachhe ami ei chithiti likhchhi er jababe apnar kachh theke byaktigotobhabe ekti chithi paowar ashay*). The addressee, or *apni*, is the singular citizen from whom he hopes to receive a "personal" reply. The letter is drafted as a private letter and is formally distinct from petitions and letters to the editor that are more familiar genres of written public communication. It is generically closer to the less common "open letters" (*khola chithi*) that appear in newspapers and are generally addressed to the head of the state and represent collective signatories. Yunus, however, expresses himself as a private citizen, thereby changing the conventional form of a *khola chithi* that is either addressed to or signed by an unspecified public.

The individualized *you* of his letter is palpably different from "the people," most commonly referenced as *janagan* or *janata*, which is ubiquitous in political speeches and nationalist texts. Finally, Yunus signs off with only his name and date. His contact information at the end includes a complete home address and two electronic mail addresses.

The preference for the singular over the plural, the second person over the first, and the "citizen" over the "people," marks a distinct shift in envisioning politics, and signals a radical break with the past. Although "people" as a term does surface a few times in the letter, (as in "I feel it with my heart that I should, showing due respect to the people's expectations of me, participate in the mission"), the responsibility of accepting Yunus, and thus welcoming the kind of politics he professes rests on the individual citizen, that is, a member of the public. He continues in the same letter: "If I get to learn about these things [the citizen's opinion and how s/he would like to help] from you in the form of a letter, my effort to realize your and my effort to have new politics in order to build a new Bangladesh will gain added strength." Note here the desire for a response in the form of a letter that would aid in realizing his dream. It is a common dream but not one that is shared by all: "*apnar amar prayas*" means "your effort and mine," an endeavor, in other words, that is not collectively *ours*. Acknowledging the dangers of "doing" politics in Bangladesh (as when he admits, "I know that joining politics is to become controversial"), Yunus seeks out the help of a citizen rather than calling on the masses to usher in a new political climate.

While the relative absence of either the first-person plural or the third person in Yunus's letters is striking, both forms are known to have played a pivotal role in the rise and the ruse of modern political language, particularly that of nationalism (Derrida 1986; Feldman and Landtsheer 1998; Rutherford 2008; Warner 1990). The eighteenth-century emergence of an American nationalist *we*, for instance, was historically connected to the making of the "bourgeois public sphere." For Emile Benveniste, whose work with pronouns is the basis of a rich theoretical debate, the third person is a nonperson, different from the other two terms that are considered personal (Benveniste 1971). Greg Urban's critique of Jacques Derrida's writing on the American Declaration of Independence makes much of the performative and constative aspects of the pronoun "we." The debate, to be brief, centers on the role of the "we" in either inventing (performative) or describing (constative) an already-existing national "we the people" (Urban 2001).

As the specific pronominal usage personalizes the letters, turning each reader into an intimate addressee, I suggest that this form of address also performatively brings an ideal citizen into being. This subject has been so far absent in a political climate known to lean more on street violence and behind-closed-doors deals than public deliberations. Simultaneously, addressing a letter to the citizen asserts the existence of a citizen, thereby indicating a suturing of its constative and performative aspects (Lee 1997). If we take Yunus's letters as symptomatic of a shift in mediating dominant political desires, one could say that by this time the Andersonian national "we," whose invocation has historically marked populist texts and discourses in Bangladesh and elsewhere had turned stale (Anderson 1991). The ideal subject that Yunus interpellates aims at leaving behind the "we" that outran its use in framing contemporary political language in Bangladesh.

The focus on choice and freedom in seeking the voice of the people or public opinion shows that one's individual choice stands in contrast to all other similarly mediated desires (Lee 1997). The mass-mediated consumerist public subject is built on the notion of choice and interest. "Its internal dynamic is that of a temporal structuring of difference that is regulated by the demands of the market and mediated by forms of consumer publicity such as advertising," according to Benjamin Lee (1997: 345). Following Lee, let us make a note of the emphasis on individual agency of the newspaper-reading citizens partaking of this grand event of democratic deliberation. In the second letter, dated February 23, 2007, Yunus reacts to the responses he received:

> You have come forward and advised me with the desire to create a new politics for a new Bangladesh. A handful of young volunteers have been struggling to keep up with the incessant flow of mails, emails, fax and sms [short message service] that you have sent to me after reading my letter in the newspapers. Your letters are continuing to flood in. The replies ranged from the people in remote villages of Bangladesh to the enthusiastic expatriates.

The citizen has spoken. Addressed as *apni* or the honorific "you," he or she is hardly the crowds of thousands or the *janata* of Huq's novel that are routinely seen rallying around their political leaders (Huq 1976). To be a citizen here is to avail oneself of the services enabled by the technological media in the form of text messages, electronic mail, and phone calls, which are designed to facilitate one-to-one communication. Nationally, the caretaker government's insistence on digital media in ensuring access and visibility was manifest in newly opened websites and email accounts through which citizens could complain about crime and corruption. Such attraction to info-technological mediation in the Indian context, according to William Mazzarella, is "generally rooted in a naïve notion of the inherent incorruptibility of digitized information, as opposed to the surreptitious modifications to which handwritten ledger entries were so manifestly subject" (Mazzarella 2006). The interconnectedness of the "people in remote villages" and the "expatriates" is facilitated by technologies, which speak to a telecommunicative fantasy in part of Yunus in realizing a new political order (cf. Rafael 2003)—"this polity without politics and media without mediation" (Mazzarella 2010b).

It is perhaps no coincidence that the tone in which Yunus speaks to a national audience—its second-person idiom—mimics the personalized, intimate voice of advertising. His post-Nobel fascination with social business as a tool to reduce global poverty aligned him closer to the sleek realm of branding and advertising than to the gritty reality of development. Grameen's partnerships with global corporate giants such as Adidas and Dannon are chapters in this unfolding saga (Muhammad 2009). "The New Kind of Capitalism that Serves Humanity's Most Pressing Needs" is the subtitle of Yunus's book *Building Social Business*. Its author's own coming of age as a Bengali of international repute was furthered by similar communicative technologies: Yunus was also elected the Best Bengali of 2006 by the people of West Bengal in India, where voting took place among Bengali communities across India through SMS votes.

The goal of Yunus's new politics—a politics that famously aimed to send poverty to the museum—was to be "non-communal, secular, democratic, good governance, free from corruption and against politicization." He explains: "The foundation of my new party will gradually build up through the same consultative process I have used to come to this decision." Politicization and consultation were thus diametric opposites; one was the undoing of the other. Yunus's advice for the grassroots party workers was to make arrangements as best they could to receive phones, letters, faxes, and emails from the people, to disseminate information, to receive people's opinion, and finally, to keep him posted. "You must continue your communication with me," he implores the reader at the end of the second letter.

By the time the third and final letter went into print (four months after the first), many theories were put forward to make sense of Yunus's "failure," which mostly meant the inability of his party, *Nagorik Shakti*, to garner enough support to become a competitive political alternative, or the much-awaited "third force" in Bangladeshi politics. The explanations ranged from pointing to the letter writer's personal limitations—most prominently, his lack of experience and political savvy (ironically, the same naïveté was once considered central to his charisma)—to a collective throwing of arms in the air regarding the incorrigible culture of politics that would refuse the entry of a different voice, even if it came with the tag of a Nobel Peace Prize. Yunus's fate was explained by a young left leader: "People in Bangladesh want to touch the person that they vote for, you see. If a politician from one of the mainstream political parties stands on the street, there's going to be a crowd around him or her. The same is not going to happen with Yunus. You need to have a physical presence. In the U.S., for example, one sorts these things out in the media, but in a place like Bangladesh, you need to have some physical presence" (personal communication, October 2009).

I do not share this explanation in order to reproduce what is a familiar binary of corporeality and immediacy versus technological mediation and, perhaps, deliberation. This distinction cannot simply be explained away as so-called Third World versus First World modes of doing politics. Rather, I believe, the opposition was very much a constitutive element of the Yunus phenomenon, wherein a conscious decision was made on Yunus's part to use media to perform an intimacy that he clearly did not share with those who would ideally vote for him. His quest for the tech-savvy, text-messaging citizen failed to resonate with that sector of the voting populace. The reason, I was told, was that Yunus was too busy courting foreign friends and expatriate followers while blithely ignoring the poor masses that his Grameen Bank was dedicated to empowering through small loans. It is worth pointing out that the one public statement that caused the most damage to the Nobel laureate's campaign, and brought down his sublime persona to the level of the mundane, was issued by Sheikh Hasina. The leader of the Awami League, and of Bangladesh since 2009, Hasina had called Yunus a *sudkhor*, a usurer. Although Hasina did not name Yunus in her comment, the invective in which she claimed to see no difference between usurers and those who accepted bribes was a direct reference to Yunus's success with the rural banking network (India-Forums.com 2007). It was hardly a novel critique of the microfinancing program of Grameen Bank that was known for charging high interest rates to its vulnerable lenders (L. Karim 2011). Still, the criticism found mass appeal, especially when leveled by the leader of a political party controlling nearly half of the country's electoral votes.[5] The relationship between Hasina and Yunus that had famously soured due to his role in leading political reforms during the emergency is said to have led to his ousting as the Grameen Bank chief.

KASU MIA'S JOKE

> A crowd thinks in images, and the image itself immediately calls up
> a series of other images, having no logical connection with the first.
> —Gustave Le Bon (2002 [1896])

In the second half of this chapter I present, as points of illustration, two other forms of media: the national photo identification card and a photograph that was censored around the same time. The ID was also considered a voter ID card and was first issued during the emergency. When juxtaposed with Yunus's letters, these two documents reveal what I have described earlier as a classic impasse of postcolonial sovereignty (Chakrabarty 2007; Mazzarella 2013a).

The ID card is of a citizen of Bangladesh. It has been circulating on Facebook as a parody of the national photo ID. The photograph features a scene of a civilian assault on a uniformed soldier. The former was introduced to accomplish a long-overdue task of making a proper list of legitimate voters and their identification, and thereby curbing electoral fraud. The photo in question was considered unsuitable for national consumption for its alleged damaging impact on the public image of the military, which provided the main support for the emergency government. It was censored in national media soon after publication.

At an analytical level, I develop a theory of "picture-thinking" as a key function of sovereignty. I take the formulation from William Mazzarella who, echoing G. F. W. Hegel and Gustav Le Bon, historicizes the opposition between reason and affect that informs classic crowd theory as well as more recent ruminations on political collectivity (Houlgate 1998; Le Bon 2002 [1896]; Mazzarella 2010a). In this theoretical trajectory, the crowd appears to haunt the modern fiction of democratic citizenship. For Ortega y Gasset, for example, the mass man is the one who "learns only in his own flesh" (Ortega y Gasset 1932). William Mazzarella explains,

> Hegel, in the *Phenomenology of Spirit*, states quite explicitly that the condition of progress toward autonomy of reason is a willingness to let the naively concrete attachments of "picture-thinking" (1998 [1807]: 64) be penetrated and surpassed (sublated) by the strain of conceptual thought. And it is precisely a slide back into the chaos of picture-thinking that defines the crowd. . . . But it is also worth noting that, within this discourse, thinking in pictures also means thinking with the body. (Mazzarella 2010b: 703)

Exploring an ethnographic instantiation of this relation between an autonomous subject and affective crowds, I argue that the sovereign, which is quick to blame the crowds for picture-thinking as characterized in Le Bon's quote at the beginning of this section, more often than not, partakes of this very act itself. I come to this understanding by examining the dialectic between citizens and crowds as played out in the juxtaposition of the ID card and the photo. To read these in relation to Yunus's letters, whose public circulation was officially sponsored or encouraged, is to point to the failure of an individuating mode of identification that is at once historical and foundational. James Scott has famously reminded us of a particular kind of "picture-thinking" that is at the core of modern state power as it aims to individualize, identify, and govern (Scott 1998). An ID card, for Scott, is a quintessential example.

With two former heads of state—Hasina and Zia—in jail and most of their political and business allies in hiding, exile, or prison, the rhetoric of change—for a change—did not sound predictably hollow. The first-ever decision to issue national identification cards for the much-anticipated elections was hailed as a necessary move in the right direction. The massive logistical enterprise of taking photos and entering the biographical information of citizens was outsourced to the military. The latter created what was to be the world's largest single database of voters by covering eighty-one million people (Alamgir 2009: 51). This ambitious plan could change the way electoral battles were fought and criminals were chased, a major news source declared within a week of the publication of Yunus's first letter (bdnews24.com 2007: 24). The card to be issued for voter identification was to also serve as a photo ID, a previously nonexistent state document in a country about forty years old. The emancipatory and democratic possibilities afforded by the ID card were comparable to the aura of the transparent ballot boxes also to be introduced for the first time in the national elections. The visual economy within which a drive to transparency took place was mediated by a sense of being looked at from afar. From foreign governments and international donor agencies to transnational media, to echo Rosalind Morris on Thailand, "the demand for transparency is thought to compel the performance of a certain honesty, and this honesty (or at least its performance) is thought to secure the possibility of smooth exchange relations in turn" (Morris 2004: 226). The following comment from a reader of an English-language daily highlights a representative sentiment:

> Ironically, as Bangladeshis we do not have any identity to prove who we are. It is even incomprehensible by many foreigners that how a citizen of a country does not have any legal means of proving his/her citizenship. There is no birth certificate or social security number for the common people . . . Most important of all is the creation of public trust in a national identity system. . . . Trust is also achieved when an identity system is reliable and stable, and operates in conditions that provide genuine value and benefit to the individual. (Ferdous 2007)

Still, performances of transparency signaled the possibility of secrets elsewhere, and trust seemed particularly elusive at a time of grand expectations and greater suspicions. Anxieties persisted around the potential success of a timely gathering of the requisite data for the elections to take place at all. In a densely populated country with inadequate infrastructure, the possibility of success was understandably far-fetched. Some wondered if it was another ploy to thwart the elections. Theories, conspiratorial and otherwise, were also advanced with an aim to unveil the political schema lurking behind the smokescreen of democratic reform. Others saw this consolidation of a graphic regime of surveillance as one of the state's first steps toward fascism (Ahmed and Alam 2008).

As was expected, the tiny piece of plastic and the process of getting it generated an equal amount of excitement and disillusionment. Confusion as to the proper function of the card in the everyday bureaucratic life of the citizen straddled the boundaries of desire and despair. One man at a voting center was optimistic: "I don't care what you all say, I'm not losing my national ID, I will get to America with this card" (Mohaiemen 2008). The confusion surrounding the card was further compounded by a technical glitch: the photographs that most cards finally displayed nearly failed to serve the purpose of recognition. Western readers would find uncanny similarities between these ID photos and the distorted, comic representations that are magic mirror reflections. A letter to the editor sums up the exasperation of a newly registered voter:

> I was awfully shocked when I received my national ID card. . . . Those who came to collect their respective national ID card were flabbergasted to see their photographs. They could not, like me, recognise their own pictures. Not a single person was satisfied with the distorted photograph in the identity card . . . The photograph in the identity card is neither colour nor black and white. It is simply an irritating and confusing picture. (*Daily Star* 2008)

The pictorial distortions disturb the classic mode of state picture-thinking, as opposed to state reason, that is an ID card. They throw the aspiring citizen back into a crowd. The technical problems of a newly introduced computerized data entry system disrupted the way in which an ID photo sought eye-to-eye interpellation, as it were, by its straight-on framing of the person. The irritation of the letter writer is partly related to the inability of the citizen to become a part of this massive project of

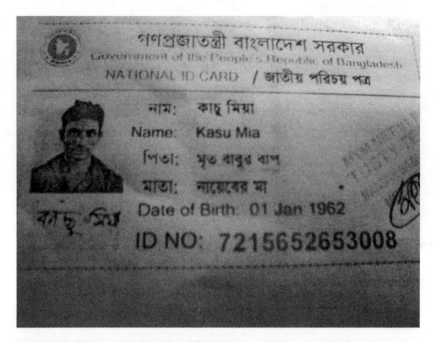

FIGURE 2 This image of a photo ID has been circulating on the Internet as a joke. *Source*: Nasrin Siraj Annie, Facebook. Reprinted with permission.

transparency, and by extension, a part of Bangladesh's political modernity. The irritation and confusion are precisely because one finds oneself unrecognizable—to the state and to oneself—and is therefore relegated once more to the primitive crowd.[6] The state's failure to engage its citizens in mutual recognition, moreover, exceeded the technical glitches in the logistics of taking photographs. I argue that the misrecognition bespeaks a deeper failure of identification that haunts most state projects of enumeration. Let me offer a photo of the ID card of Kasu Mia (see figure 2) to explain what I mean.

As per the information on the card, Kasu Mia was born on January 1, 1962. Following the typical format of the temporary card given to newly registered voters, it features a photo of its owner on the left with his signature on the bottom. The list of requisite information includes the name of the individual in Bangla and English, as well as both parents' names. In the photo, the thirteen-digit ID number in bold that appears at the bottom of the picture is displayed in English. The signature of the officer issuing the card is partially seen on the right side, while the words *Jatiya Parichay Patra* (National ID Card) are barely visible at the top.

At the outset, what is funny about the card is its failed efficacy. Kasu Mia's father is identified not by his proper name, but rather by the kin relation by which he is very likely to be addressed in his family: he is "*mrito Babur baap*"—the father of his deceased son, Babu. Nor is Kasu Mia's mother listed by her actual name; she is simply "*Nayeber Maa*"— the mother of Nayeb, who, we presume, is a male sibling of Kasu Mia. An Althusserian drama of hailing by which a citizen is interpellated, thus, comically fails (Althusser 2001). It fails simply because, in this case, the state confronts a kinship idiom that flies in the face of its bureaucratic rationality—the enumerating and individuating impetus of a national identification system. Whether this is an actual ID card of a regular citizen or a deliberately modified one is not clear from the conversations around the image. However, the fact that there is a joke to be made is adequate justification for my argument here.

The naming practices of the state require a synoptic view, "a standardized scheme of identification generating mutually exclusive and exhaustive designations" (Scott, Tehranian, and Mathias 2002: 5). The creation of a legal, fixed patronym shares long intimacy with the modern project of state building. Rural or working-class Muslim Bengalis such as Kasu Mia often partake of vernacular naming practices that are nonhereditary and context specific. In the larger South Asian context, Mian, among other things, is a last name for Muslim nobility. Its vernacular derivative, Mia, in contemporary Bangladesh, functions as a form of address for any adult Muslim male, mostly honorific but at times also comic or derogatory. The generic nature of Kasu Mia's last name adds to the little drama of misrecognition enacted in his ID card. It became a joke circulating among some members of Facebook, the principal medium through which this particular state document generated conversations and laughter. Some felt the need to clarify that the object of their laughter was not the hapless citizen. Instead, it was the state that was the butt of the joke regarding this play of, or play on, citizenship.

An ID card, a mark of the individual citizen bearing rights accorded by the nation-state, is a seemingly innocent and powerful repository of political value in the context of Bangladesh's attempted democratic reforms. When in circulation, Kasu Mia's card condenses several cultural mores supposedly characteristic of a nation and its people held responsible for the failure of democracy (cf. Farquhar 2009). The Aadhaar IDs issued to Indian residents in the early 2000s, in an effort at "de-duplicating" the nation (Cohen 2016) aimed to redress a similar problem that propelled the Bangladeshi national ID project. The larger initiative of which the Aadhaar numbers were a part rendered corruption a matter either of duplication from above or duplication from below, "the fake identities upon which persons—urban migrants, slum dwellers, landless laborers—unrecognizable within the formal archive may depend" (Cohen 2016).

Terms such as transparency and accountability are in practical terms calls to documentation. Ethnographers routinely feel what Annalise Riles (2006) calls the "pull" of documents, yet they also despise these artifacts as sources of ethnographic knowledge. For Matthew Hull (2012), this is partly because we produce and use documents in much the way the people we study do. To study documents, for Riles, is by definition to study how ethnographers themselves know. The document is at once an ethnographic object, an analytical category, and a methodological orientation (Riles 2006: 7). To top it off, bureaucracy is notoriously boring. So it is not surprising to David Graeber that documents drive anthropologists to despair, who are otherwise drawn to areas of density. Paperwork, in contrast, is designed to be "maximally simple and self-contained" (Graeber 2015: 51–52). What anthropologists have, however, explored is how the material qualities of documents inflect the character of communicative practices. Exploring the formal qualities of documents, while tracing "paper trails" (Chu 2010) and exposing "paper truths" (Tarlo 2003), helps us to rethink the instrumental or informational purposes of ethnographic writing. By treating governance as material practice, it approaches documents and similar textual objects in circulation that make up what Hull (2008) calls the material dimensions of bureaucratic semiotic technologies. Documents can discharge affective energies, which are experienced by people to the point of acquiring fetishistic qualities, where certain kinds of potency seem to emanate from their very materiality (Gordillo 2006; Navaro-Yashin 2007). Such bureaucratic techniques, of which an ID card is an ur-example, are the means by which the state governs its populace.

Yet, examples abound where the very instruments of legibility create illegibility and opacity. "Legibility," Veena Das (2004) explains, surfaces as an operative theme in the analysis of routine practices of the state because so much of the way we experience the modern state is constructed through its writing practices. Ethnographic approaches in studying the state's documentary and statistics-gathering initiatives, however, make evident the inherent illegibility—the failure to "read" on the part of both the state and its subjects—of governmental practices, documents, and words (Das and Poole 2004).

Das and Poole explain:

> In defining the state as that which replaces private vengeance with the rule of law, Weber was, of course, building on earlier traditions of Kant and Hegel, for whom the state in modernity was defined by clear-cut boundaries between the external realm of law and the internal realm of ethics and also between the realm of universalistic reason proper to the state and primordial relations proper to the family. Inherent in this imagination of the figure of law was the creation of boundaries between those practices and spaces that were seen to form part of the state and those that were excluded from it. (2004: 7)

Kasu Mia's ID card is a case in point. It is a fecund site where assumptions about the security of identity and rights become unsettled. One can venture from the name and the parental identification—or non-identification, rather—of Kasu Mia that he is a citizen of rural or working class origin. Though he is very much a card-carrying citizen, his ID nonetheless fails to effectively mediate an idealized citizenship as envisioned in the letters through which Yunus addressed the nation. The NGO charisma that Yunus aspired to capitalize for his entry into politics was framed in light of the disjuncture between the citizen of law and the infantile citizen of the likes of Kasu Mia (cf. Berlant 1997). NGOs, of course, operate on a similar paternalistic logic, as did the progressive developmentalism of the emergency, which retards democratic politics all the while claiming to usher it in. The infantile citizen is still beholden to the affective relations of kinship that dismantle the public–private divide so precious to the fiction of modern democracy. The new subject/citizen envisioned in the emancipatory ideal of the French Revolution was an abstract, unmarked individual who was the bearer of equal rights before the law (Scott, Tehranian, and Mathias 2002). Universal citizenship meant "that a citizen [could] be uniquely and reliably distinguishable *as an individual* and not as a member of a community, manor, guild, or parish" (Scott, Tehranian, and Mathias 2002: 16; emphasis in original).

The fact that these supposed borders have been flouted in the most theatrical and predictable fashion in national politics adds certain poignancy to Kasu Mia's own brand of defiance—his resistance to recognition, in other words. Bangladesh's dynastic political culture, as I mentioned, has thrived by mobilizing kin-terms, most popularly *jatir pita* as ascribed to Sheikh Mujibur Rahman, the first president. Powerful politicians are known for exploiting kin ties to further their careers. Sheikh Hasina and Khaleda Zia, both heads of state at one point, are, respectively, the daughter and the wife of two former presidents. The lateral entry of their progeny into party politics (their sons have officially joined the ancestral parties) has only signaled the continuation of a well-established pan–South Asian trend (Ruud and Islam 2016). Muhammad Yunus famously attempted to break the pattern, but it is Kasu Mia who brings to us, albeit humorously, the failure of that exception that Yunus aimed to exploit.

Kasu Mia's ID is a symptom of the failure of state modernity. It also elicits a barely disavowed discomfort shared by consumers of digital media over the feudalism at the heart of national politics. Kasu Mia's naïveté, if one could call it that, is the source of the comic effect that his ID card has for a middle-class public whose Facebook walls abound in emoticons—iconic representations of the gesture of laughter at his citizenship. Freud famously pointed out that the type of comic that stands nearest to jokes is the naïve, and went on to explain: "An inhibitory expenditure which we usually make suddenly becomes unutilizable owing to our hearing the naïve remark, and it is discharged by laughter" (Freud 2003 [1905]: 226). The state is the joke, no doubt. Yet, there is more to this laughter. The working-class, undereducated, and seemingly naïve citizen fails to perform an idealized citizenship while being subjected to state scrutiny. After all, a veritable index of identification, the photograph—devoid of the otherwise irritating distortions—is still imprinted on the card.

Is one laughing at Kasu Mia's stupidity, then? Partially, at least, it seems. Stupidity has historically remained outside the domain of the political. "The idiot is the one who is not a citizen," Avital Ronell (Ronell 2002: 41) tells us. And yet, when stupidity asserts itself without remorse, it paradoxically plays on the side of truth. Stupidity, in Ronell's reading, remains a phantom of the truth to which it points. And while saying, "in crowds it is stupidity and not mother-wit that is accumulated," Le Bon goes on to credit them with deep social truths (Le Bon 2002 [1896]: 6). Not unlike the Idiot in Dostoevsky's novel, Kasu Mia exposes the disorder and interruption that constitute the social milieu that would normally remain masked (Ronell 2002).[7]

But we must be laughing at ourselves too, we the citizens, when we laugh at—not with, mind you—Kasu Mia, or for that matter, the Bangladeshi state. Being at once native (a co-citizen) and foreign (keeping what Ronell describes as an "inextinguishable appeal" of the stranger), our idiot draws laughter from fellow nationals who align themselves, if only momentarily, with the Idiot as the "we" of a nervous modernity. Ronell's reference to modernity is a nod to the defining relationship of identity and modernity. The latter is associated with the ability to "achieve" an identity as opposed to being always defined by one given by birth (Siegel 1997). For the members of Facebook, the desire to clarify that they were not laughing at Kasu Mia implies that they felt the joke was uncomfortably close to mere classist derision. One can only have an ID if one is a modern citizen, and it is preposterous to think the poor could be that.

Freud is once more useful in pointing out the contiguity of the sublime and the ordinary as a source of comedy: "When an unfamiliar thing that is hard to take in, a thing that is abstract and in fact sublime in an intellectual sense, is alleged to tally with something familiar and inferior, in imagining which there is a complete absence of any expenditure on abstraction, then that abstract thing is itself unmasked as something equally inferior" (2003 [1905]: 261).

What, after all, could be more sublime than the idea of the modern state?[8] If Kasu Mia's ID card, the abject underside of a fetishized document, makes us laugh at the everyday, worldly affairs of the sublime state (cf. Navaro-Yashin 2007), then the laughter that it produces is at least partially one of irony. It was the emergency that forced a nation to observe from an ironic distance when the idea of citizenship repeatedly came under violent attacks from the state itself, and that, too, through its myriad technologies of citizenship. Yunus's letters, one must add, remained eerily silent on the topic.

Kasu Mia's story is tragicomic. The impersonal yet individuating effect of an ID card—its I/you mode of interpellation—is challenged by collective kin-relations passing for parental identification. Kasu Mia, at this moment of Althusserian proportions, is more a member of a generic crowd, Ortega y Gasset's "mass man" (Ortega y Gasset 1932), than an individually identifiable citizen. The generic density of kin terms in the ID card, equally impersonal because relatively unlocatable, though no less intimate than the second-person singular of Yunus's letters, protects Kasu Mia, if only in an incomplete fashion and possibly even without a conscious effort on his part. In the absence of a furtive Geertzian wink or an insider's joke shared between Kasu Mia and his fellow citizens, the laughter is an attempt to come to terms with Kasu Mia's citizenship, his subjection and ours, that can only be partial. Using this failure as a metonym, one might speculate in a more culturally grounded way, the failure of the project of the emergency.

THE KICK AND THE CROWD

That the military government's mantra of "politics without politicization" failed to effectively mesmerize a national audience was made further apparent by the events in the coming months. This time the disenchantment with the regime came from the youth, presumably a core constituency of Muhammad Yunus. A student protest movement that had started at the University of Dhaka over a skirmish between students and soldiers on campus sparked the most potent resistance against the regime. Three days of turmoil that turned into a riot reverberated beyond the capital,

FIGURE 3 The photograph of the infamous kick. *Source*: Khaled Sarkar. Reprinted with permission.

bringing charges against professors and students of public universities, and resulted in their imprisonment.

If a single image could capture the public sentiment against the emergency government, then, as the BBC wrote with unmistakable relish, it is the one of "a sandaled demonstrator in mid-air kick and a hatless army officer in terrified retreat" (Sudworth 2007). The photograph by Khaled Sarkar, a Bangladeshi photojournalist, was censored in national media soon after it was first published in the *Daily Star* anticipating retaliation from the army (see figure 3). The BBC article that carried it announced: "[The photo's] publication was seen as a humiliation, every bit as great as if that flying sandaled foot had been aimed at the behind of the army chief himself" (Sudworth 2007), the same army general that *Time* magazine called the "Boss of Bangladesh" (cited in Alamgir 2008). The photo resists the attempt at enumeration and control not simply by featuring an unruly citizen. On an analytical level, the photograph mocks state identification by indexing what I call a logic of crowd rather than a logic of citizenship.

But first, a brief chronology. Between August 20 and 22, 2007, violence spread across university campuses nationwide. It started with an incident at a soccer match at the University of Dhaka campus. A verbal back-and-forth between angry students and army soldiers (who had been camping at the university gymnasium for some time) turned into a physical fight. Most of the two hundred people injured were students. One was reported dead in the protests against military presence on campus. The government imposed a weeklong curfew to quell public unrest. Four professors at the Universities of Dhaka and Rajshahi, the latter located in the northwest, were detained along with twenty-four students for breaking emergency rules, which outlawed protests and gatherings (BBC News 2007).

The informal ban imposed on this photo and the circulation of another, featuring the public apology that one of the incarcerated professors offered later at the court premises, have since been analyzed in a Bangla language essay titled "Unruly Images: Masculinity, Public Memory, and Censorship" (R. Ahmed 2008b; my translation). The cover of Rahnuma Ahmed's essay, published as a booklet halfway through military rule, is an eloquent challenge to censorship—state sponsored and otherwise. It features the photograph of the academic under arrest speaking to a set of microphones before him. Below is a rectangular space of the same size that was originally intended for the censored image. The word "CEN-SORED," in capital letters, stands in for the absent photo. Both images are embedded in a background of blurred out newspaper print. Ahmed compares the forbidden photographs of American soldiers wounded or dead in Iraq with the controversial photo from Bangladesh, framing her argument around the symbolic emasculation of the military mediated by the images that were taken out of circulation. As Ahmed argues, for the state to domesticate the effects of the "unruly" photograph, it becomes necessary for it to publicize the photograph of the apology. Since the two images are linked to each other in a cause-and-effect relationship, despite the desire to salvage the seeming omnipotence of the military, the published photograph works as a mnemonic cue for the absent photo, which had allegedly compromised the military's image.

The reference to the military uniform in the apology that one of the professors under arrest had read aloud in public turned a civilian's kick into a metonym for the disgrace of the institution of the military. I agree with Ahmed that the discourse of humiliation brings the semiotics of a masculine corporeal aesthetic to the fore. The "hatlessness" of the soldier, I would add, is surely one crucial aspect of this perceived emasculation. Her point about the photo of the public apology serving as an index for the censored one is equally well taken.

In light of the argument of this chapter, however, I take a different tack: I want to read this photograph as a public document that resists the individuating attempts proffered in Yunus's letters or Kasu Mia's ID card. It captures a moment of resistance to the state's hailing of the citizen in the conventional mode of *I* and *You*. Here is an ordinary man, whose back faces the camera, thereby cutting an essentially defiant mode. The fleeing uniformed figure is also seen from behind. Both characters, framed this way, become archetypes in the same manner as Kasu Mia with his generic last name and elusive ancestry. The kicker and the soldier are not individual citizens, but instead are tokens of types locked in a contentious relationship that was born almost with the nation itself. With minor exceptions, the fifteen-year military rule ended with the culmination of the democracy movement that ousted the retired lieutenant-general H. M. Ershad as president in 1990.

The civilian in the censored photo, in the dominant role of the aggressor vis-à-vis the uniformed man, is not the citizen to be identified by a state document. Instead, the faceless and hence anonymous man is an element of a crowd—disorderly, amorphous, and predictably destructive. A closer observation shows more people in the photo, possibly students, shopkeepers, or passersby on the other side of the street, running away from the scene of crime while looking back at it. From Ahmed's footnotes, one gathers that the other photos of this day found in the press and in the military's own publications showed the university students with sticks (*lathi*) in hand, thus making themselves constitutive elements of a violent crowd. "Arms that are supposed to carry books and pens are carrying sticks," said one of the photo captions in the newsletter published by the military. The assertion reveals the official desire to read these actions as perpetrated by the masses who are either not students or, better yet, should not be treated as such by the state because of their actions that mimic those of a criminal crowd.[9] It is the censored image that captures the potentiality of the violent contact. It freezes the moment when a civilian is more powerful and succeeds in attacking its target and possibly hurting it. The notorious mid-air kick hints at near-certain bodily contact within an instant of the camera's click, evoking therefore an "anticipatory nostalgia" in the viewer, a suggestion that cries out actual humiliation as opposed to the possibility of an assault of a *lathi*-charging crowd (Morris 2009).

This photograph is dangerous not simply because it offers a glimpse into a moment when a menacing crowd is being formed; the latter, if anything, is a permanent fixture in everyday political performances in Bangladesh. The photo is considered harmful because it captures the realization of a potentiality that is generally attributed to the crowd. Its danger lies in depicting what the crowd is feared for but is rarely seen to do—that is, physically assault "the sovereign," or in this case, a seemingly omnipotent military (Azoulay 2008; Hobbes 1982 [1651]). Its drama is also heightened due to the viewer's inability to put a face to this figure of disobedience in spite of the vision that it creates of direct and popular sovereignty. It would be misleading, though, to take the projected anonymity of the kicker too literally or to celebrate the power of his defiance *tout court*. Indeed, a defense and intelligence report exclusive to the subscribers of Bangladesh Military Forces (BMF), which conducts research on national security, was titled "The 'Flying Kicker' Identified" (Ahmed 2008b). The title bespeaks an acknowledgment of the official effort as well as the difficulty in naming the aggressor. In this little drama of sovereignty and transparency, the army admits to overcoming the photograph's resistance to identification, albeit before a chosen public.

That none of the parties involved in the production of a photographic image—the photographer or the represented object—can seal off a photo's effects or determine its meanings is well known. In their varied observations on sense, temporality, and intimacy in the taking and viewing of photos, scholars have questioned the sense of immediacy or truth-value conventionally associated with the medium (Baer 2002; Barthes 1981; Benjamin 1977). Philosophical work has paved the way for anthropology to critically approach the fetish of photography's power, the supposed eloquence of the viewed over that of the read (Gürsel 2017; Morris 2009; Pinney 2011; Strassler 2010). Ariella Azoulay (2008) has found profound analogies between the concept of citizenship and the medium of photography. Theorizing what she calls the civil contract of photography, Azoulay approaches citizens primarily as those who are governed. Through various ideological mechanisms, the nation-state forges a bond of identification between citizens and the state. It does so, as in ideological moves of any kind, by successfully erasing this fact, thereby making the identification *seem* natural. As photography becomes a more accessible medium of expression for those who produce and consume a global visual culture, the mechanisms involved in taking photos are not mediated through a sovereign power, nor are they limited to the bounds of a nation-state or an economic contract. "The users of photography," Azoulay says, "thus re-emerge as people who are not totally identified with the power that governs them and who have new means to look at and show its deeds" (2008: 24). Similar to citizenship that is also gained through recognition, photography, as the sovereign must acknowledge, cannot be simply possessed. Hence, the desire to put an end to its circulation. Here, then, is one clue as to the need to censor this particular image. This is also one of the main points of Rahnuma Ahmed's essay in which she gestures at what I read as a vaguely Foucauldian take on censorship in which the authoritarian regime, unbeknownst to itself, enhances rather than represses the possibilities of bringing the censored image into public visibility.

What is equally riveting about the photo is its ability to speak to the fear of the crowd and its supposed immanent potentialities. William Mazzarella (2010b) has argued that canonical writing on crowds, from works by Gustave Le Bon and Elias Canetti to Sigmund Freud and José Ortega y Gasset, at face value, seems hopelessly politically incorrect. Crowds—if one were to offer a laundry list of sorts—are perpetually dangerous because they contain the danger of violent eruptions. Those who are part of a crowd are irresponsible, immature, and do not deserve all the privileges of mature citizenship. And despite the creative energies identified in them, they are ultimately the rabble that has to be kept from the gates. The crowds, in short, are the intimate enemy of constituted authority. They are the dark matter that pulls on the liberal subject from its past (Mazzarella 2010b: 697).

Mazzarella's argument also serves as a point of departure for thinking anew the social potential of group energies. For him, to restage the opposition between crowds and their more recent progressive incarnations, such as multitudes, premised as it is on a theory of an autonomous liberal subject and the multitude's supposed attachment to unmediated potentiality, is to "reproduce a misleading epochal distinction between past and present phases of modernity" (2010b: 698). I argue, and hope to have already shown through the examples of Muhammad Yunus's letters and Kasu Mia's ID card, that a certain sense of epochal distinction was very much at work in Bangladesh during the political period that is the subject and the backdrop of this chapter. The crowd as a force of politics was the intimate enemy of the military regime's agenda of effective and depoliticized governance.

One could possibly object to a reading of a photo that features a single man in violent exchange with an individual member of the military as a classic representation of a crowd. It is, however, not difficult to read the action caught on camera as a shorthand for a crowd that is by definition amorphous, faceless, and brimming with uncontainable libidinal energies (Freud 1975 [1921]). Writing on the power of a baiting crowd, Elias Canetti observes, "The victim can do nothing to [the baiting crowd]. He is either bound or in flight, and cannot hit back; in his defenselessness he is victim only" (Canetti 1984 [1962]: 49). Indeed, even the fact that charges were brought against the professors on the basis of their instigation of the student mobilizations (though the students protesting were not necessarily from the same universities or even the same cities), and of leading the masses into breaking emergency laws, points to another definitional characteristic of crowd: incapable of thinking for itself, or thinking at all, the crowd finds in the leader an ego ideal. The mass warrants issued against 82,000 anonymous persons—a veritable crowd!—bring the point home.[10] The crowd here is more than politically incorrect: it is criminal. The "unidentifiable" man in the photo defies the recognition that remains the premise of both photography and citizenship. This defiance is also an essential quality of the crowd.

It is worthwhile to revisit Le Bon's thoughts on crowds as this chapter comes to an end. If anything, the status of this photograph in the context of its circulation makes apparent that it is not only the governed who think in images, or "in its flesh," as Ortega y Gasset said of the mass man (1932). Censoring the photo of the military's humiliation shows that as the epitome of reason, the sovereign, more often than not, participates in the kind of picture-thinking of which it routinely accuses its subjects. And I do not only mean this literally. The unreasonableness with which the sovereign approaches citizens and crowds, including their various mediatized representations, shatters the fetishized boundaries between reason and affect that the sovereign continually resurrects through violence.

Surely, the irrationality of picture-thinking as opposed to the reasoned actions of an enlightened, autonomous subject is a fiction. It is still an ideological ruse that has been closely entwined with the making of the current political culture in Bangladesh. The ruse is constitutive because the sovereign must excise its own irrationality by projecting it onto both the past and the crowd that is supposed to belong to an earlier stage of political maturity.[11] This purported retardation of a democratic coming-of-age is commonly attributed to crowds. It is the picture-thinking aspect of its character that is absent in the ideal citizen hailed in Yunus's letters. The pronominal usage of the letters turns each reader into an intimate addressee and performatively brings a citizen into being. Choosing the singular over the plural and the second person over the first, the letters mark a distinct shift in envisioning politics that purports to signal a radical break with the past. A sense of epochal distinction, crafted most energetically during the emergency, was therefore bred by an effort at violent excision, which makes up what I have described here as the classic impasse of sovereignty and citizenship in the postcolony.

CHAPTER 2

SEEING LIKE A CROWD

FOR THE MOST PART, the official view of the state of emergency as a necessary disturbance to the democratic process enjoyed popular if short-lived support. Efforts to cleanse politics were left to the discretion of foreign diplomats, local technocrats, and the army, an alliance since described as Bangladesh's "civic-military-corporate" democracy (Wasif 2009). The anticorruption program of the caretaker government devoted the bulk of its energy to accounting for untaxed income, or "black money." *Kalo taka* in Bangla is a literal translation of the widely used English term. The operative ideology was transparency, as was seen in both Indian and Thai states of emergency from the 1970s onward (Morris 2004; Tarlo 2003). Indeed, transparency is routinely demanded by international financial and development organizations from poorer nations in exchange for funds and political support. Despite the focus on transparency in ranking democracies in the south, however, the popular vision of the contemporary moment is often deeply suspicious of the touted openness and accountability of the transparency discourse (West and Sanders 2003). Ordinary people observe modernity's consequences through a critical lens that is often opaque, if not conspiratorial (Hetherington 2012; West and Sanders 2003).

In Bangladesh, a democratic future where corruption would be a thing of the past—promised, ironically, by a military-backed regime—looked different from the vantage point of Phulbari where I was doing fieldwork. Against the backdrop of the transparency-fetish of the emergency, the public culture of the protest presents an alternative politics of seeing, or what I call "seeing like a crowd." This is not a straightforward attempt at distinguishing between elite anticorruption efforts and vernacular or indigenous resistances to them. As Sarah Muir and Akhil Gupta have shown, the idea of corruption has deep local roots but significant global reach (Muir and Gupta 2018). It is, after all, a category of transgression and not simply a definitional question. Neither are the anticorruption or transparency discourses reducible to an ascendant neoliberal order, with which they have been more or less concomitant. What is important is to explore the conditions of possibility for anticorruption politics, which partly means attending to the interpretive communities or publics for whom corruption and anticorruption exist as significant objects of knowledge, concern, and praxis.

The centrality of money in aesthetic productions and everyday exchanges in Phulbari was different from the nationwide drive against corruption. Here, in 2007, I had met an artist, Saiful Islam, who made signboards for a living. Islam painted extensively, and had produced more than fifty pieces of art on the protests that had erupted four months before the declaration of the emergency. Under the glass countertop of a decrepit desk in his store he displayed an old hobby of collecting foreign currency. When we met a few months after a face-off between the crowds and the paramilitary, he told me a story: In 2005, a group of men working for Asia Energy had stopped by his workplace tucked away in the township's main bazaar. A foreigner in the group became interested in the curious display of bills. Though quaint, the practice of exhibiting exotic bills as decoration is fairly common in small business establishments across South Asia. The gentleman offered him five Australian dollars in appreciation of the storeowner's little leisure pursuit of collecting and exhibiting an assortment of currency, including the dirham and the riyal (the latter more commonly acquired by able men of the countryside returning from the Middle East). "Imagine how much money these people have!" Islam, the artist, said to me, still incredulous of the casual exchange. After all, five Aussie dollars was worth more local cash than what he could ordinarily expect to earn in a day and that too without having put in any labor.

Long after the foreigner and his group had left, though, suspicions about the company they worked for, namely Asia Energy, lingered. Despite his otherwise modest background, Islam had refused to take work orders from the company to make signboards. One of his paintings (see figure 4) represents this defiance of Asia Energy's promises of fiscal compensation that the artist enacts by declining to do business with the company. It portrays a farmer holding on to his homestead while an officer of Asia Energy looks on with bank bills piled up before him. Painted in the genre of signboard art, which Islam made and sold as part of his day job, this piece vividly details the hierarchical value of labor and money that informed what came to be known as the Phulbari movement.

In Islam's painting, which I discuss in the first half of the chapter, a farmer and an Asia Energy employee are caught in the same frame. The cash in front of the company officer is its focal point. As an effort at memorializing the spirit of the anti-mining movement and the violence involved, the painting presupposes and entails politicization by addressing and thereby calling into being a protesting peasantry. Its message contrasts with the viciously apolitical and individualized desire for efficiency and good governance in a globally recognized language of neoliberal transparency.[1] In the second half of this chapter, I document the recollections of Majeda, a working-class woman who became, for a brief period of time, the face of the grassroots nature of the mobilizations. I situate the looting and burning of money that followed paramilitary violence, in which Majeda was directly involved, within the larger context of the crisis in national politics that too gathered steam around money. While still privileging visuality, these popular strategies were a form of a transparency-making enterprise, if only with different and potentially profound political effect than the anticorruption agenda of the state. Together they attempted to unmask the criminalization and contamination of social life.

Cash, in all these instances, was the most material instantiation of value. Amidst the exhaustion of routine corruption in everyday life, crowds were energized by the visibility of money. Because they found themselves in situations dictated by money, mostly as an absent presence and in sums that eluded their mental grasp, they fussed over paper bills. The focus on paper money that marked these acts, utterances, and artifacts attests to two kinds of approaches to value—namely, production and expenditure. The productive approach underwrote the movement as a political platform: it was the primary premise of agricultural labor, resource extraction, and energy generation, all of which were important considerations for the proponents of mining, as well as the organized opposition to it. The expenditure approach, on the other hand, which I explain through Majeda's recollections, brought to attention the volatility of the crowd. Expenditure was not foregrounded in the debate over energy sovereignty that was at the center of official and oppositional discourses of mining. It was, however, an important element of crowd politics in the form of plunder and waste amidst spiraling moral and ethical crises around bad or dirty money. The productive approach framed the company's cash as bad money, which was deemed sterile and therefore not exchangeable for real value. The same framing also spun out of control, as my ethnographic encounters will show, in the demand to actively eliminate money associated with the company, turning the crowds into agents of expenditure. They achieved this by a transgressive uncovering of what was "secretly familiar." Both hinged on the visibility of cash, which was fast becoming a national obsession.

THE TALE OF THE *TAKA*

"The Price of Being Bangladeshi" was a magazine article that came out in 2008. It cited directly from the annual report of Transparency International, Bangladesh:

> To begin with, every 97 people out of 100 who go to the law enforcers for some reason or the other must pay bribes. And there are specific rates for each service required. To avoid arrest you pay Tk. [*taka*]10,927, for an FIR you pay Tk. 3,983, for police verification or a clearance certificate you pay Tk. 2,605, for a charge sheet you pay Tk. 1,703 and for a general diary you pay Tk. 795. An average interaction with law enforcers costs Tk. 3,940. (M. S. Khan 2008)

The petty fiscal exchanges listed here are supposedly well known but rarely documented, such as the fixed rate of bribery in the life of an average Bangladeshi citizen. The numerical specificity with which the article highlights the minutiae of routine corruption is telling. Not only is corruption an open secret but it can also be calculated with utmost precision.

This kind of scaling down of the state in relation to its citizens, according to Kregg Hetherington, is the goal of the project of transparency that ostensibly aims to empower individual citizens. This correlates with the advent of what Hetherington calls the "seeing" individual—a citizen-subject who is endowed with the ability to see, thus realizing the promise of transparency (Hetherington 2012). In the annual reports of international anticorruption watchdog groups, from which the above article borrows, transparency continues to animate civilizational discourses. As a set of policies and an ideology that gained global currency after the Cold War, transparency ensures redistribution of political agency to individual citizens "who could rise from under the yoke of communal and dictatorial regimes" (Hetherington 2012). Wider access to information is said to promote economic development by stimulating innovation and empowering market actors to make more optimal choices. This freedom of the rational individual, in the neoliberal imagination, is deemed as good in and of itself (Hetherington 2012).

Every year between 2001 and 2005, the time leading up to the emergency, Bangladesh was ranked the most corrupt country (Hashmi 2017). The thrust of the opinion piece cited above reflects this scenario and resonates with the caretaker government's fight for transparent governance, which was waged most energetically on finding hidden money. The government had filed charges against hundreds of politicians, civil servants, and members of the business community, including Tareque and Arafat Rahman, sons of the former prime minister Khaleda Zia. The ex-prime minister and the leader of the opposition, as we saw in chapter 1, both were in prison for allegations of tax evasion, bribery, and money laundering. Beyond the high-profile graft cases, scores of low- to mid-ranking public employees were caught with money stashed away not in foreign banks but in their pillowcases and under their beds. "'The King of the Jungle' Osman Goni, his bed and bedding a mine of money" (*Boner raja Osman Goni, leptoshoke takar khoni*)—was the title of a comic strip, published by a weekly satiric supplement of a national daily, about the infamous chief conservator of forests, Osman Goni. Goni was arrested on the charge of destruction of forests under his authority. He had amassed an obscene amount of wealth by felling and selling state-owned trees. The ill-gotten wealth, including seven apartments in the capital and land in his ancestral village, amounted to millions. More than Tk. thirty million was retrieved from inside the mattress and pillowcases in his bedroom and from a drum of rice in his kitchen, prompting the title of the satirical comic strip.

Finding bank bills in unlikely and intimate spaces was in effect a macabre introduction to the vicissitudes of transparency. Mass-mediated spectacles of "primitive accumulation" played in a loop where "primitive" caused more irk than accumulation itself. Indeed, the act of hoarding is historically considered the heights of greed and backwardness of the hoarder, and not just in Bangladesh. The individual's long-standing desire to keep a watch over his or her money has been deemed barbaric since at least the nineteenth century. Gustave Peebles tracks a history of the processes through which people everywhere needed to be taught the difference between solipsistic hoarding and "civilized" saving (Peebles 2012). In colonial South and Southeast Asia, to be specific, money was a pedagogical medium, its proper use a gauge of the users' adaptability to modernity. Robert Foster shows how the moral educational projects of first the Australian colonial state and later the postcolonial nation-state of Papua New Guinea sustained a fetish discourse through explicit teachings about money and wealth. In newspaper columns and educational films, native Papuans were taught the conveniences of paper money, its production process, such as the mint (in order to dispel the myths around the magical sources of the indigenous tokens of value), and the benefits of "growing" money in a savings bank (Foster 1998: 67). Or consider the "primitive" lack ascribed to the indigenous people in colonial India because of their inability to manage modern money. For Prathama Banerjee, it was the rationality of money that made the primitive absolutely different from historical societies. The former lacked the temporal foresight required for the comprehension and management of money as credit (Banerjee 2006: 119). "It is a remarkable moment in history," Peebles writes, "when countless people were gradually convinced to 'draw their money out of the mattresses', separate it from their individual surveillance, and hand it over to a trusted social institution that would provide surveillance for them (and a profit, as well)" (Peebles 2012: 236). The national currency that much of the globe relies on today, Peebles adds, emerged out of this transmigration of the private hoard into a public one—a giant national mattress, so to speak.

In Bangladesh, the televised attempts at mass sensation—finding money literally in mattresses or with foodstuff in pantries—kept the other financial arrangements comfortably hidden from an enthralled national public. Case in point—the contracts of work or memoranda of understanding between the government and various multinationals (including the one between the government of Bangladesh and Asia Energy) or the inflated value of (expatriate) "expert knowledge" were never publicly disclosed, either during democracy or dictatorship (T. M. Khan 2006; Muhammad 2011). The energy sector in particular thrived on behind-closed-doors deals and hefty kickbacks for incumbent politicians and bureaucrats, exemplifying a recurrent trend in the global extractive industry (Apter 2005; Coronil 1997, 2011; MacLean 2014). A paltry 6 percent royalty rate in the contract for the Phulbari mining project, with provisions for export of 80 percent of the coal, was but one example among many in a familiar story of foreign direct investment, joint ventures, and production-sharing contracts in the Bangladeshi resource economy (Gardner 2012; Muhammad 2014b). The Phulbari movement's struggle to bring such invisible agreements into the national consciousness must be situated within this dialectic between transparency and secrecy.

I call this a dialectic because secrecy is constitutive of publicity, especially the neoliberal version of it (Dean 2002). It is deeply implicated in the everyday functioning of late capitalism. Transparency's constant demands for visibility frequently hide bigger or bitter truths, evoking a noticeable public feeling that something is not as it is said to be, "that power remains, notwithstanding official pronouncements, at least somewhat opaque" (West and Sanders 2003). Its language may be recognizable across contexts, but transparency also recreates subjects and objects in surprising ways (Hetherington 2012). Martin Webb has shown that for India's poor on whose behalf transparency activists work, the mechanism that is supposed to guarantee transparency has become a bargaining tool that the poor use to pressure bureaucrats. This is different from demanding a fundamental shift in the practice of governmental accountability through the Right to Information Act 2005. In Webb's words: "The apparition of transparency manifests more as a familiar politics of connection than as new politics of voluntarism" (2012). In other words, the ideology of accountability inherent in Right to Information activism is shaped by a familiar and long-standing culture of clientelism rather than transparency. These cultural insights are in effect calls to explore the social life of the transparency discourse rather than accept it as a universal ideal or a mere political ploy. Similarly, the fact that a state-sponsored and internationally sanctioned drive for transparency in Bangladesh homed in on the fiscal nature of corruption is perhaps not all that unique. What is of relevance is to understand the popular fixation with money's materiality and its effects on popular politics around energy and democracy.

Cash itself has a curious status in the neoliberal economic arrangement. The flow of invisible value makes up the world of finance capital and the culture of contemporary capitalist circulation (Lee and LiPuma 2002). In the wake of the Bretton Woods era, then, what we see is a transformation from Marx's production-based dynamic of self-reflexivity, time, and labor to "a metatemporally based dynamic of circulation" (Lee and LiPuma 2002), at least in the social imaginary (Maurer 2006: 18). Stock markets in the post-Fordist age stand in for markets while cash becomes its moribund material form, a fetishized figuration of value. Thanks to new communications technologies, meaningful economic value circulates in and as numbers, in the form of risk and finance capital. In the current paradigm, providing services and manipulating information are at the heart of economic production, a process also known as informatization (Hardt 1999). The global resource scramble is sustained by conjuring numbers and creating an economy of appearances (Tsing 2000). The frontier-making impetus of capitalism, surely as old as capitalism itself, presents a different relationship between capital, value, and money in neoliberal times. Asia Energy's lucrative stint at the London Stock Exchange, for example, aided by the promise of Phulbari's coal, follows such movements of capital. Similar intangibility and obscurity in the accounting of profit or personal wealth in the Bangladesh emergency mobilized governmental and popular efforts at making money more visible, or to take it out of circulation, as it were.

Money may also be considered tainted due to its proximity to foreign remittance (Gamburd 2004) or mineral extraction (High 2013), as seen in Sri Lanka and Mongolia, respectively. In the collective Bangladeshi imagination, paper money had also become the most tangible sign of secret (if predictable) machinations of power, which were not restricted to Phulbari or coal mining. My exchanges in the early days of fieldwork were instructive. The year 2007–8 was a politically sensitive one, and the exaggerated nature of state surveillance during the emergency affected fieldwork. When I thought of introducing myself to the local authorities, friends and allies well acquainted with the scene warned me of the prevailing political unease. The potential futility of my effort at presenting documentary legitimacy to the authorities was caricatured in a story. An activist with a top-level position in local anti-mining leadership asked if I was familiar with Krishan Chander's writing. Chander is a well-known progressive Hindi-Urdu fiction writer of the mid-nineteenth century whose work has been translated into many South Asian languages, including Bangla. The story was called "*Chapapora Manush*" (The trampled man). His version of it went something like this:

> A man was stuck under a felled tree during a storm. When other people came to help him out from under the tree, they noticed that the tree that had trampled the victim was no ordinary tree; it belonged to the Forest Department. The government office had to be alerted of the accident before any measure could be taken to save the man. Upon being notified of the event, and following the established chain of command, the Forest Department informed the police, who felt obliged to report to the Home Ministry. Ultimately the prime minister had to be made cognizant of the accident. After all, it involved a human being. At the end, the person who cut the branches to help relieve the man of the weight of the tree was greeted simply by a skeleton.

"So, this is how the Bangladeshi administration works," my interlocutor said following the story's morbid punch line. "By the time your information gets to the [office of the] District Commissioner, they might seriously wonder if you are a representative of Tata [the Indian business giant] or if you are a spy," he explained, smiling. His was a knowing smile, generated as much from contentment in possessing knowledge of how the state *really* worked as from satisfaction in being able to show the naïve outsider the ropes, so to speak. After all, state-sponsored violence, including death, was dangerously close to their everyday lives. People got randomly killed when protesting against the corporation; a well-known leader was publicly humiliated, beaten, and held up by the military on account of fabricated charges of theft; a young Internet activist and the founder-moderator of a web forum on Phulbari was interrogated by members of Rapid Action Battalion, the elite police force. After a relatively soft display of might, they "suggested" that young people like him should go abroad for PhD's and not get their hands muddied in such antinationalistic initiatives as stopping coal mines and discouraging foreign direct investment.[2] Power worked not in unpredictable and capricious ways but in a precise and exacting fashion, its banality and absurdity notwithstanding.

The story of death in this caricature revealed the violence of routine bureaucratization. The corpse was the evidence of power, whose physical locations were never easily traceable: "I die, therefore I am," the subject of stately being, crushed under the government-owned tree, may very well be saying (Taussig 1997). The material remains of the man was a visual shorthand for the circuits of power that worked through a strategy that many people described to me as "eyewash." "Eyewash," used in English when speaking or writing in Bangla, is best understood as the conceptual other of transparency. If the latter is aimed to make the state visible to an individual citizen, then eyewash points out the collective inability to see. In 2006, when the government of Bangladesh declined a much talked-about Policy Support Instruments treaty initiated by the International Monetary Fund, eyewash was again on offer as a ready explanation. This rare resistance to a powerful donor organization surprised many observers, including some of my friends in Phulbari.[3] They smelled conspiracy and invoked eyewash that countered transparency's claims to inclusion and visibility.

Money, I soon realized, was simultaneously out of place and all over the place (Rafael 1997); it was found in unexpected places and destroyed as bad money in acts of protest. Its unsettling ubiquity became unstable grounds for oppositional politics. Money's emplacement is crucial as new political potential inheres in the creative exchanges in which commodities stray from their specified paths—when they are "out of place," as it were (Appadurai 1986). But money is also a commodity unlike any other. Its power is an effect of a gigantic system of coordination of human activity, and in situations of radical change, a revolutionary moment in which a larger system itself is being transformed, this ceases to be the case (Graeber 2001). In moments like these, the commodities themselves become pivots between imagination and reality; this is when money reflects forms of social power like magic and sorcery, or as Bill Maurer puts it, "when the not-seen is suddenly thrust into light, the agencies animating value can receive new social scrutiny" (Maurer 2006: 28).

On a quiet afternoon in early 2008, I was sitting at the only tea stall in the main marketplace of a village near Phulbari. It sold meals, snacks, and betel leaves to the men who came in and out of the village for work. As I was paying for my snack of chickpeas and sweets, the young boy who regularly waited on me looked at the two 10-*taka* bills and exclaimed, "Each time this *apa* [older sister] gave me money, the bills have been so clean and shiny, just like *paka* [paved] roads!"[4] I was keenly aware of how striking the crisp bills (carried all the way from the capital) must have appeared to him, and was embarrassed to be the source of such an alien commodity. Rickshaw-pullers in Phulbari had trouble coming up with change for a Tk. 50 (about 75 cents) bill. It was easy to imagine the tea-shop boy's dealings with regular clients who had mostly tattered notes to exchange. Bills were carefully taken out from the folds of their *lungi* (sarong) or shirt pockets where they nestled with loose change and a roll or two of *bidi*, filterless cheap cigarettes consumed by the masses. The *taka* was generally old and frail from the intense circulation to which it has been subjected. The long-worn creases often gave way, which were then mended with cello tape. The creases signified overuse. They were also indices of a lack of circulation of big capital.[5]

Despite the rice that grows in relative abundance three times a year, businesses in Phulbari were mostly small-scale. Only a handful of local entrepreneurial types were said to have made big money by supplying goods and services (through legal and informal channels) to the nearby granite and coal mining projects and through the black market sale of scrap metal and other factory by-products. The rest of the well-to-do were either some sort of beneficiary of the mainstream political parties (mostly AL and BNP, and to a lesser degree, Jamaat and Jatiya Party) or they owned lucrative businesses such as brickfields or rice mills. More often than not the two categories overlapped. The richest man in Phulbari, I was told, was poor a mere fifteen years ago. Owner of a humble *paan* stall in the market, he lived in a crammed two-room house with his extended family. His impressive rise and cutthroat business acumen were envied, but nobody I came across ever questioned the source of his income or the amount of labor he had long invested in his monopoly business as a supplier of consumer items to the local market.

The metaphor of the paved road stayed with me. On my way back from the market, sitting on a rickshaw on the dirt road that wound its way through paddy fields and thatched huts, I thought about the company's plans for paving these roads. Asia Energy's SUVs had zoomed past the same tea stall where people now sat idly yet cautiously, not knowing fully what the future held. I had heard stories of drilling expeditions in the nearby fields that had started since 2005. Villagers had contributed to these projects at times with their labor and at other times simply with curious attention as they gathered in large crowds around the drilling sites. Then there were times when they protested violently, beat up people, or stole parts of the machinery. What did a paved road mean in this context? And what did one make of the desire and distrust so neatly captured in the image of "clean and shiny" money?

AN ENERGY EMERGENCY

Some more details on the mining project, the protests, and their role in shaping energy politics before and during the state of emergency may help answer some of these queries. Phulbari sits on the northwestern tip of Bangladesh, roughly 180 miles from the capital city. The township falls under Dinajpur district and is close to the northwestern border with India. It is also locatable, figuratively speaking, on a decades-long path toward the privatization of the energy sector (T. M. Khan 2006; Muhammad 2014b). Large deposits of bituminous coal attracted a mining project supervised by Asia Energy Corporation Pty. Ltd., a British company.[6] The coal sequence is 14 to 45 meters thick and 150 to 250 meters below the surface, which is

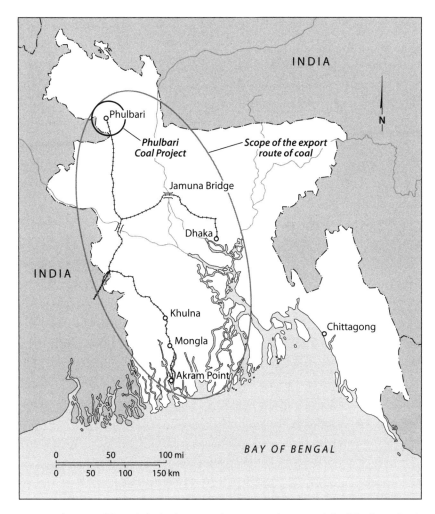

MAP 1 A map of Bangladesh showing the potential scope of the Phulbari Coal Project. *Source*: Adapted from "Phulbari Coal and Power Project: Location and Ownership," GCM Resources. http://www.gcmplc.com/phulbari-coal-project /project-description/location-ownership.

most profitably extractable, as expert knowledge would have it, by opencast mining.[7] Phulbari was one of the four *upazilas* (subdistricts) to be directly affected. It would also be the hub of the mining operations (see map 1). Using this coal for power generation would mitigate the energy deficit for the next fifty years, or nearly half of the national daily energy production.

The region is low-lying and densely inhabited, making the human and ecological costs of the coal project steep (Kalafut and Moody 2008; Muller and Moody 2009). It is still the only mining operation of Asia Energy, a fully owned subsidiary of Asia Energy PLC. It was founded in 1997 and renamed Global Coal Management Resources (GCM) in 2007, presumably to tackle the image crisis that followed the Bangladesh protests. Among the ordinary people in Phulbari, the company is still known as Asia Energy, which I maintain throughout the book. The project received fiscal support from equity investments of well-known private financial institutions and at one point sought public sector funds from Asian Development Bank (ADB). Between 75 and 80 percent of the coal was planned for export through the Sundarban mangrove forests in the southwest (FE Investegate 2007; Muhammad 2014b). This meant relocating 55,000 to 250,000 people to make coal pits a few kilometers in diameter with a lifespan of about thirty-six years; the number of affected people is projected to be much higher than the corporation's conservative estimate (Asia Energy Corporation 2006; Bern Declaration and BankTrack 2007; Nostromo Research 2008). A 500-megawatt power plant would sit at the mine face, and the project was primarily export-oriented (Nostromo Research 2008). The royalty rate in the contract was initially 20 percent, the minimum required under existing mining regulations of Bangladesh. To move the deal forward, the rate was later lowered to 6 percent. The issue of blatantly disproportionate national gains has been a key rallying point for the protesting lobby. The host country would also bear much of the infrastructural expenses, along with the ADB, for ensuring safe and efficient transportation of coal by rail to India and by waterways to the coastal terminal in the south for seaborne export.

In 2015, a report of the United Kingdom's National Contract Point found breaches in GCM's obligation to "develop and apply self-regulatory practices and management systems that foster a relationship of confidence and mutual trust" (Haigh 2015).[8] In Phulbari the feelings of betrayal ran deep. The resulting mobilization has been the only success story among other similar efforts to lay bare the collusion between multinationals and Bangladesh, a country that has been unabashedly loyal to neoliberal policies for decades (Gardner 2012; Muhammad 2015; Sobhan 2005).[9] Both the European Union and the U.K. government were openly lobbying for the company. The Parliamentary under-secretary of state for trade policy with the Department for International Development (DFID) and the Department for Business, Enterprise and Regulatory Reform (DBERR), Gareth Thomas, MP, went on record to say that they have provided support to Global Coal Management Resources PLC through the British high commission in Dhaka. They have lobbied to ensure that the government of Bangladesh takes the company's interests into consideration and does not prohibit opencast mining. He also added that the Bangladeshi caretaker government's new draft coal policy leaves the way open for opencast mining in Bangladesh in the future.[10] In 2010, Wikileaks confirmed the implication of the United States as well. It reported correspondence between the U.S. ambassador to Bangladesh, James Moriarty, and the energy advisor in which the former aggressively pushed the government of Bangladesh to realize the project. His interests were not surprising given the 60 percent of U.S. ownership in it (F. Karim 2010). The leaked cables confirmed the suspicions that many people in Phulbari shared with me about the kinds of invisible alliances that they imagined to be at work in deciding their fate. It was a story, they believed, where the places and agents in question remained beyond their purview, the signs for which were there for all to see.

And still, coal remained invisible to the naked eye. The knowledge of its existence did not come with any material trace for those who happened to live above the accumulated source of value.[11] Phulbari was still a vast expanse of lush paddy fields dotted by shady villages. As a site of development, it was framed in terms of potentiality, a projection of prosperity into the future that tied its coal mines inextricably to the prosperity of the nation. During 2007–8, the state's list of failed services included a huge deficit in power-generating energy. It caused "load shedding"—to use the term familiar across South Asia (Kale 2014)—for hours on end. In the summer months, it plunged the country's major cities and peripheries into routine bouts of darkness, thus calling forth a visual aporia in yet another sense.

The incessant power cuts became proleptic signs of a dark national future. Like population, poverty, and other indices of delayed development, load shedding emerged as a source and a symptom of a malaise that afflicted a nation better known for natural disasters than natural wealth. A former state minister for energy condensed the two when he stressed the urgency to mine coal at a roundtable on energy crisis I had attended in the capital in 2008. "I have been experiencing load shedding since my school life," he exclaimed, "but now it seems like a real Sidr." Sidr was a Category 5 tropical cyclone that made a landfall in the coastal areas of southern Bangladesh in November 2007 and claimed around ten thousand lives. Not allowed to get near the boring holes, villagers in Phulbari talked about seeing coal shining bright out in the fields. They mentioned the gold mines that they had heard lay deep under the earth across the country. Confusing two kinds of subterranean wealth, they appraised coal using the standard of gold, the more familiar fetishized mineral. The confrontations between curious or angry villagers and the company guards at the drilling sites, or the generous gifts of cash, seeds, blankets, television sets, greeting cards, and calendars distributed to the local clubs and the residents of the mining area, generated suspicions about the company's motives. Over time, the gifts became telltale signs of the heightened precarity of a future yet to come (cf. Papadopoulos, Stephenson, and Tsianos 2008).[12]

The political future of the nation was also on shaky grounds. The army takeover was pitched as the only viable option for bringing democracy and development back on track. Power cuts became metonymic of much that had gone astray in the way of development. Despite the less than 40 percent of the population who enjoyed access to electricity, ever-rising consumption had created serious lags between demand and supply—a gap of 1500 megawatts daily as calculated in 2010 (Asian Development Bank 2011). The World Bank added to the woes by estimating a 10 percent loss of business sales due to load shedding (Gunter 2010). Technical and commercial inefficiencies accounted for a waste of nearly 45 percent of generated power (Gulati and Rao 2007). The numbers translated into intermittent but insistent power cuts that divided up everyday life into more or less predictable grids. As the hub of a deeply centralized political and economic system, Dhaka received better services than the rest of the country. Still, in August 2010, a five-hour shutoff of air conditioners and a six-hour closedown of natural gas stations per day were slapped on the capital city to tackle the peak summer-month crunch (Ethirajan 2010). Provincial towns like Phulbari felt the brunt of severe outages.

At the same venue where Heytens spoke, the World Bank representative Ellen Goldstein found Bangladesh "in the grips of a serious energy crisis of multiple dimensions." She repeated the phrase, "transparency and efficiency" three times to make her point about how to tackle it, adding that permanent solutions required large, long-term investments, spanning election cycles (World Bank 2011). Despite donor institutions avoiding politics in policy recommendations (cf. Ferguson 1994), Goldstein's speech acknowledged the electoral considerations of most development projects that parallel the life cycles of political regimes. Both speakers addressed the energy advisor and the secretary of the power division present in the audience. "It is important to ensure that the energy sector is structured and led on sound technocratic principles," Goldstein announced in a spirit resonant of a global, generic development paradigm (Mitchell 2009). "There must not be any politics here," a local expert later announced as he laid out the "anatomy of the failure" that was the energy crisis (Saleque 2011).

One of the more effective energy-related state measures was introduced in 2009 with daylight saving time. After Pakistan as the other neighboring country to have taken the step a few years before, Bangladesh moved its national clock an hour ahead to cut down the use of power. It was aimed at realizing the new government's electoral promise of efficient power supply. Caricaturing the much hyped "Digital Bangladesh by 2021" mantra of a successful electoral campaign, the new temporal reality quickly came to be called, unofficially though popularly, "digital time." It was widely resisted in its first months, more so in the peripheral towns like Phulbari, where people refused to adjust their watches and clocks, thus resorting to cumbersome translations to accommodate the one-hour lag created by a new, national standard time.

Energy was becoming a political issue on a scale far more spectacular than subaltern resistances to "digital time," which was scrapped within a year. Though the hierarchical and antinomial status of technocracy and politics was not novel to this developmental state (see Gupta 2015 for the

Indian case), spontaneous uprisings for equitable service of power and water brought policy and politics together in unexpected ways. Popular unrest in Kansat in the northwest was a precursor to Phulbari. Kansat had mobilized a considerable portion of local villagers with long-standing grievances against ineffective and corrupt energy management. The 5,000 new electricity lines that the company was obligated to connect every year were not backed by adequate power. Since April 2006, police had killed seventeen people, including farmers, day laborers, and children, and physically attacked their families. Largely dependent on power for irrigation, the villagers objected to paying for services that they never availed and in consequence produced the country's first "electricity martyrs" (*bidyut shahid*) when they organized under the Action Committee for Rural Power Development.[13] The forces that opened fire on the rally and later tortured their leaders in custody were never put on trial. The crowd politics in Phulbari and its success, however mitigated by the shifting positions of those who came to power following the emergency, needs to be situated against this background.

A PEASANT UTOPIA?

I hearken back to Saiful Islam's painting (figure 4) as an artistic response to this larger landscape of violence, betrayal, and distrust. About two feet by three feet in size, the artwork is a juxtaposition of opposites. On its right is a farmer with his muscular back turned to the viewer. He is wearing a *lungi* with a *gamchha* (cotton towel) tied around his waist. A traditional straw hat, or *mathal*, completes the archetypal attire of a Bengali peasant. His arms, fantastically long, are wrapped around a hut. The farmer sits in a lush green paddy field that surrounds the house he is protecting. The vegetation on the horizon draws from stock images of rural Bengal. On the left of the painting, in what looks like an office space, is a man visibly marked as urban. Reclining on a chair with his legs crossed, he wears Western-style trousers, a shirt, and a tie; the sartorial conventions of this elite, educated man contrast starkly with the naked torso of the peasant.

The man has a cigarette lit in his left hand and a bundle of cash in his right. He stares at the farmer as he puffs out smoke. The wall behind displays an Asia Energy calendar. Copied from actual calendars that the

FIGURE 4 Saiful Islam's painting on the Phulbari movement. Photo taken by the author with permission from the artist.

company gave away as gifts (or bribes), it shows a disembodied hand of an apron-clad laboratory worker holding one of several test tubes. The test tubes were kept in the company laboratory in Phulbari to store soil samples that were collected from the coal-mining zone. I saw many of them crushed on the floor when visiting the company's vandalized (though still guarded) premises a year after the events. When Islam first showed me the painting in his house in Phulbari, he needed to explain: "This man was the *boss* of Asia Energy," using the English word for emphasis. He went on to produce an imaginary dialogue: "[The officer] is saying, '*Bhai*, come and take this. Give away the house.' But the peasant is replying, 'No, there is no need for money.' He is holding on to the house. They cannot force him." The persistent theme of resistance to commercial exchange with Asia Energy ran through Islam's paintings. This was also reflected in his anecdote about the Australian money in which he accepted the token of appreciation but declined the possibility of further business.

The people with whom I spoke in Phulbari were well entrenched in a monetized economy. Indeed, wage laborers from the region had already participated in the *Tebhaga* movement in the mid-twentieth century. *Tebhaga*—literally "three shares"—is one of the best-known peasant movements in South Asia (Hashmi 1992). Sharecroppers across East Bengal (presently Bangladesh) demanded the reduction of rent paid in kind to the *jotedars* (land owners) and *mahajans* (money lenders) from one-half to one-third of the yield. By challenging the dominance of petty landlords, including middle peasants and the *bhadralok* (the educated classes) who sublet their land to sharecroppers, the movement had the direct agenda of eventually destroying all intermediary interests that came between the cultivator and the state (Hashmi 1992). Some of the prominent communist leaders of Bengal Kisan Sabha, the regional peasant front of the undivided Communist Party of India, were from poor, rural backgrounds and included Rup Narayan from Phulbari, who became a member of the lower assembly (MLA) in 1946.

In *Pakistan as a Peasant Utopia*, Taj ul-Islam Hashmi gives a rare glimpse into Phulbari's location in the wider canvas of South Asian peasant politics. The region, then a part of undivided India, was directly caught up in the pre-1947 volatility of the subcontinent as well as the Cold War dynamic of a world beyond reach. "Under the influence of the [Communist Party of India] a section of the peasants learnt about the revolutionary activities of Chinese peasants under Mao Tse-Tung. They became familiar with the names of Chiang Kai-shek and President Truman, as has been depicted in some songs composed by Khabir Sheikh, a poor peasant in Dinajpur (of Phulbari village)" (Hashmi 1992).

When Chiang Kai-shek went to meet President Truman in the United States in late 1945, the "poor peasant" from Phulbari wrote the following song: "The frog (Chiang Kai-shek) is boasting that it can destroy mountains by kicks. Listen, you idiot Chiang, if your 'big brother' Mao Tse-Tung hears this he will simply kill you."

Clearly, the "poor peasant" from Phulbari was aware of and firmly located in contemporary geopolitics. *Tebhaga* itself was waged to retain the use value of grains, pointing to a world that was distinctively agricultural. Actual ownership notwithstanding, peasants in general are known to nurture bonds with cultivable land (Adnan 2013; Hashmi 1992; Sartori 2014). As Michael Taussig has noted of Colombian plantation workers facing wage labor in the 1970s, and as farmers in Phulbari have repeatedly brought to my attention, use value and the peasant mode of production often stand outside of and in opposition to selling and buying things with money (Taussig 1977).

The elevated status of productive labor in Islam's painting and the many others that he has drawn is, therefore, familiar. The importance given to agricultural labor at the core of the protesters' argument against mining that threatens peasant life is also convincing. Together they constitute a moral narrative in which cash is a symbol of immoral and corrupt exchanges. In the painting, this comes through in the exaggerated contours of the peasant's muscles, which are iconic of a physique that can only result from the toils of his daily existence. The relatively thinner, fully clothed body of the company employee, on the other hand, features the bourgeois dress code of the educated South Asian salaried class, a familiar if mildly comic product of an erstwhile colonial bureaucracy.[14] Still, the message in Islam's painting is not simply a transition narrative like the one Taussig describes for 1970s Colombia. Money here is neither alien nor only alienating. Rather, its use as bribe, incentive, or mere compensation indexes a bigger and more permanent loss. "This land is going to give us returns till the *keyamat* [the apocalypse]. Money gets used up just like that," one farmer replied when asked about the company's promise of reimbursement.[15] The farmer did not consider the multiplication of money as capital as a power inherent in money itself. Rather, the offer to buy the land was seen as corrupt because this was the land in which the peasant had invested his labor, thus potentially rendering his body as exchangeable for hourly wages like that of the miner. He who was now an agriculturalist, but potentially a miner as well, understood the affective truth of mine labor, "that the miner—unlike the capitalist to whom surplus value accrues—does not experience his work as a process of accumulation, with productivity enabling consumption" (Morris 2008b). The miner himself was consumed in time. In many South African languages, mines are referred to as the place of cannibals, as they are also in the South American mining cultures documented by June Nash (Nash 1993). In

Phulbari's dialect, as I explain in the conclusion, the word for "mine" (*khoni*) sounds identical to the Bangla word for "murderer" (*khuni*).

The peasant who aggressively guards his wealth sees through the ruse of monetary compensation. To him, value is created by labor alone. Money's corrupting powers are not seen from the perspective of exchange value because the reproductive aspect of capital or "its capacity to make its own vitality" (Comaroff and Comaroff 2002) is denied by the peasant who questions its dubious origins. The body and demeanor of the Asia Energy officer, on the other hand, speak of his distance from an economy where the path from labor to value has not been contaminated. Money is a sign of that contamination. The five-dollar bill from Islam's anecdote was iconic of such corruption of daily life and the disparity between foreign and local money (cf. Senders and Truitt 2007). It indexes an incredible amount of cash that is vividly imagined but never actually seen—hence, the artist's disbelief, "Imagine how much money these people have!"

Saiful Islam's art is focused on this archetypal cultivator. Its central figure is squarely located in the agrarian politics of nineteenth- and twentieth-century Bengal, wherein the concept of property is grounded in labor. It represents the core of peasant aspirations to self-determination as found in early twentieth-century Muslim Bengal (Sartori 2014). Its invocation in Islam's painting is recognizable as resistance. The crisis of labor and value that it depicts, however, takes on new meanings in the time of venture capital. The leading edge of contemporary capitalism is no longer the mediation of production by labor but rather the expansion of finance. Capitalist social relations are facilitated by risk, along with labor (Lee and LiPuma 2002). Thus, in its faith in a thriving circulation-based capitalism, the hierarchy between the peasant's labor and "dirty money" as a basis of resistance in Phulbari may seem anachronistic or at best misdirected. In a world where capital increasingly moves as numbers, the peasants' perception of the crisis is still framed in terms that seem more relevant to an earlier phase of capitalism.[16]

In its most recent iteration, what the Comaroffs have termed the "Second Coming of Capitalism," consumption has eclipsed the primacy of production: "For many populations, in the upshot, production appears to have been replaced, as the *fons et origo* of capital, by the provision of services and the capacity to control space, time and the flow of money. In short, by the market and by speculation" (Comaroff and Comaroff 2002). Under such conditions, it is only to be expected that there would be an intensification of efforts to make sense of the hidden logic of supply and demand, "to restore some transparency to the relation between production and value, work and wealth" (Comaroff and Comaroff 2002). I argue that the preoccupation with money during the Phulbari movement and, for that matter, the state of emergency, was precisely a result of the way contemporary capital functions. Ordinary people were unable to fathom the amount of wealth that was in circulation, and therefore demanded a way of seeing this wealth by relying heavily on materiality, which functions as an antidote to the invisibility of capitalist circulation. Islam's painting, in this sense, has an added efficacy. Unlike institutionalized efforts to maintain transparency, such as the emergency government's rabid anticorruption agenda, Islam's artistic attempt to make corruption visible was not rooted in a lofty, liberal idea of citizenship said to be responsible for voting out autocrats, generating market efficiency, or investing in private and public forms of capital (Hetherington 2012). Instead, the painting represents collective political agency, the kind we saw in action in Phulbari, even as it draws from a well-worn script of an idealized peasant life. The artist's desire to make the company's ploys transparent echoed the general political tenor of the protest. It stemmed from an inability to envision fiscal exchanges that hovered just beyond the ethnographic imagination. The *taka* was the medium through which that invisibility was challenged.

REVEALING POWER, UNMAKING VALUE

Islam's painting essentializes the peasant as a political figure. His art, therefore, is familiar and readily valorized as resistance. My conversation with a woman that I recount in this section posits a different configuration of money, morality, and politics that unsettles this recognition. It does so, I argue, by foregrounding crowds as political agents and expenditure, as opposed to productivity, in the manner in which they approach and appreciate value. Destroying objects of value is a kind of spending that cannot be confused with mechanisms of utility, mass production, or mass consumption (Bataille 1985; Stoekl 2007). This personal recollection is of an episode of collective vandalism and attack on Asia Energy, including its offices and employees. It was representative of many others that took place soon after violence was unleashed on the villagers.

A working-class woman from the township, whom I shall call Majeda, was party to the burning of cash as protest. Majeda was already quite a celebrity when I met her in Phulbari (more details on Majeda are in chapter 3). In 2006, she, along with a few other women from her neighborhood, had come out on the streets to challenge the brutality of the border patrol guards that had led to the deaths of three men the day before. Interviewed multiple times by journalists and activists who thronged Phulbari following the killings, she was by far the best-known representative of the women of Phulbari, a potent and eminently utilizable token of local resistance. An op-ed article, first published August 26, 2006, and reprinted on the same date the following year, had the following to say in a section titled, simply, "The Women": "It is rather ironic that a woman who has been utterly neglected by society, who is detested by and large for not being honourable, was the first woman to strengthen our social cohesion. It was [she] who prompted other women to come out on the streets too. In plain English, [she] is a prostitute and often remains outside of Phulbari on 'business'" (T. Ahmed 2008). The activist cited here iterates two well-known facts about Majeda—her political participation and her profession. She was one of the first to have come out of her house with a machete to confront the paramilitary. Majeda's profession, though not so subtly handled in this piece, was a public secret. My research assistant, a local resident in his late twenties who was also a good friend and confidant, went to great lengths to euphemize what Majeda did for a living before giving a name to her profession.[17]

In our interview, Majeda's husband reminisced about the events from a year ago: "[Hussain] was the one who fled first, you understand? He left on his motorcycle. . . . Why would I run away if there was no weakness in me?" he asked rhetorically. Majeda interrupted her husband. "I set Hussain's house on fire," she said abruptly. Her husband tried in vain to change the course of the discussion. Undeterred, Majeda continued: "Then Hussain's house was set on fire. The sack of money burnt down.

At last when there was a light wind, one could only see the seals on the notes." Addressing the older woman standing at the doorstep, she nearly shouted, "He kept money in the turmeric, *Nani* [grandmother]!" Our conversation at the time of her interjection focused on how to tell if someone was a collaborator or a traitor. Locally known as a *dalal*, the collaborator was a ubiquitous figure in Phulbari, rife as it was with suspicions of profiting from the energy company and its myriad forms of corruption. Hussain was suspected to be a collaborator. (See chapter 4 for a longer discussion of collaboration.)

The audio recording of our exchange is hard to decipher with Majeda's voice drowning in the parallel conversations taking place among her husband, the older woman, my friend, and me. It is not clear if she said, "*Holdir moidhye taka thuise*," meaning, "he kept money *in* the turmeric," or "*Holdir moto taka thuise*," "he kept money *as* [he would keep] turmeric." It is a productive confusion either way. In both cases, Majeda was describing a sack that was a shockingly improbable place for storing money. The shock was comparable to a television public's collective awe at the spectacle of hoarding cash in the forest officer's house in drums of rice. In both cases, there is an indecent mixing of bad money with foodstuff, where the latter signified distinctive (use) value. Kofirul, a farmer from a nearby village, further affirmed the point when he explained to me their collective sense of betrayal: "All they [the company and its allies] want is money. We will stop [supplying] the paddy. Now whether they want to eat money dry or eat it by soaking it in water, it's up to them." Majeda's immolation of this sterile money interrupted a theory of value that privileged production, the kind we saw aestheticized in Saiful Islam's art. Hiding money with food grains, for people whose livelihood had been integrally tied to the latter's production, made hoarding much more scandalous than simple accumulation.

Shrill and almost jovial, Majeda's voice betrayed both the shock and humor at this scene of plunder. The first sentence, "*Hussain er barit agun disi*" ("I set Hussain's house on fire") claims individual agency. When she repeated the assertion, "*Tarpore Hussain er barit agun dewa holo*" ("Then Hussain's house was put on fire"), the sentence assumes a collective agent. It applies an indirect and passive form to simple past tense that in most cases identifies the speaker as a member of a group. The reason behind the switch in the narrative register—passive substituting for active—had at least partially to do with the careful policing by her husband. "There was no accounting for how people thought at the time" (*tokhon loker mathar kono* station *chhilo na*), her husband added as a justification for her act. His wife got caught up in the events. The thoughts of the vengeful had no rational coordinates, thereby displaying the quintessence of crowd behavior.

The reason behind Majeda's clear excitement in seeing the fire was not simply that money could be stored like a condiment; money, when put to fire, also burned in flames like any other object. "How did you know that there was money there?" I asked her. In response, she almost repeated her answer: "Because all the sacks burnt down! Only the seals were there. If you blew lightly on it, the sack would be all ashes." She went on to describe how the ashes were flying around in the wind, showing enough proof that the bills had indeed burned. What was offered as the ultimate evidence was the "seal" (for which she used the English word), the symbol of paper money's source of authority, its national indexicality (High 2013). The seal is the hidden if enduring feature of bank bills issued by national treasuries or state banks. For Majeda, this was visible even when the rest of the bill was consumed by fire. In the absence of ritualistic immolation of bank bills to be found in other cultural settings,[18] Majeda's use—or abuse—of paper money was a political act lodged in a system of meaning that tied productivity with morality.

This explanation still does not completely account for Majeda's excitement or joviality in telling us—a couple of strangers—the story of being in that fateful crowd. Money, we must remember, is also fun to play with (Maurer 2015). The magical or fetishistic nature of money is routinely brought into relief by the fact that magical tricks themselves often have money as a favorite prop. Bill Maurer explains the proximity of money and play: "Coins are satisfying to hold, flip, throw, spin, hide, and recover. Paper bills can be cunningly folded, ripped, burned, drawn upon, and modified in a host of ways . . . The act of destroying value by tearing up a bill or making a coin disappear always creates excitement in an audience, and the relief at seeing the value restored always draws applause" (Maurer 2015: 91).

So, what kind of value did Majeda reveal or restore by burning down the money at Asia Energy's office? In the most mundane sense, what was revealed in Majeda's act were the acts of betrayal by Hussain, who had kept sacks full of money in his pantry not unlike the forest officer arrested during the emergency. Majeda's joining the pillaging crowds in this "burn-off" stemmed from anger and grievances that she had nurtured because of the violence committed by the state on their bodies, neighbors, and kin. More generally, there is something more profound and fundamental about spending that cannot be identified with a calculation, planning, or goal orientation in a commonsensical conception of resistance. Unlike in mass destruction or consumption, in the kind of expenditure described by Majeda, there is always something left over, some excessive element, some energy "that is burned off and that sets us afire" (Bataille 1985). The remainder, literally, was locatable in the ashes flying in the wind. Equally important, Majeda's excitement and humor spelled out an excess of energy that was not fully recuperable in a familiar script of popular protest.

Michael Taussig tells us that when the human body, a nation's flag, money, or a public statue is defaced, a strange surplus of negative energy is likely to be aroused from within the defaced thing itself (Taussig 1999). What he calls "negative energy" is similar to George Bataille's concept of "heterogeneous" energy. In the energy regime of Bataille, ritual or sacrifice entails a production and consumption of energy that is not stockpiled or quantified in the same way as are raw materials or energy resources used in industrial societies. It is different from the "homogenous" energy, which is merely the power to do work and generate (apparent) order (Bataille 1985; Stoekl 2007). The energy stored in and released from a strip-mined mound of coal, for example, is qualitatively different from the bodily energy discharged at the contact of an eroticized object. Money, no doubt, falls into the category of potent things that can be defaced as do many other symbols of state power.

Georg Simmel has famously drawn an analogy between the erotics of sex work and the money form. Of all human relationships, Simmel says, "prostitution is the most striking instance of mutual degradation to a mere means." This is the most fundamental factor that places it in a historical relationship to the money economy, "the economy of 'means' in the strictest sense" (1978: 408). This particular episode from Phulbari, however, adds a different meaning to the so-called isomorphism of the two of which Simmel has written (409). No more a mere means, Majeda's burning of cash elevated both her and the money she had burned from their "purely generic content," another common feature Simmel identifies between currency and sex work. Their individual distinctions were produced anew by an act through which the identity of the collaborator was sealed, while that of Majeda's was refashioned. She transformed and transcended her previously established role as a "public woman," albeit as a part of a crowd whose ability to reason and efforts at seeing were suspect. Caught in the midst of an emergent crisis of representation when allegations of collaboration saturated the public sphere, through this collective act of plunder, Majeda created value as an individual as well as a member of a protesting crowd.

The ethnographic moments in this chapter are moments of encounter; in one way or another, they lead to revelations—of an uncovering of things and processes that were hidden from plain view or were "secretly familiar," as Taussig would say. For Saiful Islam, the foreigner who had offered five dollars out of amusement and appreciation inadvertently revealed a dangerous potentiality about him and his foreignness. The spectacle of plunder that Majeda remembered unmasked Hussain as a collaborator: why would anyone try to hide money in sacks *with* or *as* condiment, she wondered. And the teashop boy, who reacted positively but pointedly to the Tk. 10 bill that I had given him, proved what was already circulating as public knowledge. Revealing the secret only compounded the suspicions of collaboration and the dangerous power of money that it relied on. It was in the burning of money that defacement took its most spectacular form. Money was burned *because* it was valuable. And it was more so as its charred remains were scattered in the wind, offering further evidence of its expenditure.

Despite being touted as a universal form of value, not all money is equal or interchangeable. Anthropology has been particularly effective in demystifying the commonplace about money being a transcendental object unmoored by cultural norms (Parry and Bloch 1989). The elaborate rules by which people use and earmark monies evidence how money is

infused with doubts, fears, and desires that are specific to the cultural contexts in which it circulates (Foster 1998; Senders and Truitt 2007; Zelizer
1994). Certain money can be associated with the foreign and therefore suspect, but it is also often incorporated, encompassed, and relocalized or
resacralized (Maurer 2006). Collectors' money is carefully kept out of
circulation, as my artist friend in Phulbari reminded me. Its value lies
precisely in the nonexchangeability of the bills or coins—secure, station-
ary, and on display like objects of art. The episode was also telling of a
different kind of relationship to money that I believe has been symptomatic of the movement against coal mining in Phulbari, and to a certain
extent that of Bangladeshi political culture immediately following the
declaration of the state of emergency. Its significance exceeds the mere
observation that people value different monies differently.

At one level, in the transaction between the artist and the Asia Energy employee, two parties of extremely asymmetrical power relations met
in a chance encounter. Their interaction was an exchange in which certain value was created at the cost of others, as in the refusal of future commercial exchange with the mining company. At another level, the artist's
coming face to face with the five-dollar bill, offered casually and uncon-
ditionally, garnered suspicion that was stoked by a gift whose origin was
partially known, a form of expenditure unaccounted for by productive
labor. The bill stimulated speculations as to the very motivation of giving. For our artist, the bill was a symbol of the powers of reckless capital
and the notorious energy company that channeled them. It was a token
of the type of corrupt exchanges for which important people, such as the
former heads of state, were sent to jail. Its momentary unveiling made
people wonder about that which remained unseen.

Because of her profession, which was widely known but rarely discussed, Majeda herself was a public secret. The act of defacement, which
she performed again in her narration, was a gesture whereby she achieved
certain publicity in the community that was quite different from before.
Her jest and laughter as much as her thoughts and memories warrant a
more situated analysis of the contours of crowd politics. Majeda's memories or the paintings of Saiful Islam were texts that aided their authors in
ethical, moral, and political self-fashioning. Still, there were significant

differences. While Islam's artwork was an elegy to productive labor in-commensurable to wage labor, Majeda's involvement in the destruction of something as valuable as cash disturbed the preeminence of economic concerns in both the discourses for and against mining. In both cases, however, the impetus was to restrict or destroy bad money. With Majeda, unlike with the painting, there was no counterpoint to the evil of dirty money; there was only destruction. The plunder made possible a shift in which her heroism, as opposed to abjection, was publicized.

Following David Graeber, I have suggested earlier that in moments of revolutionary upheaval, commodities turn into pivots between imagi-nation and reality. In Bangladesh, at least during the period of the emer-gency, cash had become the commodity whose disconcerting presence revealed varied imaginations of the valuable. By focusing on the minu-tiae of crowd politics in Phulbari, I argue that while the productive ap-proach to value turned the anti-mining movement into a familiar though important form of resistance, the expenditure approach brought to atten-tion the excess, volatility, and political agency of the crowd. It was premised on a different mode of "seeing" than that proffered in the state-led project of transparency.

In 2014, in response to governmental plans for a new price hike in con-sumer electricity supply, an opinion piece came out in a prominent national daily (Muhammad 2014a). It panned the Bangladesh Energy Regulatory Commission's proposal to increase the price of electricity for the sixth time in a span of a few years. In 2009, the average price of electricity production was Tk. 2, which became Tk. 6 by 2014, the year the article was published. The author, who is one of the most ardent spokespeople for Phulbari and a noted public intellectual, identified corruption, un-necessary dependence on foreign companies and expertise, and poor main-tenance of infrastructure as reasons for the higher price of energy produc-tion. Interestingly, a cartoon accompanies the article that, in the spirit of Saiful Islam's painting, also stages an unequal encounter (figure 5). The corpulent figure in suit and tie on the left with his distended belly, a telltale sign of excess consumption, faces a peasant on the right. The lat-ter holds a machete, though more as a tool than as a weapon. Bank bills are peeking from the pocket of the well-heeled man. In place of a head,

FIGURE 5 *Source*: "বিদ্যুৎও চাই, অযথা বেশি দামও নয়" (translation: "More Power, but Less Price Hike"). *Prothom Alo*, http://www.prothom-alo.com/opinion/article /167037/বিদ্যুৎও_চাই_অযথা_বেশি_দামও_নয়. Tuli/*Prothom Alo*.

the man has a bulb lit with a sign of the national currency. He is unrecognizable. Defaced, one could say.

The headless man's power emanates, as it were, through electricity that is still out of reach to many rural and urban Bangladeshis, and it is about to get costlier, the article tells us. Electricity is increasingly not a service that the state provides for its citizens, but a product sold to citizens turned consumers. Here, then, is yet another representation of an encounter that demands defacement. What is unclear is whether this would lead to the kind of productive resistance Saiful Islam had ascribed to his peasant, or the plunder in which Majeda and the crowds had participated. The demeanor of the two characters suggests, however, that what we are seeing here is in fact a deferral of politics. In a changed national scenario with an ostensibly democratic government in power but a rise in the privatization of basic services and ordinary violence, what possibilities of the political remain are yet to be revealed (Hashmi 2017). That money is obstinately at the center of these iconographies of encounters is worth our ethnographic attention.

CHAPTER 3

ACCIDENTAL POLITICS

A MYSTERY DEATH AND A TOWN IN UPROAR

Accidents have been constitutive of the protest culture in Phulbari. The tragic and by some accounts accidental death of Nasreen Huq, a well-known human rights activist, is now an important episode in the anti-mining agitations. A senior employee of Action Aid in Bangladesh, Huq had been vocal against Asia Energy's activities in its early days long before the deadly climax of August 2006. She had "stumbled across" a dossier with important information about the corporation's controversial dealings regarding the Phulbari Coal Project (P. Karim 2006). She had even met with its country representatives in February 2006. According to reports, including one that quotes her sister Shireen Huq, the U.K. Department for International Development had expressed concerns about Nasreen Huq's involvement in the coal-mining issue. David Wood, the head of the organization, is said to have personally asked her to stop campaigning for the cause. Shireen Huq reminisced soon after her sister's death: "I remember [Nasreen] was furious. She said, 'They think they are the East India Company, telling us to leave Asia Energy alone because Action Aid is a British organization'" (Doward and Haider 2006). Nasreen Huq was killed in April 2006 when her chauffeur, also a member of Action Aid staff, hit her as he was backing up the car in the driveway of her home in Dhaka. Head of media at Action Aid Jane

Mayo referred to Huq's death as a "tragic accident." She believed that the driver's foot had slipped and gone down on the accelerator instead of the brake.

The case of Nasreen Huq's death has become the proverbial litmus test of one's ideological allegiance in regard to foreign investment and its effects on development. Overshadowed in this overdetermined confusion is the centrality of accident, which often characterizes crowd politics that encompasses the ideological and the affective. The accident serves as a portal from the neighborly to the state and the intimate to the political. While accidents become enframed in local political and cultural logics, they are also generative of them. Existing cultural frameworks seek to recuperate the accidental, but each accident also evokes a sense of the force of the accident as an event open to contingency. Accidents, then, bring our attention to the indeterminacy and excess of crowd politics, and in so doing, show how "the accidental" contributes to a more comprehensive understanding of embodied political engagement.

Many well-known participants in the Phulbari movement were what one might call "accidental activists," whose bravery or loss was later sublimated as political activism. And yet, to foreground accident in relation to a political movement runs the risk of trivializing it. Here I do so not in order to suggest that the densely charged and largely successful mobilization in Phulbari was a mere culmination of unintended convergences and chance happenings. That would be ventriloquizing the voices of its most vehement opponents—the energy company, the state, and the transnational allies of both, namely a group of powerful financial brokers such as investment banks, hedge funds, donor agencies, and a handful of developed nations, each with its own stake in the mining project.

In the aftermath of the violence in Phulbari and a few months after Nasreen Huq's death, the U.K.-based *Observer* wrote in a tone that was worthy of the controversy surrounding this event/accident:

> The truth died with Nasreen Huq on 24 April, the day a car rammed her against a wall, expunging a life in the 48th year. The private conversations she had with senior governmental officials in the weeks before her death went with her to the grave. But the ghost of the popular human rights activist has

since continued to weave a haunting narrative which sweeps back and forth between Whitehall and the Indian sub-continent, and seems to have come straight from the pages of a John le Carré novel. (Doward and Haider 2006)

The title of the piece, "The mystery death, a town in uproar and a $1bn UK mines deal," along with the rest of the write-up. plays with the generic conventions of blockbuster fiction. In that very gesture, however, the article betrays an affect that is emblematic of rational disavowals of rumors that are said to traverse a hypermediated globe at dizzying speed. Though sympathetic to the cause for which Nasreen Huq had fought and possibly died, the report, regardless of its final, emancipatory political message, reproduces the binary of rational explanation and unsubstantiated speculations—between crime and accident—that informed the social life of this event. Naturalizing an apparent cultural trend, it reports in the self-assured voice of secular reason: "The manner of Nasreen's death has fuelled conspiracy theories in a country where they are as common as rain" (Doward and Haider 2006).

Accidents have cropped up in Phulbari in unexpected ways. Its polysemy was apparent in the ways in which people shared their experiences of the political turmoil. Many of them had become involved in the mining agitations in a manner that can only be described as accidental. These chance happenings resulted in individual and collective politicization. To understand the political possibilities of accidents and to assess their ethnographic significance, here I approach "the accidental" both literally and conceptually. Can accidents be political? Are they gendered? What kinds of politics take shape in the wake of an accident? To put it differently, what are the ethico-political possibilities that are made available, or are foreclosed, within various discourses of the accidental? Anthropological perspectives on accidents, I argue here, could rescue the concept from its usual modernist and technicist moorings while opening up spaces of radical contingencies. I suggest that rethinking the accidental demands a rethinking of the political.

Here, I follow two figures that had become linked in intimate ways to the protests in Phulbari. The first is Majeda (pseudonym), who became popular due to her express conviction and actions against the coal mines; the second is Tarikul, who was shot dead when he joined the giant procession on August 26. We met Majeda in chapter 2, when she spoke about her joining a crowd of protesters. This chapter centers on the theme of accident that dominated her retelling of the events in Phulbari. Unlike Nasreen Huq, who, as an elite development worker, was publicly vocal against the mining venture, neither Majeda nor Tarikul was a trained activist. Majeda was a well-known protester who directly challenged state power and the muscle flexing of the mining company; Tarikul was primarily known and later iconized as one of the three martyrs of Phulbari. Majeda's accidental entry into politics and subsequent celebrity made it possible for her to articulate grievances that went beyond the violence around mining. In that sense, it had revolutionary effects. The reminiscences about Tarikul, particularly those featured in my conversations with his mother, on the other hand, generate a more ambivalent set of meanings around the accidental that are not reducible to either progressive or counterrevolutionary politics. Together, their narratives point to the affective, intimate, and contingent nature of crowd politics.

At a literal level, the word "accident" in circulation in Phulbari followed its conventional usage in English as well as in Bangla where the English original is habitually inserted in everyday speech. The Bangla synonyms for "accident" are *durghatona* or *aghaton*. Both are ill-fated events. They are happenings that are exclusively bad, negative, or evil depending on the various connotations of the prefixes *duh-* and *a-*. For instance, the first is a common everyday word for road traffic accidents; the latter covers mishaps of all kinds, minor or significant, violent or harmless. Accidental does not have a single-word equivalent in Bangla, but accident, in the English original, inserts itself frequently at unexpected places and at inopportune moments, thereby mimicking the phenomenon it signifies.

Theoretically, accidents point to the frequent and unexpected convergences that interrupt the temporal sequence and conceptual coherence commonly assumed in the notion of an event. Accidental is that whose agent remains uncertain and whose meanings cannot be completely recuperated in a temporally coherent narrative, thus opening up a space for radical, or at the least, imperceptible politics. The ethnographic value of the term lies in its capacity to span the temporal and the affective qualities of "things that crop up" (Stewart 2007). In other words, it contains within it the germ of its own disruption. When applied to ethnographic situations, it forces us to pay attention to the intimate nature of public events, and to consider the political potential of the sudden, the uncontrollable, and the unexpected.

Brian Massumi calls the time of accident as criticality: "Criticality is when what are normally mutually exclusive alternatives pack into the materiality of the system." But it is a system that no longer acts and outwardly reacts according to physical laws unfolding in a linear fashion. "It is churning, running over its own possible states" (Massumi 1998). Accident for Massumi is pure, senseless urgency. Yet, the "chaotic" interlude is in fact a super-ordered state. Paul Virilio sees accidents as what lies beneath any knowledge, or more particularly technoscientific knowledge (Virilio 2007). Virilio concerns himself with accidents that happen in the course of its progress, "as though this 'temporary failure' was not itself programmed, in a way, when the product was first put to use." The local accident located here and there, Virilio notes, is trumped by the great accident, "the global accident that integrates, one by one, a whole set of minor incidents along the way that once characterized societal life" (Virilio 2007: 49). Both Massumi and Virilio discuss accidents in terms of the technicity and modernity of our times. They render "societal life" if not a thing of the past then at least one subsumed in or potentially undermined by a global system. My argument, emerging from both routine life and spectacular violence in Phulbari, rests instead on the cultural work that accident does in forging or splintering societal life. For the purposes of this chapter, the accident is a descriptor as well as an organizing principle.

"THEY WENT DIRECTLY INTO *ACCIDENT*"

In Phulbari, the coal itself was not seen, but a bleak horizon signaling a disemboweled land was reflected in the murky water of the canals that cut through the dense paddy fields. They carried the coal-soaked water from Barapukuria, an underground coal mine ten miles away. The contrast between the gray of the water and the green of the crops added luster to a surface that was already overwhelmingly lush. The canals brought along the dirt to dump it into a river in Phulbari. Farmers standing ankle-deep in the slippery mud of well-watered rice fields yelled out their answers to my question about whether fish survived in the water: they did, but nobody ate them. The mining company itself acknowledged that the untreated water that passed through farming areas contained phosphorous, arsenic, and magnesium.

Violent traces on the bodies of people and their land made up this political landscape, which was also a storied cultural real (Stewart 1996). Here, facts became rallying points for unmet demands and long-standing grievances, but the stories that people recounted and those they claimed to have heard straddled that stubborn divide between information and imagination. It is through their (re)telling that events became accidents and the latter retrospectively became originary moments in a clear-cut sequence of cause and effect. People at the forefront of the struggles publicly swore on the blood of those who were killed and promised to retaliate with violence when necessary. "We'll break your leg if you're a *khonir lok*" (a person of the mines), a woman yelled at me while cleaning dishes in a village courtyard. Elevating the fallen to the status of martyrdom, the three names—Tarikul, Salekin, and Amin—have been permanently etched on a monument that stood as a concrete reminder of state terror.

The marks left on the environment were even less subtle where the canals originated. Because of a steady pumping out of underground water for use in the mines, the land in its vicinity had been sinking at an alarming rate. The starkly uneven surfaces inside houses, in the courtyards, and across agricultural land already looked like a minor earthquake had left marks in its wake. The houses were so close to the restricted zone that television sets and glass surfaces of furniture inside them shattered in the reverberations from the explosions targeted to open up underground mine faces. Still, the similitude to a natural disaster could hardly mask the reality of a man-made crime. Officials estimated, no doubt conservatively, that an area spanning four square kilometers would sink about two meters in the foreseeable future.

In 2007, a British mining expert who was visiting the same coal mine was killed in an accident. This was months after the paramilitary violence. Four hundred and thirty meters under the surface, he was said to have been exposed to poisonous gas leaks, which have since hindered coal extraction from one of the mine shafts, thus locking in over a million dollars' worth of machinery. According to news reports, in April 2007, the sixty-two-year-old mining ventilation expert Albert Brains Davis and a fellow British visitor both fainted during a tour of the No. 1110 coalface. It had been abandoned for almost a year due to high carbon monoxide emissions. Davis was pronounced dead at the hospital, and a "high-level" committee was set up by Petrobangla to investigate the reason for his death. Activists and locals who kept up with the news were adamant in calling it sabotage, resisting the emplotment of the event as accidental. The deaths in the belly of the mine, otherwise fairly common in underground mines, could bolster the case for open-pit mining, which despite its disastrous effects on the environment is considered safer for the miners. Because the shock of a foreigner's death would bring home the dangers of underground mining, it would work as the perfect alibi for giving the final nod for the open-cut method. Or so did the reasoning go. Another mishap in 2010 that killed one worker and injured nineteen others, if anything, revealed the deeply flawed and severely inadequate safety provisions at the 2,500-acre underground mine, portending a bleak future for those who would be working in the deep and sprawling craters.

On my many trips around the township and the surrounding villages, rickshaw pullers and fellow passengers volunteered to point to the exact spot where someone was hit by a bullet on August 26 or from where it was shot. But these facts only made sense by paying heed to what Michael Taussig calls "terror's talk." "What matters for terror is how it is passed from mouth to mouth across a nation, from page to page, from image to body" (Taussig 1997). A young and friendly rickshaw puller barely in his twenties remembered an event as he stopped the rickshaw on the side of the highway that ran from the capital through to the country's northern border. The incident he recalled involved twelve or thirteen corpses that were taken out from the mines on a truck in the dark of night to cover up a terrible accident. The bodies were those of miners. The Chinese who oversaw the mines were involved, he was confident. I heard the story only from him, but the deep paranoia that accompanied his retelling was proof enough that in this "state of emergency," the matter-of-factness of production became anything but matter-of-fact, and facticity itself was rendered marvelous (Taussig 1997).

Take Majeda's recollections, for instance. A poor woman in her forties living in the Phulbari municipality, she had inspired her neighbors to physically challenge the paramilitary. They had come out of their houses to protest the intrusion into their neighborhood and the local mosque, and started a procession chanting slogans, which significantly helped in ending the impasse that had debilitated regular life in Phulbari for a few days after the confrontation between the crowds and the armed forces. Majeda was a highly celebrated figure in the narrative of Phulbari's resistance, as I have explained in Chapter 2. She was also pregnant during the 2006 violence when she fell down after the BDR[1] had pushed her. It is the theme of physical and other violence that she picked up again in our conversation the second day, but through a detour: "Listen, the bottom line is, we didn't have any problem [that led us to] this movement. We didn't have any headache about it. It became a headache when they were beating up the *commissioner*. It was only out of the responsibility of a sister toward her brother. Apart from that, we had no other problems."

Majeda made a point that surfaced repeatedly in her memories of how she came to join the agitations. It began with the physical harassment of a local benefactor. Originally from the same neighborhood as Majeda, he and Majeda shared fond memories of their childhood. At the time of our conversation, he had been in charge of one of the wards of Phulbari Municipality (*pourosabha*). Wards are the administrative units into which urban space is divided across Bangladesh. Let us call him Akhter.

Majeda's deep affinity with Akhter that bordered on kinship was one of the main reasons for her involvement in a struggle in which she saw her own membership as an accident rather than as a premeditated, ideologically driven intervention. And this despite her admission that at this point the movement had already acquired a kind of mass character. Satellite TV channels, print media, and independent Internet activists had not missed out on the potential import of the powerful imagery of rural and working-class women protesting or taking to the street (see figure 6). Despite an unsure beginning, when she had no desire to join the cause

FIGURE 6 An anti-mining propaganda calendar featuring the women of
Phulbari. The slogan calls for resisting foreign capital and protecting Phulbari,
the land, and the environment. Photo by the author.

but only decided to confront the forces because they were harassing a close acquaintance and a patron, she now saw herself as an integral part of it. Over time her accidental entry into Phulbari's political life had become a token of collective actions, although the two factors that had motivated her actions were anger against injustice and intense courage.

> Everybody had become mute (*stabdha*). These people, these people [pointing around her], they had become mute. There was shooting. People were killed. Everything became mute . . . Even if they went ahead with the coal mine, nobody was going to come out because of fear, you know? . . . When Akhter *Bhai* [brother] got beaten up, anger rose in me. Then having seen me . . . everyone else . . . they said, "If a woman can come out how come we, the men are sitting back?" All the women came out, you know! They could have taken this opportunity to . . . "Why did you [referring to the paramilitary] have to enter the village," right? They were some ruffians [*badmaish*].

Chronologically speaking, on August 27, 2006, when Majeda charged back at the BDR with a machete and became the voice of the crowd that had become "mute" (*stabdha*) in fear, she was pushed and shoved by the border patrol guards. She still managed to mobilize crowd support (although at first when she looked back "there was not even an ant" behind her), and in the process, violated the Section 144 rule that was unofficially invoked in the township following the killings.[2] She and a few other neighbors then went on to vent their anger by attacking the properties of *dalal*s (agents or traitors). *Dalal*s were people suspected of maintaining ties with Asia Energy and benefiting from those connections. This atmosphere of collective agitation lasted for a couple of days. It was the "victory procession" (*bijay michhil*) on August 30 celebrating the treaty that marked an end to her stint in politics.[3] She was then sent to her husband's family home outside of Phulbari. In June 2007, ten months later, when we were talking, her husband was still wondering if something could happen to Majeda should the government give a final go-ahead to mining.

The careful and caring act on her husband's part notwithstanding, Majeda's involvement was by then a public fact, which even caught her by surprise. She enacted a comical back and forth between her and the strangers who now recognized her as a political figure:

> Wherever I go, whether to my in-laws in Natore, whether I go to Natore, Jaipurhat[4] . . . go home, people just look at my face and ask me questions. Many people ask me: "*Apa* [older sister], where is your home?"
>
> "Why, *bhai* [brother]?"
>
> "Do you live in Phulbari?"
>
> "No, *bhai*, I don't live in Phulbari."
>
> "No, no, your home is in Phulbari! We have seen you on TV."
>
> "Eh, you have been mistaken." . . . Many times, when I'd get on a train, I'd see people staring at my face. . . . Akhter Bhai says, "She is world, world famous [*bishwa parichita*]." Akhter Bhai would say, "Majeda, why do you worry? Why? I have made you world [famous]."

The technomediatic environment cocreated by television, mobile phones, news coverage, and voice recorders helped Majeda become a celebrity in her own eyes and those of others. The communicative circuitry proved crucial in convincing her of the significance of her contribution to the movement that now overcame its deeply personal beginning. Mass mediation helped social actors such as Majeda in becoming aware of their own massness (Morris 2008a). When I asked her how she knew what happened in Phulbari while she was gone, she mentioned being in regular correspondence with her mother and with Akhter Bhai over "mobile." Her in-laws had been aware of what had happened because they saw her on TV. She herself saw the events unfold on television.

> They beat up the son of that fisherman's wife in our neighborhood. They beat him. We saw it on TV. They showed it towards the evening. [The journalists] are the ones who recorded [the scene]. Otherwise how could we have seen it? They beat up that boy. He was killed by a gunshot. The boy fell down. Even then with their shoes, they propped him up with their shoes, then again with their gun, with the pistol [I think she meant bayonet] of their gun they hit him again, although he was already dying. We saw it on TV. Now you see how much they tortured people. They became animals and were not humans anymore. . . . They couldn't have done this if they were humans. They had become animals.

At one level, Majeda had accidentally stepped into history when she became witness to an injustice that nobody else protested. This inhumanity challenged regular communication. At another level, the succession of the events, her getting caught up in them, and her becoming aware of the role she played were articulated by a delayed temporality that was retrospective because it was telemediated. Paul Virilio puts it well when he elaborates on the relationship between television and accident. On television, he observes, "history becomes accidental through the abrupt telescoping of facts and the collision of events once successive that have become simultaneous, despite the distances and time lapses once necessary to their interpretation" (Virilio 2007: 26). Media changes the speed at which one views time. This not only overexposes accidents but also causes more accidents in the future. Contrary to her seeming desire to remain incognito, people far and wide recognized Majeda for who they thought she was—a courageous activist from Phulbari. She kept up with the news through regular phone conversations. And, even from up close, her experience of violence was technologically enhanced: she saw the atrocities of the BDR on television, which made her aware of the profundity of the events. Her stumbling into politics acquired significance through similar mediations that included a collective gaze that she shared with innumerable strangers in the empty homogenous time of TV watching (cf. Anderson 1991). At the end, it made her "world famous."

In a curious substitution, Majeda used the word "accident" to mean what could best be translated as "action." An accident, as I said before, is that whose agent is uncertain and whose meanings are difficult to be completely recuperated within coherent terms of representation. Explaining, for example, what she would do if the mines forced them to relocate, Majeda complained that the energy company, instead of helping them out, "went directly into accident." That was the reason behind her current ideological position regarding the movement.

> This was not part of the deal . . . First we heard that we would be given some money. A little bit of money. And they said if they didn't give us money they'd find us some refuge; like they have offered in *guchhagrams* [model villages], they would make homes for us, they said. But, no, they went directly

into *accident* [in English]. That's not what they did. If they benefit from all sides, they need to offer some benefits to us, the poor people, too. But they are not giving us any.

For Majeda, accident is the name for the unexpected and uncalled-for violence unleashed by Asia Energy or the BDR (the two become one as "they" in most of our conversations) against ordinary people that ranged from indiscriminate bodily harm to broken promises of relocation or compensation. The physical attacks were not part of the deal. Majeda and the other people directly affected by mining were waiting for the promised compensation, in cash or in kind. What came instead were shootings and beatings, unsolicited and unnecessary, just like an accident, as Majeda herself revealed through this semantic substitution.

THE GENDER OF THE ACCIDENT

If the accidental, yet revolutionary status awarded to Majeda helped strategically recast gender for the sake of the movement, it came with a cost. The persistent invocations of husband, *shoshurbari* (affinal home), marriage, and family may have been her way of mitigating a public persona to make it more congruent with the image of an average wife. These concepts are crucial nodes in the progression of an adult woman's life whose ideal place is the home of her husband.[5] "All that we women want is a little happiness [*sukh*]," was one of her pronouncements that aimed at universalizing and downplaying the needs of her gender with small-scale desires and ordinary affects (Stewart 2007).

Majeda's narrative revealed an ongoing tension between her personae that vacillated between what I call "ideal feminine" and "public political." The constant movement between the two, one in which Majeda highlighted her role as a wife and the other in which she owned up to her revolutionary status, was symptomatic of the difficulties of the deeply gendered context of her politics. The exchange below, which follows the sequence of a longer conversation, exposes the tension. Here, Majeda was expressing her displeasure at various injustices that took place after the confrontations on August 26. She was upset that some people had lied and asked for monetary compensation from the authorities for damages

that had nothing to do with the protests. These little acts of disingenu-
ousness made her angry:

> There's a [proper] place to show anger. If ten people consider you bad [*kharap*],
> even Allah will consider you bad. If ten people don't love you, Allah won't
> love you. . . . Sometimes I get so angry, so angry, but look at him [pointing
> at her husband], he has no anger. No anger. . . . And the husband with whom
> I had that daughter . . . I used to earn a lot. I got beaten up as much as I used
> to earn. I have the scars of his beating on my body. And then my hands and
> feet got wounded in the coal mine [incident]. The BDR pushed me and I
> fell down. Then consider these other problems that I have. . . . Here, here
> [shows me the bruises].

Both public and domestic violence left visible wounds the same way
accidents leave traces—on both minds and bodies. Accidents that happen due to unfettered expansion of resource-based capital leave wounds
on the earth. Perhaps this is why shock and trauma have both been used
to describe injuries that take a toll on the mind, the body, and the lived
environment (Caruth 1996; Freud 1950 [1920]; Klein 2007). Wounds in the
psyche manifest themselves as neuroses, as untimely, anachronistic, and
unexpected outbursts or symptoms. Language takes the brunt of this.
There is either no language or too much of it. Environmental accidents
are also often spectacular, but like the workings of the mind, the workings of nature too may remain invisible for some time or take forms that
may not be identifiable as disaster yet.

For Majeda, the scars from an ill-tempered husband's abuse overlapped
with those she acquired in a more recent and public struggle, which in an
ironic turn of events also made her famous. The importance of the public
gaze is pivotal to all this. The approval of "ten people" (*dosh jon*) was as
important as that of the divinity. *Dosh jon* in Bangla is a symbolic collectivity that conventionally indexes a representative section of society;
as a collectivity, it is a form of anonymous public. In Majeda's enuncia-
tion, it was still modeled on the face-to-face sociality of village life. As
such, it captures the traffic between intimacy and anonymity that is inherent to any form of effective political communication (Mazzarella 2009;
Warner 2002).

The bruises on Majeda's arms from BDR's beating were discursively inseparable from older wounds that she insisted were still visible in places where her husband had burned her. Her body was a palimpsest of injurious signs where previous wounds survived despite the treatments she had received for them under—and along with—fresh injuries. These bodily marks due to domestic and public violence served multiple communicative functions, turning her body into a field of communication (Aretxaga 1997; Feldman 1991; Scarry 1985). Political violence is a mode of transcription, Allen Feldman writes, but this transcription requires agency, "both the communicative activity of the transcriber and the transcribed 'object'" (1991). Struggles occur between the "adversarial transcripts" that accelerate the body's subjectivation. What unifies the photograph of the placard-bearing Jew made famous by Walter Benjamin and the bodies violently staged as political texts in Northern Ireland described by Feldman is "the process by which an entity violently expelled from the social order is transformed into an emissary, a cultural donor and bearer of seminal political messages" (1991). Begoña Aretxaga has found that gendered bodies and sexual violence added more elements to the production of subjectivities through violence in her research on women's political practices, also in Northern Ireland (Aretxaga 1997). Rosalind Morris reaches a similar conclusion when she describes sexual violence working as a metonym of political violence in post-apartheid South Africa (Morris 2006).

While making her body available to a similar reading, one in which gendered violence and accidental violence become one and the same, Majeda was worried about being considered *kharap* by others. *Kharap* (bad) is habitually tossed around to refer to "wayward" women, similar to the way "loose" serves the purpose in English. The struggles over the body's textuality were clearly reflected in Majeda's use of categories that are routinely mobilized to describe, define, or discredit women.

> But I am not good [*bhalo na*] myself, you see. My mother wanted to protest. I didn't let her. I am the one who is not good. To whom would my mother complain? My mother took me away and tied me down with a chain. My father beat me up. They put me in chains. They locked me up. I cut the chain with my teeth and came out. Who am I? I am not good either. So who doesn't have pain in her life?

"Who am I?" she asked rhetorically, but only as a ploy to enact an ab-jection. Majeda's self-image, her insistence on presenting herself as "not good," *bhalo na* or *kharap*, was foremost an admission of guilt in not being a proper wife. This discursive self-berating was a part of a larger effort to present herself as an ideal woman who deserved a husband's wrath when "bad" and an adult daughter who was perpetually disciplined by parents where the family was clearly a metonym for society (*dosh jon*). It judged and punished those who strayed from sanctioned social trajectories. A constant struggle made itself known through her words between a politically aware self and a model feminine self. The latter in its ideal-typical form was extra-political, or "juxtapolitical" as Lauren Berlant would have it (2008), although Majeda's political persona relied fundamentally on her gender.

But lest we privilege this aspect of the narrative and take her abjec-tion at face value, here is a snippet of the exchange that took place be-tween us within the next minute:

> Author: How did you get rid of that husband? [Literally, "How did you get him off your shoulders?"]
>
> Majeda: How did I get rid of him? I went directly to the court and divorced him. It's impossible to tolerate this. I am getting old too.
>
> Author: You should have done it sooner.
>
> Majeda: My life, I didn't get a life partner like [I wanted]. . . . See, if one man does wrong all men get blamed for it, but men are by nature greedy [*lobhi*]. . . . Now, you are working. You are putting a lot of labor into this. But if your husband today, like if you get 10 *taka* for this work and your husband hits you and takes it away from you, then how can you stay at that home? . . . So these are the stories I have in my life. My husband bothered me a lot. Seriously bothered me. . . . That's men for you. Men are inherently greedy. Now you'll get to work and you'll take a good boy along with you, like the one you've brought here [pointing to my research assistant]. You have taken a boy to accompany you. Their [men's] gaze is so bad that they will start seeing you differently.

This was not the first time that Majeda invoked the law during our conversation. At one moment in their mutual bantering (common between her and her husband during our meetings), her husband mockingly threatened to take off with their daughter after Majeda claimed, rhetorically, that she was strong enough to live without her child. As he challenged her declaration of such extra-human mental strength, she reciprocated with a threat cloaked in legal-speak that betrayed a clear understanding of the workings of the law; all she would have to do, she said, was to go to the court and make them issue an order. The husband would be bound by law to bring the daughter back because she was the mother and their daughter was still an infant.

And here again she claimed to have sought recourse to the law when her previous husband's torture had become intolerable. *Ami soja court-e gesi*, "I went straight to court," she said with the confidence of someone well versed in a discourse of rights and familiar enough with the state that backs it and gives it potency by inscribing it in/as law. This is the same person, we may recall, who charged back—armed—at a state agent, was part of a plundering crowd, and at one point confessed that she nurtured a distinct urge to fake love and then poison all those greedy men who lust after women, bribe them into relationships, and then deprive them of physical intimacy.

Majeda was not unique in embodying what may well be described as the constitutive ambivalence of liberalism. Similar everyday invocation of the discourses of the law has been observed in relation to sexual and political violence in a South African mining community as well. Echoing Rosalind Morris's reading of subaltern relationships to law that in post-apartheid South Africa had themselves become spectralized (Comaroff and Comaroff 2006), one can describe Majeda as someone who transgresses the law while summoning it; she is convinced of her own sovereignty while simultaneously believing it to emanate from law, and despite her bravado, seeks recognition of it from the state (Morris 2006). But as is apparent in Majeda's case, this invocation did not stop at the level of a threat devoid of practical consequences. She did succeed in divorcing an abusive husband. There was no doubt that she would pursue a similar course of action in the future should her present husband try to deny her child custody.

Law was only one part of this discourse that moved precariously between empowerment and abjection. While it is important to remember that men are universally greedy and women should be aware of this, as women "we" are perpetually under "their" gaze, according to Majeda. By using "we," Majeda extended me a membership in this wronged collective. Despite being a city-dwelling, foreign-educated, professional woman (she thought I was a journalist), I was hardly beyond the gendered sign-system of Phulbari's everyday life, as Majeda was honest enough to bring to my notice. In this "regard," the professional relationship between my male research companion and me was still tainted by a universal, masculinist perspective that generated scandalous speculations.

The politics around Majeda's public visibility—her accidentally becoming a member of a pillaging crowd and later a dedicated activist—is to be understood in an anxiously moralizing cultural backdrop. Majeda, for example, was not the only one to hint at the rumors circulating about me, my socializing with the activists (almost all men), and my friend, a young man from Phulbari, in whose company I was constantly seen in public. As the months went by and my participation at the early-evening gatherings of activists became somewhat ritualized, I became privy to a genre of humor that revealed the gendered perspective of which Majeda spoke so passionately. "Wives are like a ball of yarn; the harder you try to pull it in, the more tangled it gets," a man joked as he and his friends were teasing one another about their investment in marital life. This was gauged by the husbands' involvement in or distance from such domestic chores as shopping. The bantering, I should add, was taking place toward the end of Ramadan, a time of frantic shopping for Eid (the end of the month of fasting), when both men and women are socially and religiously obligated to give to family, friends, and charity.

While in the realm of the domestic women boasted of feminine righteousness, in public gatherings of male activists, womanly virtue was reified and suspect at the same time. Once a middle-aged male political activist talked about how he urged people to join the anti-mining cause. He said he distinctly remembered trying to humiliate and provoke them: "I said we would make them wear bangles taken from a prostitute." Wearing a piece of feminine jewelry, especially bangles, is a culturally embedded trope of emasculation; wearing a bangle of a sex worker must be all the more disgraceful, a double castration that raises the specters of other taboos and their unspeakable transgressions.

This is why Majeda's accidental entry into politics had to be told in a gendered register through which she became an ideologically driven activist and not simply an anonymous member of a crowd. Her accidents were celebrated on a distinctively feminized register of spontaneous outbursts and instantaneous surge in emotions. Or, to be more precise, in the case of Majeda, accidental was one of the only paths to politicization. Her politics was perceived to have played out on an affective mode that was befitting of her gender. The wounds that she incurred through an accident were brought to public attention; it earned her, at the least, modest monetary returns (Tk. 3,000 to be exact)[6] and unforeseen fame. The wounds that she insisted were still visible on her body were due to accidents that were best kept hidden until they could be tolerated no more. However, it should be noted that in this landscape of emotion, women's protests are primarily articulated as what James Wilce calls "troubles talk." They include small linguistic acts of resistance like criticism/accusation (*nalish, abhijog*), crying (*kannakati*), lamentation (*bilap*), and chanting or calling "God, God" (*Allah, Allah kara*) (Wilce 2003). "Bangladeshi troubles talk is emotion talk," Wilce argues, "reflecting not only on problematic external realities but also on inner states" where grumbling, for many women and certain men, is still safer than shouting (2003). Majeda's presence in public political matters was momentous because it was rare, accidental, at times even tentative, and therefore, authentic.

THE ACCIDENTAL ACTIVIST

As an analytical framework, accident provides a particular vantage point from which to appraise how and why Majeda had become a powerful token of Phulbari's revolutionary women. The recuperation that had happened in her case, however, was continually denied to another person whose life is also tragically, and accidentally, tangled with the same events. I am referring to Tarikul, or more specifically, his mother, with whom I had the opportunity to speak. Tarikul was a twenty-year-old from Phulbari who was one of the three young men killed in 2006. He was a part of the *michhil* that was trying to get to the office of Asia Energy and eventually confronted the paramilitary. In contrast to Majeda, Tarikul was the son of a well-heeled member of the local elite whose role in the mining issue was at best dubious, as was widely believed by my politically active friends. Among Phulbari's elite, local government officials and big landholders and business owners were mostly supportive of the mining project. Poor peasants, often with little or no land, small traders and laborers, such as Majeda or her husband, and some indigenous groups opposed the mines due to the potential loss of land and the insurmountable problems they generally faced receiving compensation in the absence of proper documentation and powerful kin or patrons. Tarikul's mother, in spite of being the mother of a *shahid*—a martyr—had failed to become a part of the resistance culture. The suspicions around her husband's alliance with the mining company tarnished her public profile as the one who sacrificed her son. This despite the fact that the martyr's mother is a quintessential mourning subject (Mittermaier 2015). It did not suffice in guaranteeing her an elevated status in the representational economy of the movement.

In Tarikul's mother's narrative of her son's death, accident was the single operative theme. It overwhelmed her version of how her son had become a victim of the day's events. Tarikul had no desire to join the procession. He was there only to see what was going on. After all, it was not every day that 40,000 to 50,000 people (some would say many more) congregated in Phulbari to attend a public meeting. In the midst of the chaos, his cell phone fell out of his pocket. As he was about to pick it up, a member of the BDR shot him. Had he not bent down to retrieve the phone, he would have been alive. A minor accident of a phone slipping out of his pocket eventuated in a fatal accident that was to become a critical event (Das 1995). The young man, as per his mother, was only accidentally a part of the crowd.

The role of the cell phone in setting off a deadly event could not be underestimated. From artistic representations to popular remembrances, Tarikul's mobile figured distinctively. The phone, as a source of the accident, became the pivot around which sentiments and actions took on their respective shapes. The headlines in major national dailies of the day came with large, color photographs of dead bodies on *vangaris*[7] being rushed away. Being the most readily available means to remove bodies or to carry wounded individuals to relative safety, *vangaris* were of frequent use on that day of crisis. A painting by Saiful Islam, whose work

I discussed in chapter 2, is intertextual with that other genre of visual mediation (figure 7). What readily grabs the viewer's attention about the painting is the exaggerated and undeniably surreal status of the handset. Its relative size compared to Tarikul's body, its foregrounding in the overall composition, and the details that mark its artistic reproduction enframe the death as accident. We could say of Tarikul's phone what Kathleen Stewart has said in relation to another accident at the heart of a mine-ravaged community in the Appalachian mountains, "that it stood as a graphic, literalized metaphor of the sheer impact of events on lives caught, through no fault of their own, in a local space of contingency in which things happen" (Stewart 1996: 167).

The cell phone was the cause of Tarikul's death because it stopped him from leaving the scene of danger in time. The accident, it seems, happens when ordinary communication fails, as is signified by the misplaced cell phone. Still, as an inanimate object and lacking agency of the kind ascribed to human actors, the cell phone's role in the fatality was accidental. This in no way diminished either its power or its significance, both of which were noted by Majeda and her husband:

> Husband: The son of the commissioner was killed . . . I heard his
> mobile fell off . . . [sounding unsure].
> Majeda: That was it! It fell from his pocket and when he went to pick
> up the mobile, the BDR thought he was about to throw stones at
> them. People couldn't stand the BDR. They used to throw stones
> at them. He was going to run away and the mobile slipped off.
> He was about to pick it up and they thought he was picking up a
> stone. . . . The people there who were dragging away the boy, they
> are the ones who told me. I only heard it from them. I didn't see it.
> Only heard about it.

Like any accident, Tarikul's death too was a culmination of missed cues and misrecognitions. When he bent down to pick up the phone, the BDR thought he was picking up a stone to hurl at them and reacted preemptively. Majeda could offer this explanation because she had heard eyewitness accounts of the course of events. The source of Tarikul's misfortune was still a matter of speculation between the couple who relied

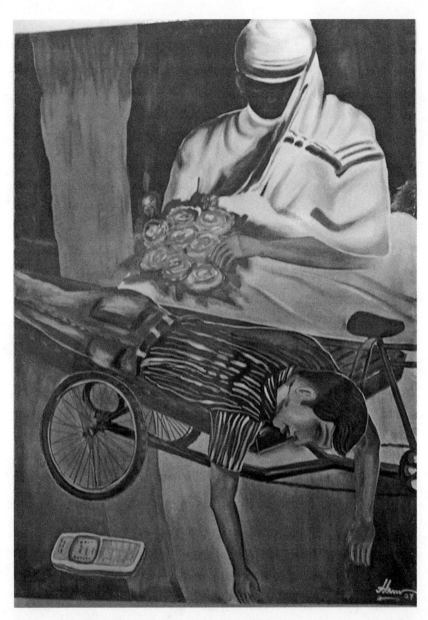

FIGURE 7 Tarikul's death as painted by Saiful Islam. Photo taken by the author with permission from the artist.

on hearsay to come to terms with an inconceivable accident: "I only heard it from them. I didn't see it. Only heard about it," she clarified.

Throwing stones at the police and other state agents was as common in this agitation as it has been elsewhere in Bangladesh and South Asia. The gesture is generally recognized as a counter-hegemonic, albeit violent and potentially dangerous strategy that crowds employ when faced with an enemy of unequal force and might. Often it is a mere tool for evoking reaction or getting attention from the powers that be. In Shahid Amin's thick description of Chauri-Chaura, stone-hurling features in a subtle yet significant fashion. Chauri-Chaura was the site of the peasant violence of 1922 perpetrated in the name of Gandhi, which in its own way changed the career of Gandhi and the course of Indian nationalism. Dissimulation was at the heart of that incident as well. Facing a crowd that just attacked a police station yelling "death to the red-turbaned bastards," the chauki-dars (watchmen) and constables were running away while shedding visible markers of state power: red turban, uniform, lathi, belt, and *mirzai*: "Siddiq ran for another six miles to the next police station and filed the first report on the riot. Badri scurried out half-clad and picked up a fistful of stones to appear like your average rioter. Jeodhan threw off his uniform and turban 'and went out with *kankar* [stones] in both hands pretending to be one of the rioters and calling out "Hit him, hit him"'" (Amin 1995).

Phulbari's Tarikul, however, was no average rioter. Devoid of any express political will, according to those who outlived him, he was a bystander who got caught up in the motions and was in a hurry to leave. The simple act of picking up a phone looked like it had a subversive motive. The accidental seemed intentional and in turn solicited violent intervention. As Majeda's husband pointed out, Tarikul had a more priv-ileged social standing than most of the people who were a part of the protests. This made his death even more extraordinary. A young boy of a rich father could only find himself in the middle of this stone-hurling crowd by accident. It had made his death all the more tragic in the eyes of Majeda and her husband.

The line between death and martyrdom is rarely settled. From the "unintentional martyrs" in Palestine who were killed while carrying groceries or looking out the window (Allen 2006) to the suicide of Mohammad Bouazizi, the fruit vendor in Tunisia, the making of martyrs often has little do with their own intentions. As the crowds in Tunis, Tahrir Square, or Phulbari, for that matter, have made evident, martyrdom is ad hoc, improvised, uneven, contentious, and precarious (Mittermaier 2015: 585). Had Tarikul survived unscathed from the day's events, had he been able to come back home like thousands others across Phulbari, would Tarikul have become conscious of a coherent political project? It is impossible to know whether and how his curiosity and attraction to spectacle would have set the stage for future politicization. Beyond his mother's lament for his untimely death and the ascription of martyrdom and retrospective inclusion of Tarikul in the core script of the movement, one can only speculate the possibilities that exist in such exposure to situational convergences that may, and indeed have, led to political awakening for other people in other places.

The interpretive possibilities raised in the thematic of the accidental demand that we take them seriously. Rather than symptoms of deeper truths, they are constitutive elements of a culture that makes itself known in this space of contingency where things happen. In the narratives of the woman-activist, there are encounters. The wounds of these various run-ins, some more overtly gendered than others, coexist on her skin. The wounds caused by crowd politics confront the affect, intimacy, and urgency that belong to the other causes of wounds, such as the loss of land and domestic abuse. Their relationship to politics and its various accidents is articulated in a voice that is simultaneously public and intimate. To bring them together, to read the political and the affective as instantiations of what I term accidental politics is to charge mass mobilizations with more encompassing and more intimate valences.

What the discourses of accident also offer is a fresh way of thinking about affect and intimacy. It gives us a renewed appreciation for the way ordinary people such as Majeda and Tarikul's mother experience the political structures of global commerce and the state through sensation, emotion, and personal experience. The impersonal and excessive nature of crowd politics, as we have seen, also generates intimate moments through which politics is embodied and performed by those on the fringes—bystanders like Tarikul and those "disreputable" like Majeda. For the latter, the discourse of accident was also a means of negotiating a moral self. I agree with Rosalind Morris that the potential force of an accident depends on the recognition that it cannot be simply relegated to the past, because accidents can happen anytime (Morris 2008a). Accidents, as Morris admits, may not be the model for radical politics, but surely if my ethnographic accounts from Phulbari are anything to go by, recognizing them as accidents, with the particularities that I have assigned to the term, can be the ground on which a progressive political future may very well be envisioned. In this understanding of the political, resistance extends beyond insurgencies and public unrest and into a state of mind where affect and accidents converge with powerful and lasting effects.

EPILOGUE: ACCIDENTAL ENCOUNTERS

The sun was already setting as Dipu came up in his wheelchair to greet us at the entrance to a group of huts. He lived there with the rest of his family. In his thirties, Dipu had lost sensation in his lower body when a paramilitary's bullet hit his spine, forcing him permanently to a life in a wheelchair and to give up his job as a *vangari* driver. He had spent months at a rehabilitation center near Dhaka and had undergone multiple surgeries. A bench and a couple of chairs were hastily produced to seat the guests. His wife, children, mother, and neighbors surrounded us, offering answers to the questions about their collective well-being asked by this group of important people visiting from the capital. Their polite replies were supplemented by nervous smiles and what I perceived as expressions of sincere gratitude. The mood was somber and yet there was something mildly festive about the meeting, which I realized over time was common to such visits.

One of Dipu's sons recited a poem for the appreciative audience. It was a popular rhyme that students of his age learn at school. Around this time someone pointed out the *tabij* (amulet) worn by one of Dipu's younger sons. The boy had recently seen a witch (*petni*). Hardly eight or nine years old, he was scared and wore the amulet as a shield against the malevolent force. A few in our group laughed out loud. A guest from Dhaka, a reputed activist, advised the boy to talk back loudly next time he saw her; that should chase away the witch, he said.

This story of haunting that we heard sitting in Dipu's courtyard in that sticky May evening haunts my own memories of that day and often of Phulbari more broadly. The allusion to the witch brought up the uncanny, which I still see written with a question mark in my notebook. Dipu was maimed by the armed forces, which worked to protect a foreign corporation. His son saw a dark and long-haired witch. While the foreignness of the company and its arrival in the lives of those like Dipu animated popular thoughts and actions that I have flagged at multiple places in this book, the witch signaled something beyond the category of foreign, at least in the narrow sense in which Asia Energy, for instance, was thought of as a foreign presence in local life. This is partly because the *bhutpetni* or the ghost-witch duo is intimate to Bengali cosmologies, cultural productions, and daily practices across faith. *Bhut*, commonly translated as ghost, can take many forbidding forms, while *petni* (witch), like the one that accosted Dipu's son, is a quintessentially feminine version of the occult. Residing on specific trees and always an evil character, the witch in the local life world, unsurprisingly, has survived its encounters with modernity and monotheism. Both are accommodated alongside and accorded a status similar to the jinn or spirit in Muslim cultural traditions (Callan 2008; N. Khan 2006). Ghosts and jinn can possess humans, one is "being held" by them, as the common expression goes; a *petni*, though fearsome, does not generally use humans as media of contact between different worlds. Despite being anthropomorphic, *petnis*, unlike ghosts, are not the dead reappeared in the world of the living, but they often act jealously by stealing objects of value or by causing bodily harm. Witches hold a venerable place in our disciplinary production spanning the canonical and the contemporary (Comaroff and Comaroff 1993; Evans-Pritchard 1976; Siegel 2005), and ghosts have a special kind of presence, an absent-presence that is by definition a reappearance and haunts Western intellectual thought more broadly (Pemberton 2009).

"The ghost makes itself known to us through haunting and pulls us affectively into the structure of feeling of a reality we come to experience as a recognition"—Avery Gordon thus explains her affliction by the ghost in sociological analysis (1997). Haunting recognition, she says, is a special way of knowing what has happened or what is happening. Gordon channels Max Horkheimer and Theodor Adorno while following them to a note in *Dialectic of Enlightenment* where the sociologists ruminate on civilization and its own haunting:

> Individuals are reduced to a mere sequence of instantaneous experiences which leave no trace, or rather whose trace is hated as irrational, superfluous, and "overtaken" in the literal sense of the word. . . . The respect for something which has no market value and runs contrary to all feelings is experienced most sharply by the person in mourning, in whose case not even the psychological restoration of labor power is possible. It becomes a wound in civilization, asocial sentimentality, showing that it has still not been possible to compel men to indulge solely in purposeful behavior. (Horkheimer and Adorno 1972)

Instantaneous experiences produce signs that are dismissed as excessive and irrational. One could say the same for accidents. Haunting has deep affinities with mourning, though the relationship is hardly causal. Everybody at some point is haunted, the authors seem to be saying, but the one who is in mourning feels it the most, or most sharply. Being haunted, which also means having respect for that which lacks any market value, runs counter to the logic of capital and its driving force, which is labor power, leading to an "asocial sentimentality." Indeed. An otherwise sympathetic group—*dosh jon*, as Majeda would say—laughed at a boy wearing an amulet to chase off a witch. This public disavowal, I submit, did not necessarily disclose the personal beliefs of the men in the group. Given the intimacy shared with *bhut*, *petni*, and *jinn* in mundane exchanges across social, religious, and class divisions, it would be naïve to ascribe complete disbelief to the members of the visiting delegation. It was the performance of reason and skepticism instead that was revealing about this brief encounter centered on another encounter of a different ontological nature. "Speak back loudly at her," were the words of advice on offer.

"Speaking back," so to speak, is what people in Phulbari were known to have done quite effectively. Indeed, they did it more effectively than a lot of other groups in similar conditions of exploitation and terror. Phul-bari, people here claim, did what others, such as the victims of a disas-trous blowout in Magurchhara gas field run by Occidental in the Sylhet region in the northeast had failed to do. In 1997, the fire from the explo-sions raged for months, burning down 6.9 billion cubic meters of precious resources while wiping out the betel leaf canopies that sustained the local *khasi* population and disrupting rail connections to the area for about six months—and all this before calculating the irreparable environmental damage caused by the so-called accident. In 1998, Unocal, the California-based corporation that took over Occidental's interests, got away with paying $6.3 million in compensation in response to the demand of $650 million by the government of Bangladesh for an environmental and hu-manitarian catastrophe for which it was directly responsible.[8]

Collective actions in Phulbari, in contrast, had chased off, if only for the time being, a foreign company, high-profile politicians, and big capital. Many people have paid a high price for it. Dipu was in a wheelchair. He had lost his livelihood because his erstwhile profession of a *vangari* driver relied solely on his now-inert lower body. His family lived off random acts of generosity from strangers and a steady though inadequate support sys-tem from the National Committee. While I was still there, the activists had collected enough money to buy Dipu a cow that he could put to pro-ductive use. "We need to make sure there's some money stashed away, money that is not easily accessible, like a fixed deposit, otherwise his young wife would leave him," an activist voiced his concern about Dipu's well-being. Dipu's political involvement—and the larger violence to which he was a victim—reverberated within his domestic life in ways that often took the form of an accident, like his son's encounter with the ghost.

Ghostly matters "are often the case of inarticulate experiences, of symptoms and screen memories, of spiraling affects, of more than one story at a time, of the traffic in domains of experience that are anything but transparent and referential" (Gordon 1997). It is a case of modernity's violence and wounds, and a case of the haunting reminder of the com-plex social relations in which we live. Gordon's reading of "ghosts as wounds" follows from Horkheimer and Adorno's preoccupation with the wounds of modernity taking apparitional forms. To make a place for ghosts in our own scholarly imagination, it seems, one still reads "ghosts" as a means to get at something else, a different or alternative kind of knowledge that is scarcely available to us in broad daylight (for an exception, see Morris 2008a; Pemberton 2009). When it comes to ghosts, one needs to look askance, as it were, as is the case with the uncanny (Weber 2001). As Gordon (1997: 17) reminds us: "To write stories concerning exclusions and invisibilities is to write ghost stories."

The story of seeing a witch was as much about seeing as it was about not being able to see, a relationship that governed Phulbari's public life as well as the political life of the nation with which it was intertextual, a point I have elaborated upon in chapter 2. The boy whose shy admission to seeing the apparition, his "asocial sentimentality" that generated awkward laughter from an audience of relatively powerful men, was asked to speak loudly in order to dispel ghostly matters by raising his voice and thereby finding a voice of resistance. This voice is akin to the celebrated voice of protest that propelled and popularized the Phulbari movement. He was asked to gather courage in face of evil by finding a voice that would be audible and comprehensible to an audience similar to the one sitting in his courtyard.

Whether or not the moment of confronting the witch was uncanny, I cannot tell. My first impression of the encounter was still framed in a highly charged oppositional relationship between the local and the foreign with all their attendant connotations. I am not sure if, and how, the dark, feminine figure with flowing hair conjures the *unheimlich* nested within which is the forgotten aura of the home, for the boy's worldview, if anything, is opaque to me. The little that I know about him centers on a combination of extreme poverty, social vulnerability, and traumatic encounters/accidents that make up the span of his short past. What was uncanny, as I see it now, was the minor drama around the boy's vision of the witch. The advice of speaking back was offered as an antidote against the residual, the trace of which was visible as apparition, fleeting and anachronistic at the same time; both could be said of accidents. It was familiar, too, as the image of the witch described by Dipu's son is formally congruent with scary occult characters that thrive as much in indigenous fairytales (*rupkatha*) as in mass-mediated cultural products, in these other fairytales of late modernity. Horkheimer and Adorno, of all scholars, would have much to say about those.[9]

I am tempted to leave the *petni* seen by Dipu's son alone and refrain from reading it as a social figure in the way Gordon suggests that we do for ghosts. The interpretive possibilities that are raised in the thematic of the "accidental," however, demand that we take such encounters/accidents seriously. They are not simply symptoms of deeper truths but are constitutive elements of a larger system that makes itself known in this space of contingency where things happen. I was reminded of it again a few years later. In June 2011, a protest march in Dhaka against governmental plans to export natural gas was violently tackled by the police. The memories of a similar event two years before in which a public intellectual (and the member-secretary of the National Committee) was targeted by riot police with charging batons, leaving him with a fractured limb, were haunting this day of resistance too. The committee and its allies were resisting the government's decision to sign a production-sharing contract with the American energy giant Conoco-Philips. The latter was handed two gas blocks in the Bay of Bengal for exploration. In 2009, the agitation that I was a part of aimed to dissuade the government from signing the deal that left provisions for selling up to 80 percent of natural gas to foreign buyers. Two years later, it was to vent anger at what was by then a fait accompli.

I was on the phone in Chicago with a good friend in Dhaka, a leading member of the protesting lobby. We were discussing a photograph of Rahnuma Ahmed, a Bangladeshi anthropologist, writer, and activist whose work I have cited on multiple occasions in this book. The photo was a close-up of her face showing a wounded forehead with fresh blood streaming down her right cheek. It soon became iconic of escalating tensions between the state and the protesters that were being staged on the streets of Dhaka and other urban centers with due regularity. Ahmed was hit by a stone hurled from the same protesting crowd of which she was a part. In the messy and chaotic space of a *michhil* halted and roughly handled by the police, the stone of a picketing member hit the forehead of one of their more ardent representatives with bloody repercussions.

I teased my politician friend, as I had often done before, about banking on a mishap and using it as a political strategy. It was innocent banter. Being physically present in the 2009 procession where the police were beating up activists with ruthless precision, from which I ran and took shelter in a grocery store, I had some idea about how nasty such confrontations could get. The politics of dissimulation around pelting stones, from Chauri-Chaura to Phulbari, was fresh on my mind as I joked to provoke a reaction. "Maybe," my friend replied with all seriousness, "but it's only in times of war that such accidents can take place."

The invocation of war and accidents brought back, in a flash, the tragic and still unresolved death of Nasreen Huq, with whom I began this chapter. When I had first become interested in writing about Phulbari, Huq's death was one of the more prominent news items in circulation. Years later, after dwelling on the topic to some length, I came across people who wondered, upon learning my research interest, if I was writing about Nasreen Huq. Clearly, who gets to relegate politics to the domain of the accidental is a question of power. To mobilize the idea of politics simply as accident is a constitutive element of late liberal economic logic that points repeatedly to the impossibility of political change. To dismiss mass uprisings as "ephemeral mobilizations" is to invalidate the claims of those who take part in them and deny them any ideological commitment. To say this is not to make a tragedy out of all accidents but to finally start taking them seriously (Virilio 2007). As is common in mass movements elsewhere, many people who joined the anti-mining agitations in Phulbari were at some point accidental activists, or as Rosalind Morris would say, "curious observers of inadvertently gathered crowds" (Morris 2008a). To deprive their actions the force of politics is to undermine presences that open up possibilities for complex appropriations, resistances, and excesses (Stewart 1996). The gesture does violence to the very idea of politics.

CHAPTER 4

CROWDS AND COLLABORATORS

> The [intriguer] stands as a third type alongside the despot and the
> martyr. . . . In all circumstances it was necessary for the intriguer
> to assume a dominant position in the economy of the drama.
> —Walter Benjamin, *The Origin of German Tragic Drama* (2009)

"I HAVE NOT EVEN *seen* Asia Energy" (*Asia Energyke chokheo dekhi
nai*), he said dismissively, but with a determined movement of his hands
for added conviction. The well-respected, elderly organizer and I were
chatting near Phulbari's main bus stand, a few minutes' walk from the
Chhoto Jamuna, the river that runs through the township. Asia Energy's
office stood on the other side of the bridge that connected the two parts
of Phulbari municipality, sliced by the river. The bridge was the battle-
ground in 2006 when armed paramilitary took positions to block the protesters from crossing the river to place a *gherao* at the company's office.
The first of the gunshots that killed three men were also fired from atop
the bridge. Sitting amid lush paddy fields and boasting an array of radio
and satellite antennae with air conditioners jutting out of its windows,
the unusually urban-looking two-story building that served as the company's office was, if anything, impossible to miss. Hordes of security
guards were still protecting the building when I saw it nearly a year after
Asia Energy's activities were put to a halt following the uprising. What,
then, could possibly explain such passionate disavowal?

The denial only makes sense against the backdrop of accusations of
collaboration that pervaded everyday talk about coal mining and corruption, and by extension, the immediate survival and possible future
of those around whom I lived in Phulbari. Widely discussed and debated,

collaboration, in the sense of working for the enemy and benefiting from such exchange, produced narratives and threats of violence, some of which were actualized over the years as the protests got more heated. From the vantage point of Phulbari, a collaborator could be anyone, ranging from a next-door neighbor to the adviser to the Ministry of Energy sitting in the distant capital. It was a figure known to straddle the boundaries of the community and whatever stood beyond or against it. The activist's claim to have never seen the company was an attempt to stave off accusations of collaboration. One who had *seen* Asia Energy—meaning a person who has had any direct relationship with it other than antagonistic ones—was exposed to denunciations often aided by verbal or physical attacks.

A collaborator, by definition, was a local, although his (and at times, her) ties to the foreign were exposed within the community through suspicion, gossip, jokes, and assaults. Barring a few prominent men who made up Phulbari's small but influential elite—namely, the member of Parliament elected from Dinajpur district (who later became a state minister for environment and forests) or the chairman of a nearby union council—collaborators were mostly ordinary people who all lived very similar lives. Perhaps for this reason they required added surveillance in order not to escape notice (cf. Siegel 2005). In informal interactions and within the ritualized space of interviews, the collaborator was referenced more frequently and with far more palpable passion than the *shahid* (martyr), the mining company, or state administration. They were also frequent targets of crowd violence. Crowds were at arms against the collaborator, who, for all intents and purposes, was often a part of the crowd.

A sustained look into this vibrant, if violent culture of accusation illustrates the entangled effects of aggressive resource extraction, collective sovereignty, and popular and state-initiated attempts at settling the score with the nation's past. In Bangladesh, the individuals indicted for crimes against humanity and collaboration in 1971 are called *dalal*, among other things. Largely of Bengali origin, they had conspired with the Pakistani state against the idea of a Bengali homeland. These individuals' status in the nation's public life has been a thorny issue for mainstream politics and a deeply personal one for activists and family members seeking justice for over four decades. The much-awaited war crimes trial that started in 2012 and the protests and politics that preceded and followed it have permanently altered Bangladeshi politics (more on this in chapter 5). A closer look into how the dalal figured so prominently and productively in contemporary political movements, at one level, brings Phulbari's reality into dialogue with national political discourses. At another level, it reveals how collaboration also surpasses questions of national politics and political economy and hints at foundational cultural anxieties around identity, recognition, and betrayal.

In this chapter, I attend to the minutiae of a landscape of resistance in which the collaborator, though liminal by definition, came to occupy the center stage. As figures of suspicion, dalals dictated every action of the activists. They were topics of idle talk and targets of jeers, social censure, and bodily harm. Their property—whether a small store in the village bazaar or a big *paka* house at the heart of the township—was often the first target of retribution. They made it possible to externalize popular grievances, even though as individuals they were hardly marginal social types. In other words, they were unlike the witches among the Zande (Evans-Pritchard 1976). Nor were they always the rich landlords or landed farmers whose granaries and cattle herds were attacked during peasant insurgencies in colonial South Asia, so vividly documented by Ranajit Guha (Guha 1983). Dalals in Phulbari needed to be constantly recognized and accused, and thereby revealed by their neighbors, but were also continually coopted back into social life. In this sense, they enabled the strategies through which ordinary people undermined and accommodated the enormous efforts by the energy company and the government at turning their home into a thriving mining town. The culture of suspicion that cohered around these outliers of the existing moral economy shows that collective sovereignty was activated through a fear of otherness within.

In the crowd of peasants and farmers, day laborers, shopkeepers, and rickshaw pullers, the dalal had to be identified and marked precisely because it was often impossible to tell one apart. Although a personification of moral laxity and transgression, a dalal's origin and location remained mostly within the boundaries of the local. The latter was variously anchored in the neighborhood, the village, the township, the district, or the nation, each of which could be described as *desh*, the everyday word for sovereign country. The foreign or *bidesh* loomed just beyond its borders, both literally and figuratively. Ranu was the first one to bring this point home. A young woman in her twenties, Ranu was the daughter of the first person who was shot by the paramilitary. Months later, she described an incident on her way back from a shoe store at the local market. Its owner, knowing who she was, started making snide comments about the anti-mining movement. He said the mines would be beneficial for the area and that the struggle of Ranu and others like her was not going to amount to anything. "You don't belong in this *desh*. You have no business living in this country. You must be a No. 1 dalal," Ranu ended up saying to the shop owner. Her outburst evoked laughter and appreciation from the little crowd that had gathered at the time Ranu was telling the story. Her retort at the shop owner's comments was no doubt a response made from exasperation, courage, and political conviction. Still, her reply was far from a direct accusation. "You must be a No. 1 dalal" (*Apni nishchoi No. 1 dalal*) is not the same as saying, "You are a dalal" (*Apni ekjon dalal*). The latter has the capacity to name someone a collaborator without revealing a trace of doubt in the mind of the speaker. What Ranu said, although accusatorial, only divulged the suspicion that she maintained about his role as a collaborator and a lack of material proof. It was at best an *attempt* at recognition.

The presence of a multinational company in an out-of-the-way corner of a global resource scramble and the opposition to it had refigured the boundaries of the foreign and the local, infusing both with added meanings. Foreignness in the guise of experts or employees of the company, or as university-educated activist types from the capital, was prominent on the streets. Although suspicions about their direct involvement in the crisis were rampant, they were not the first to be labeled as dalal. Not unlike the intriguer in Walter Benjamin's writing, a dalal could and often did have access to the highest echelons of politics, though he or she was frequently of native and at times modest origins. As a figure, the collaborator embodied the most concrete evidence of the traffic between inside and out, even when nothing concrete could be said about it. The collaborators' roots remained in the community against which they had turned.

Dalals were everywhere, as enemies but also as family and neighbors, in everyday speeches and actions, thus forging a field of communication whose primary mode has been violence.

A year or so after Tarikul and the others were killed, I found myself sitting in the courtyard of a village house that I visited often in 2007–8. The politically conscious older farmer couple, who had long aligned themselves with local left politics, lived in a modest mud hut. That particular afternoon as I was talking to the woman of the house, facing her and occasionally taking notes, my host suddenly stopped the conversation. Another woman from the neighborhood had been standing quietly behind me and now just silently walked away. My host said casually that she was a dalal. She was a next-door neighbor, who had been watching and listening in on our interaction all this time, leaning on one of the bamboo poles supporting the thatched roof. She had left because she did not want to say anything in favor of the mines in our presence, I was told. This neighbor, who had accepted seeds from Asia Energy, always went around saying, "What's the point of protesting? The mine is bound to happen [*Khoni habei*]." It was a strong assertion of inevitability that denied the power of political organizing and thereby revealed her true nature as a traitor.

This line of talking was characteristic of a dalal. People got paid by the company, I was regularly told, to sit at public places like tea stalls or restaurants in the bazaar and the bus stand to speak in a dismissive manner in order to cast doubt on the fate of the movement and to convince others of the inevitability of mining. While talking was a sign of collaboration, not being able to speak marked its end. "Dalals can't speak with their heads held high anymore, at least not in Phulbari. Outside [of Phulbari] they may be conspiring with Asia Energy," a man once told me. Many others echoed the same sentiment. Although clearly on speaking terms with her neighbor, my host had neither acknowledged her presence nor accused her of collaboration in our presence.

The allegations of collaboration that filled Phulbari's public and intimate spheres could not be separated from the absolute normalcy with which dalals were also accepted as neighbors and kin. This is because a sense of betrayal more often than not takes place within the sphere of the intimate. This intimacy is not oppositional to but constitutive of violence (Thiranagama and Kelly 2010). As a "continual, potential self" the traitor could be anybody, and therefore set in motion a larger problematic of recognition (Thiranagama and Kelly 2010: 10). As a part of the crowd they activated minute and careful strategies of identification, which in turn incited crowd violence. This dialectic has been symptomatic of the politics of recognition at the center of Bangladeshi nation-formation. It was during the turbulence of the war and its immediate aftermath in the early 1970s that the categories of freedom fighter (*muktijoddha*, or *mukti*, for short), traitor (*dalal*), radical Maoist (*Naxalite* or *Naxal*), and *Bihari* (Urdu-speaking refugees to East Pakistan) bled into each other. Such ethnopolitical entanglement was vigorously denied in post-independence years in order to realize discrete nationalist visions.

What political and ethical possibilities did the neighbor or the outsider enable when the allegations of collaboration, at times direct but frequently retrospective and indirect, were also the basis of and the medium for popular sovereignty? I address this question by heeding the call to rethink neighbor-love. Modern day horrors have to a great extent robbed us of the innocence of the concept (Žižek, Santner, and Reinhard 2005). Unlike or beyond the friend and the enemy, the neighbor is a figure located not in a field totalized by sovereign exception—a definition of which we get from Carl Schmitt (Schmitt, Strong, and Strauss 2007)—but rather within an infinite series of possible encounters, and as Kenneth Reinhard argues, without the stability of margins. The border between friend and enemy—and between public and private realms they are associated with—is fragile, porous, contestable, and to this extent, the Schmittian discourse collapses. Reading the figure of the neighbor in relation to that of the intriguer or plotter in Walter Benjamin's writing offers a robust analytical framework in thinking through the centrality of collaboration and its relationship to everyday forms of popular sovereignty.

The intriguer—and the dalal, in our case—is a powerful figuration of the *third* type, which, sociologically speaking, has been the case in Phulbari. Two aspects of collaboration in Phulbari highlighted the fecund nature of collaboration and its ties to popular violence. First was the curious role of the cell phone. As the preferred technological medium of collaboration, "the mobile" emerged as a fetish object both in its power to facilitate illicit exchanges and in its status as a highly coveted commodity for most people in Phulbari. The second was the collaborator's ability to confuse and collapse binaries of local/foreign, friend/enemy, or neighbor/dalal, which shared metonymic links to the charged topic of collaboration that emplots the originary narrative of the Bangladeshi nation. During fieldwork, the latter surfaced in the memories of a group of people who had migrated to the Phulbari area right before the 1971 war and was later collectively vilified as collaborators. This was the same group whose wide participation in the mining protests was more fervent and committed than others. Once suspected of colluding with the West Pakistanis, they were now intent on rooting out any sign of collaboration among them. Suspicion was the lingua franca in these exchanges, and it is to suspicion I first turn.

A SUFI OR A THIEF?

Contemporary political mobilizations are often energized by suspicion, mistrust, and fear rather than hope and idealism. The negative dispositions ultimately reveal a tension between a subject and that which is doubted, suspected, or mistrusted (Pelkmans 2018). Suspicion, Mathijs Pelkmans explains, denotes a direct and active engagement with the object, entails an affective position toward knowledge, and carries aesthetic, moral, and political dimensions. He further writes: "What we are observing is how people strive to create liveable situations, about how they navigate landscapes that are replete with unknowns and uncertainties, in which they focus their doubts and suspicions on certain objects, leaving issues that are less immediately problematic or threatening for what they are" (2018: 173).

Most people in Phulbari suspected each other of collaboration, which related to a general distrust with the mining project. Partly, the accusations stemmed from not understanding the fuss around coal since the villagers who questioned its value were mostly bystanders to this theater of operations that involved the building of infrastructure, visible circulation of cash, and inflated promises of prosperity. Ranu's father, Ranjan, voiced a similar concern. Though keen on talking about his near-death experience after being shot by the paramilitary on August 26, Ranjan, an elderly farmer, was not as thrilled to talk about coal. And he was hardly alone. As if to please me, while presenting himself as a knowledgeable participant in the protests, he began on a standard note. He brought up the unequal royalty arrangements between Asia Energy and Bangladesh (6 percent for the host country) and the high-level governmental corruption that would make such an arrangement even imaginable. Still, he did not stay very long within the parameters of a well-rehearsed story, and refused to accept Phulbari's fate as simply a story of unequal exchange:

> We cannot be sure that there is nothing more of value [*mulyoban*] here other than coal. We have been seeing very high-quality coal. It shines. When they did the boring, the tests, we went and stood there at the front to watch. They didn't let us in, of course. But you can see it before you as they bring it above ground through the pipe. Then you could see. Now, is it easy to say what else is in it? How could we see? Do you think they'd let us see? They blocked off the area with red ribbons. Their guards did. So that nobody could go in.

Because of the tight security around the boring holes, Ranjan valued the coal from a distance, from where he stood with the rest of the crowd. Phulbari's coal was prized for its quality by the company and the experts and politicians who were demanding its speedy extraction. The "high volatile bituminous" coal (Asia Energy Corporation 2006) is deemed superior in quality than metallurgical and thermal coal imported regularly from India (Saleque 2011), a fact that was publicized to significant political effect. It bolstered the case for exploiting local mines to save foreign currency and curb foreign dependence. Indeed, Phulbari was slated to add 1 percent to Bangladesh's annual GDP. Ranjan thought it was of good quality as well, but he appraised the coal on its visual rather than material value, not by scarcity but by aesthetic abundance. The mineral was good because it was glittery. The expression Ranjan used, *chokchok kora*, to shine, was the same as one would use for gold, precious gems, and other objects with surfaces that reflect light. Equally significant was the slippage in his use of the verb *dekha* (to see). When Ranjan said, "We have been seeing very high-quality coal," he meant seeing in a literal sense. This was the shiny coal that was there for all to see, particularly those who stood on the other side of the guarded area. The second use of *dekha* was of a figurative nature. "Now, is it easy to say what else is in it? Do you think they'd let us see?" he asked, unsure of the motives behind the extraction of coal and other assets that were possibly more valuable (*mulyoban*). These were hidden behind the facade of digging up coal. People like Ranjan could not possibly see this process because it was not even meant to be seen. The relationship to coal that many people in Phulbari had was different from what Katy Gardner (2012) had heard around the gas fields in the northeast of Bangladesh. "Under our fields is gold," a local woman said to Gardner when she was doing fieldwork in Sylhet in the northeast. For Gardner, this meant that the residents were aware of the price of the wealth in their proximity. "Savvy entrepreneurs that the locals are," she writes, "everyone is aware of the economic potential of the gas that the foreigners discovered" (Gardner 2012: 3). While people in Phulbari were made conscious of the resource underneath, they were not convinced as to why coal, and what all this official interest in the mineral *actually* signified.

The power of the secret bears on the lives of ordinary people, but its recognition has also been foundational to the social sciences. Émile Durkheim, Georg Simmel, and Sigmund Freud were all great theorists of secrecy, who knew how to locate the secret and study its psychosocial effects. The tension produced by withholding secrets is productive in every sense, Joseph Masco notes, "not only in defining insider and outsider status but also by energizing the social, allowing identifications and misidentifications, confessions, gossip, conspiracy theory, speculation, and belief" (Masco 2014). It is precisely the secret as a *limit* case that functions to enable the public, which constitutes these theories of social order, he says.

It is not surprising that mistrust with the workings of extractive industries is rampant and surfaces regularly in ethnographic encounters with resource politics. Andrew Walsh writes about the sapphire trade in Madagascar where people never understood what made the gems so important to their foreign consumers. Sapphires had no local use value, making many Malagasy miners and traders speculate that they must have some other use that is being kept secret from them (Walsh 2004). In this *bazaar* economy, the most valuable knowledge of all was that which was withheld (Walsh 2004: 231). Similar knowledge differential affected the artisanal coltan miners in the Congo. Price uncertainty added to vast temporal and material dispossession among the Congolese, who learned to believe that the minerals after all had no price (Smith 2015). It was the collusion between powerful foreign nations and the president of DR Congo that influenced the fluctuations in value to serve the interests of the various stakeholders. The case of Phulbari was similar, but the anxiety about the dalal, though akin to the suspicions around resource extraction in other places, still exceeded the political economy of resource exploitation and the unequal distribution of knowledge. It is the script of Bangladeshi nationhood that provided a culturally and historically determined space for accommodating the Other—in this case, the collaborator—in one's midst.

For example, in early 2008, a few miles south of where I lived, a cinema hall had its film posters plastered on nearby walls, *paan*-cigarette stalls, and rickshaw stands. A couple of them that stood out due to sheer number and catchy titles were *Ora Dalal*, which I translate as "They Are Dalal,"[1] and *Kathin Prem*—"It's a Different Love." The English translation for the second film was conspicuous and got almost equal billing as its Bangla title. There was nothing comparable for *Ora Dalal*, a shortcoming that I realized over time had significance beyond simply being a proper noun.[2] *Dalal*, in the Persian from which it entered Bangla, means an agent or a broker. More frequently and mostly disparagingly, it refers to a collaborator, a pimp, or a tout (Ghosh 1987; Huberman 2010). The absence of an English title for the movie *Ora Dalal* in the poster and the original Bangla, which uses the third-person plural, *ora* (they), captures some of the ambiguity of a dalal's curious status as a culturally familiar, though sociologically elusive figure.

Although no dalal was known to have been killed in the course of the few days of violent reprisals that followed the death of civilians in 2006, many people told me that they regretted not having killed the more active and potentially more harmful collaborators when the time was "right." A few of them vowed to do so in the future should such urgency ever arise. Despite such strong views, ordinary people in Phulbari never

found it easy to explain what it was that made one a dalal. One clear definition was outlined by an intellectual and reputable activist: "Anybody
who talks about adequate and timely monetary compensation for land is
a dalal." The idea was this: anybody who would opt for open-pit mining
in exchange for monetary recompense was suspect because of the dubious desire to broker potentially lucrative cash distribution. But this description was simultaneously overdetermined and inadequate: it fit way
too many people in Phulbari to be meaningful while leaving out many
others who were suspected or named collaborators. My questions about
dalali or collaboration regularly met with initial reticence if not outright
denial: "There is no dalal among us" or "Nobody serves the company
around here. Not anymore." The need therefore, one might argue, is for
the third-person plural, "*ora*," as seen in the movie title. It displaced the
accusation directed at oneself, such as the activist leader who denied ever
seeing the office of Asia Energy cited at the beginning of the chapter.
The disavowal, difficulty, and desire to name were instructive; they outlined a political topography where the interface of native and foreign,
however defined, stoked collective vengeance although in ways not always
comfortably aligned with the discursive framework of the anti-mining
movement.

The stories of revenge that I was hearing were given credence by the
signs strewn across town. There were graffiti on the walls lining the highway leading to and from the capital that echoed the popular demand of
punishment for the dalals of Asia Energy (figure 8). Once in a while, as
we traveled by a rickshaw or *vangari*, my friend would point to a motorcycle that just zoomed past us. He would call its rider a "marked dalal"
(*chinhito dalal*). Marked meant that this individual's relationship with the
company and ill motives were either public or at the least not difficult to
prove. Identifying a handful as "*chinhito*"—marked—also suggested that
most collaborators were not. On my regular walks around the township,
I came across the concrete ruins of an ornate cement arch on the side of
a busy street. Clearly impressive at some point, it was now nearly stripped
of all the ornamentation by attacks from pillaging crowds. The arch was
intended to be the entrance to Hussain's mansion that never got built.
Hussain and Alam, as I name them here, were two of Phulbari's most

FIGURE 8 "Down with the dalals of Asia Energy." This graffito, on the outside wall of a house, has a collective signatory: *Phulbarbaasi*—"The residents of Phulbari." Photo by the author.

prominent "*chinhito*" dalals. Their relationship to the company, I was told, went further back, to at least around 2015. People rarely expressed doubt or sympathy about the motives or actions of these two well-known members of the local elite.

A journalist by the name of Shaon, who was the editor of the only pro-movement publication in Phulbari, suggested that the problem of collaboration found its early beginnings when tensions around mining had just begun to surface. In fact, this was more so the case when an arm of the area's political and social bigwigs began negotiating with the company in the name of protecting Phulbari. They founded the Phulbari Rokkha [Protection] Committee in 2005, ostensibly to streamline the sporadic discontents against the mines. Though BNP was in power at the time, the elite men of Phulbari had overt or indirect ties to both mainstream political parties, as is often the case. In Shaon's words, a member of the local elite—then vocal against the mines, but soon a turncoat—had banned Shaon and a few others from the local press club. This was followed by the publication of three issues of a monthly magazine, *Satya Kantha* ("The Voice of Truth") in which some unappetizing facts were printed about these individuals and their possible collaborative roles. The blame of collaboration was then squarely placed on the journalists. "They said, 'You are the ones who went to the office of Asia Energy first,'" Shaon said, citing one of these men who implied that the journalists themselves were negotiating with the company and were, therefore, dalals. This is how Shaon explained the nature of the blame game:

> A Sufi [he meant a devout Muslim] once went to a pond to do his ablutions before the prayer at dawn. He spotted another man already sitting there and thought of him as more pious than himself. This man, who happened to be a thief, upon seeing another person so early in the morning, thought instead that the Sufi was a thief like himself. As a thief, he suspected that the other man could only be a thief.

Likewise, as a dalal, Shaon said, this powerful man from the Rokkha Committee could only think the same of others. Beyond rehashing a familiar tale of "it takes one to know one," the story reproduced a binary of good and evil that had enormous purchase in everyday life in its various manifestations as *us vs. them*, *local vs. foreign*, and in this case, *pious vs. criminal*. More significantly, however—and as was typical of Phulbari—the demarcation between categories was tricky business. When faced with each other, both the Sufi and the thief in the story mistook each other as one's own because the enemy was most likely a neighbor who not only looked like oneself but also lived a life that was intimate and familiar. This confusion, as anthropologists have been particularly effective in noting, is productive; it is characteristic of disparate cultures of accusation, be it of witchcraft, collaboration, or crime (Evans-Pritchard 1976; West and Sanders 2003; Siegel 2005).

In *The Origin of German Tragic Drama* (2009), Walter Benjamin highlights the same by guiding our attention to the role of the "intriguer." In German baroque drama or the mourning play (*Trauespiel*), the *Intrigant* occupies a curious position. In the complex figure of the intriguer, Benjamin finds a window onto a literary world without any stable authority. In historical terms, this would be sixteenth-century, Counter-Reformation Germany. The character becomes central to the argument that Benjamin ultimately makes about *Trauespiel* specifically, and the emergence of modernity more broadly (Benjamin 2009). The function of the intriguer, from Latin *intrigare*—confused and confound—is to in-trigue, to confuse; the condition of such confusion is the particular spatialization and localization of processes that are usually temporal or historical in character (Weber and Benjamin 2008). Samuel Weber, paraphrasing Benjamin, explains: "Power changes character; it detaches itself from rulers and devolves upon those who know how to exploit the weakness of others, whether strong or weak; which is why perhaps the most characteristic figure of the baroque, who completes the triad of its 'political typology,' alongside the tyrant and martyrs, is the intriguer, schemer, or perhaps better: plotter" (Weber and Benjamin 2008: 141).

Despite the obvious limits to such intergeneric translations, the intriguer presents itself as a literary counterpart of the collaborator. Unlike the great criminal who inspires the shudder of admiration by taking unto himself the stigma of the lawmaker, the intriguer, vested as he is with demonic qualities, has no proper place. He has no home outside the court, which is the exclusive showplace of the tragic drama (Benjamin 1978, 2009). Not inhabiting the role of the tyrant or the martyr (the shadows of these antinomial figures also hovered over Phulbari's everyday life), the plotter is not the master of this place; and yet, he "remains the one who best knows how to move in it" (Weber and Benjamin 2008).

If the journalist, unbeknownst to him, exposed his links to the company by telling the story, then Mahbub volunteered similar information. In his mid- to late forties when we met at a tea stall, he was a former employee of Asia Energy. He had worked as a night guard for about three months in 2005 when grievances against the mining company were only starting to cohere as a movement. "They make you work for twelve hours," Mahbub began on a grudging tone:

> They don't even let you sit for five minutes in those twelve hours. . . . One day there was severe fog and cold. . . . I thought that I'd get some hay and sit under the bridge. It hadn't even been two minutes after I sat down that one foreign officer and one Bengali one came in their car. The Bengali officer asked, "Why is there hay there?" I said, "Sir, sometimes I sit [on it]. It gets really cold." . . .
>
> He said, "You can't sit for even a second. You don't have the *capacity* to sit for a second here."

There were at least two other similar incidents—one about not getting paid on time and the other about not being allowed to walk freely in his own village—that Mahbub recounted in our conversation. Tired of such abuse, he had decided to quit and join the movement. "Now I won't give up my land even if my life is at stake," he said twice in the same interaction. Mahbub felt comfortable introducing himself as a former employee of Asia Energy (to me and many others who were eavesdropping on our conversation) because of his firsthand exposure to the unjust practices of the company's officers. Though he had once drawn a salary from the company, he now volunteered to reveal his involvement by asserting a moral position through victimhood that included both physical suffering and righteous indignation. Unlike the respected leader quoted at the beginning of the chapter, Mahbub did not need to deny *seeing* the company and open himself up to allegations of collaboration.

A group of dalals had indeed visited Mahbub's village around the same time. One of them claimed to be a friend of a fellow villager. He was distributing money from house to house that had been provided by the company. When I asked if this man was doing so publicly, I was given the example of corruption during local and national elections. "Everybody knows who is paying whom to vote for this candidate or that, but you don't *see* anything," a friend of Mahbub who was following our conversation explained. "A dalal would be exposed exactly like that," he said. One did not need to see the actual exchange in order to know that cash had indeed changed hands. I was curious: Would working for the company be enough to turn one into a dalal? Mahbub replied excitedly in his own defense: "Just because someone has a job doesn't make him a dalal. We didn't start the job as dalals. We entered the company for employment. . . . Here dalals came from outside. Those who have a job are not dalals. They were employed in exchange for a salary. That's the truth."

Mahbub's friend added another explanation: "A dalal is someone who didn't put in any labor. They hung out at the office. They were paid. [They were told:] 'Go convince the people, convert them secretly. Take whatever you need.' These are the people who are dalals. . . . They used to go to the office, give attendance, and then leave."

Mahbub's explanation raised crucial and seemingly contradictory aspects that pointed to the difficulty in reducing a dalal to a social type. For instance, when narrating an incident of humiliation in which Mahbub was asked to get off the road as an Asia Energy car was going by his house, he called the driver *bideshi*, the Bangla equivalent of foreigner or outsider—literally, one who is not of *desh*.[3] Yet, when I was curious if the foreigners working for the company were worse than their native counterparts, Mahbub categorically said that the officers—*bideshi* or no—were all the same. It became obvious that the main difference between Mahbub, who had sustained close economic ties to the company (though as a low-ranking employee, which he made sure to point out), and a dalal was the kind of economy in which they participated. Mahbub earned his salary in exchange for the physical labor that he was obligated to put in as a night guard. A dalal would simply go to the office, take money, and then take off. In his moral universe, differential valuations of wealth and labor played a decisive role in naming a dalal: they worked in secret, although others eventually found out who they were the same way they were cognizant of other open secrets, such as routine corruption during elections. And a dalal did not put in any hard work for what he earned, thus making the nature of his occupation and remuneration at best dubious. Saiful Islam's painting in chapter 2 may very well be a visual shorthand of the scenario Mahbub and his friend presented. Our tea stall conversation ended with the following thoughts from Mahbub:

> We cannot really say that there is no dalal in our area. Maybe they are communicating separately [with the company]. Maybe. This is the issue. We cannot say that there are no more of them. We cannot say that. But we don't really see them. Before, the dalals of Asia Energy from this area tried so hard to convince us. They tried to convince me too. . . . Now, that is no more. With Allah's *rahmat* [kindness], those boys, those men are now behind us. And maybe others are doing [*dalali*]. That is hard to say.

OF MOBILES AND MOTORCYCLES: THE CURRENCY OF COLLABORATION

A spate of attacks on the property and person of collaborators took place in the few days between the paramilitary leaving the streets and the signing of the Phulbari treaty on August 30, 2006. These included the burning of cash found in at least one dalal's house, which helped concretize suspicions about the secret nature of the source of their wealth (see chapter 2). Motorcycles and shoes were also common targets, as were shops and other property owned by suspected dalals. The pillages were often just that, pure destruction, although looting also frequently took place. Narratives that circulated of these episodes stressed the importance of the cell phone both as a technology that enabled communication and as an object of consumerist desire. It was invested with powers that made possible the hidden exchanges in which dalals were thought to participate. Seen as such, cell phones were similar to the bank bills that were located and collectively destroyed, but also repeatedly referenced in textual productions of all kinds. Like money, the cell phone was a sign of the power of collaboration. It served a "double duty" as is typical of indexical icons. The mobile set was an icon of economic mobility or, in the case of some dalals, of the quick fortunes that they had amassed as collaborators. It was a luxury item whose aura exceeded the utilitarian logic behind its use. It stood out as the preferred technological device for the secret communications in which dalals were suspected of engaging and the type of physical movement they enjoyed by virtue of it. The cell phone entailed indexical iconicity because of its perceived ability to facilitate exchanges; widely and wildly growing suspicions endowed the icon with added signification. Although regular folks were also variedly dependent on their use of cell phones, the telephonic capacity to mediate hidden contracts verging on criminality accorded it occult powers peculiar to collaboration. The "mobile" enabled mobility of both kinds— upward and spectral. Just like cash, it was at once a medium and a proof of collaboration.

Kamal was part of a mob in an incident of vandalism where cell phones were in abundance. He was in his late thirties when we stayed at his house a few times during our trips to his village. We spent one such evening chatting in a room lit by a single candle since there was no power supply in that or any of the neighboring villages. That evening we talked about many things, including Kamal's imminent departure to the Middle East as a migrant laborer, common among many of his contemporaries. Soon, as expected, collaboration came up. "Alam [a *chinhito* dalal] should have been killed that day," my friend who traveled with me said out loud, his voice betraying a familiar tinge of agitation and regret that I had sensed in others too when remembering the same events. Kamal did not seem to care or completely agree with the statement. Instead, he went on to recount his memories of attacking Alam's house:

> When we went to Alam's house that day his wife came out and opened the door. I've known [his wife] through a different connection. When she opened the door, I asked her, "Why are you here?" She said, "This is my house." Suddenly those who were behind me entered in a rush and went up to the second floor. From there they picked up about thirteen or fourteen mobile phones. *What does Alam do with all these phones?* There were at least fifty pairs of shoes in his house. Everybody took off their own sponge sandals and came out with Bata shoes.

This violent episode began with a relatively agreeable encounter. Kamal did not elaborate on his relationship with the woman whose house he had vandalized as part of a group of protesters, but there was admission of mutual recognition. No sooner had that interaction ended, the crowd forced itself inside. One could say that the exchange was cut short due to the onslaught of the crowd. Kamal described the scene as a bystander, one who was pushed aside by the mob and left to watch the scene of plunder. His mode of storytelling switched to a style that distanced the narrator from the destructive crowd that looted not only cell phones but also shoes. Their unusually large number shocked Kamal. *What does Alam do with all these phones?* was the question that was on his mind. Lacking an "I," the question took a collective form that Kamal and others as members of a crowd must have asked themselves. He inserted this reaction, which, though personal, went beyond individual shock and gave his story a semblance of objective remove. This was what he and others like him had thought to themselves at the time. Kamal, for one, was clearly not over the awe of that excess even at the time of our conversation.

He narrated this episode with a hint of a smile that occasionally broke into a muted laugh. For instance, when I asked him who might have led these crowds to destruction, he replied cryptically, smiling: "The one who makes the call stands still, the one who hears it runs" (*Je daak dey se daray thake, je shune se douray*). This was Kamal's pithy insight into how a mob was formed. It was not important who headed a violent crowd or who called it into being. Once formed, the one who gave the call of action ended up not doing anything, meaning perhaps that the caller ensured his own safety by not participating in the unlawful actions. The person who received the message, often not the intended invitee but simply an overhearer, rushed in without premeditation, as crowds are wont to do.

I had often heard activists complain that these high-profile dalal types incurred no serious damage in the end despite all the stories of pilfering. For instance, Hussain, the alleged collaborator whose house was set on fire by Majeda and others, had apparently left a couple of his old motorcycles out on the veranda so the crowd could destroy those if they wanted to. This could not have made any serious dent to a rich person like Hussain. I can imagine the activists having similar thoughts regarding

Alam's shoes as well. The number of shoes was shocking to Kamal. He noticed the many pairs *and* their high quality and called them "Bata." The crowds quickly decided to exchange their cheap sandals for what they thought were Bata products, which are generally held in high regard across South Asia for their durability and popular brand identity. No matter who manufactured Alam's shoes, for Kamal they stood out as Bata and had to be better than the footwear everybody else must have been wearing that day.

Insofar as objects were concerned, motorcycles and cell phones were by far the most desired and expensive commodities in Phulbari. Motorcycles (commonly called *gari*, the word for automobile) were the preferred mode of transportation for Phulbari's middle and upper classes. Cell phones represented a more democratic ownership. The latter are as omnipresent in Phulbari as they are in the rest of the country. Cheaper and infinitely less bothersome to acquire than landlines, mobile phones in less than a decade or so had become the only dependable tele-medium in rural Bangladesh.[4] Aside from—and in spite of—their everyday usage, cell phones had also become an effective mediating technology in petty to mid-level economic crimes such as extortion and bribing. The Flexiload program of Grameenphone, a company that to date boasts the largest subscription rate, proved particularly conducive to invisible fiscal exchanges. Offered to both prepaid and postpaid accounts and therefore making it virtually impossible to trace the user of the account in question, Flexiload gave its subscribers the freedom to load any amount between Tk. 10 to Tk. 5,000 by buying scratch cards or paying instantly to a retailer locatable, seemingly, on every street corner.[5] The escalating threats of extortion in which victims were forced to pay directly to a cell phone through Flexiload had adequately displeased those in power before and during the emergency. In 2006, the home minister acknowledged the problem at a high-level meeting on crime and security. He promised to make recommendations to the company to bring down the amount of reloading from Tk. 50,000 to 10,000 to reduce the rate and severity of extortion cases—a suggestion that most likely reflected the company's current policies. Years later, in 2015, the government of Bangladesh made biometric information a prerequisite for registering cellular phones. This has been a part of a vamped-up governmental surveillance scheme ostensibly due to the rise of religious extremism and cybercrime.

In the first decade of the twenty-first century, "Flexi" (a shorthand which later included similar offers by other mobile companies), the invisible and quasi-magical mode of exchange, enthralled all, including those living in Phulbari. In a place where daily fiscal exchanges happened exclusively in cash—and that in petty amounts—the invisible movement of money through Flexiload had an added aura due to the rumors of monetary incentives offered by Asia Energy. Even the activists were hardly immune to allegations of profiting from such arrangements. One of the persistent themes in the regular evening gatherings of activists at the township bazaar was the state of the national economy, collective speculations about which never failed to pay attention to individual financial conditions. Though concerns were expressed and advice and other help were offered, jokes were regularly made about certain members sliding into economic hardship where a little Flexi-like magic had become necessary for survival. Snide and facetious comments abounded regarding the so-called anonymous patrons whose generous Flexi contributions boosted someone's mobile accounts and elevated its owner's power to maintain necessary social ties as befitting of a leader of the movement.

Humor hardly ever masked the feelings of distrust about the potential of such ghostly technologies, of which Flexiload was but a more tangible manifestation. Senior activists were often uneasy in the face of jokes made by their junior comrades. In a context where gossip surrounding the acceptance of bribes offered by the energy company, such as blankets, seeds, motorcycles, televisions for youth clubs, calendars and diaries, and cash had continually proliferated, even the activist leaders did not find themselves beyond reasonable doubt. In fact, the anxiety was more pronounced in their case as rumors of selling out to the company carried serious threats to their political careers.[6] Stories of virtuous refusals to these offers were in public circulation as powerful counternarratives.

The stories were still inadequate. My friend and research assistant— young, vocal, and at times harshly critical of some of the activist leaders— was visibly frustrated one evening after attending a typical social gathering of the anti-mining activists. He vented as soon as we were on our own:

Who pays for somebody's mobile phones? Who doesn't need money? Is there anybody who doesn't need money? Money moves. You cannot come to *Nimtola Mor* [the center of the township] if you don't have enough to spend on tea and cigarettes. You need a lot of money to do politics, like a constant source of money to be able to do what X *bhai* or Y *bhai* does [he mentions the names of two senior leaders, hence the honorific, *bhai*].

My friend's questions, though rhetorical, were not unfounded. Clearly, prominent figures were equally vulnerable to accusations of petty corruption, and collaboration, as always, lurked on the horizon. Mahbub, the former Asia Energy night guard, drew a direct link between virtual crimes like Flexiload cash influx and Phulbari's reality. "How did they give out money?" was my insistent question, to which he replied nonchalantly, "They sent [the money] to mobiles by Flexiload. They can't give out money just like that, you see. They give it via mobile. When they gave away like Tk. 200–400 [*dui-charsho taka*, a generic expression for a modest lump sum amount] that's how they gave." Or consider what Mahbub said about dalals toward the end of our tea stall conversation in light of this brief foray into Phulbari's cell phone culture "They [dalals] are people of a separate class. They did everything over mobile phones" (*Era alada srenir lok. Era mobile-e sabkichhu kaj korto*). The word Mahbub used for "class" is *sreny*. It has near-identical connotations as "class" in English. In this context and as is true of the English equivalent, it did not refer exclusively to economic class. One could say that by using *sreny*, Mahbub meant something akin to the expression "As a group, dalals do things differently." The first utterance of Mahbub, "*They are people of a separate class*" was formulated in what can be described as an unmarked tense; like historical present, it imparts a sense that the claim made in the sentence continues to be valid in the here and now of the interaction, the social time-space of the speech event (Lee 1997; Silverstein 1976). The second sentence, "*They did everything over mobile phones*," was in the past tense. He was speaking of actual individuals and their specific actions that were perpetrated via cell phones. While the first assertion was a categorical statement of the way the collaborators generally were—a judgment, more accurately, on their behavior—the second was an account of how an act of collaboration took place within his earshot or eyeshot, hence, the past tense. As Mahbub observed for three months while working for the company, it was *because* dalals did everything over cell phones that they comprised a different class.

The mobile might have cast its spell in ways that universally evoked awe, but the wonder did not always translate into submission to its powers. A group of women in a village when speaking of their experiences with the survey routines of the company in its early days (carried out by other agencies on contract) also brought up the cell phone. They did so not to wax on its ability to mediate mysterious exchanges but to point to a basic technical attribute—its power to photograph—to steer attention from what was *really* going on. The cell phone, then, was a prop; it was successful in diverting focus from the ulterior motives of the company. The realization, however, was only retrospective. When I asked how the surveyors explained what they were doing, like going around asking the price of people's homes, the number of trees or cows that they owned, or the exact dimensions of their ancestral land, the women remembered not being told anything about the mines. But they also collectively reminisced about how the surveyors took photos of *everything* because people did not remember and could not provide details of their life's possessions. The following exchange was instructive:

Author: They took your photo too?
Woman: YES [*laughs out loud*].
Author's friend: How did they take photos?
Woman: With mobiles. . . . [The surveyors] said NOTHING! Only there was this hullabaloo. You know, about taking instant photos. They were showing [the photos] to us right away. That became a thing. Crazy Bengalis [*hujuge bangalee—hujug* meaning a craze or fad], you know. Nobody understood anything, listened to anything. Old and elderly, young people and little children, all were getting photographed.

Mahbub's insistence on the intimacy of collaboration and mobile telephony, Kamal's awe at the handsets found in abundance in a "marked" dalal's house, and these collective pleasures and suspicions around instant photography spelled out a kind of telecommunicative fantasy. This version of it, however, was different from the one Vicente Rafael has observed in the Philippines. I borrow the expression from Rafael's essay, which explores a set of fantasies around communication against the backdrop of a civilian-backed coup in the Philippines nicknamed "People Power II" (Rafael 2003). The Philippines, like other developing countries, shows the paradox of being flooded with the latest communicative technologies while being mired in deteriorating infrastructures. Bangladesh is no exception, as I explain in more depth in chapter 5. Communication made possible by a medium such as the cell phone acquires a fetishistic quality, seen as possessing power to transcend sheer physical density of the masses through technology. In the event described by Rafael, the middle classes of the Philippines projected such fantasies onto the crowd—"while telecommunications allow one to escape the crowd, they are also seen to bring about a new kind of crowd that was conscious of its own movement" (Rafael 2003). Self-consciously tech-savvy, the middle-class members of the youth in Rafael's observations identify themselves with the latest technological novelties while celebrating their location within a physical space known as the text messaging capital of the world. When the time came to oust the president, now established as corrupt and unacceptable to large portions of the educated bourgeoisie, it was the crowd that became invested with the power of the cell phone. And the latter, as a technologized *thing*, was idealized as an agent of change powerful enough to bring forth new forms of sociality.

What exactly is this power and what kind of sociality does it forge? Rafael ventures an answer through an insightful foray into the history of telemedia in the Philippines. Telephony, when introduced as early as 1885, already provoked fantasies of direct communication among the colonial bourgeoisie—the desire to hear and be heard by the state. The telecommunicative ideal was, however, shaped by another aspect of telephonic capacity that it shares with print—to reveal what was once hidden, to repeat what was meant to be secret, and to pass on messages for a particular circle (Rafael 2003). It is no surprise that the cell phone, because of its increasingly diminutive stature, the mobility that it ensures, and the secrecy with which it can be handled, not to mention its increased affordability, condenses a few centuries' worth of colonial, nationalist, and developmental desires surrounding communication, wired or wireless. The founder of Grameen Bank, Iqbal Z. Quadir, echoes similar thoughts, if from a political economic angle, when he identifies "unimaginable possibilities" of the widespread wealth created by the use of cell phones in low-income countries (Quadir 2013). Cell phone technology, he argues, contributes to Adam Smith's goal of inclusion through the potential of universal usage and cost-effective communication, and therefore, higher productivity. increased economic engagement of citizens, and less poverty (Quadir 2013).

Text messages further add to this aura of communication, an aura that we have seen Muhammad Yunus of microcredit fame invoke in a comparable fashion and to similar ends as have the middle classes that Rafael describes (see chapter 1). Such was the strength of this medium that the Philippines coup was popularly known to be spurred partially by cell phones in which they became weapons, enabling their user to be "in the groove, in a fighting mood" (Rafael 2003). The power of the people, presupposed and entailed in mass political events like the anticolonial mobilizations in the Dutch Indies or more recent communal riots in South Asia, has also been ascribed, partly though crucially, to the powers of communicative technologies (Mrázek 2002). The Digital Bangladesh campaign by the ruling Awami League in Bangladesh is but a latter-day iteration of fantasies of unhindered communication. As we shall see in the next chapter, cell phone imagery has become a new tool of disaggregation and identification when faced with crowds and the face of crowds, its power paralleling and at times overshadowing that of the state.

A COUNTRY UNDECIDED

> Sometimes the people counterfeits fidelity to itself. The mob turns traitor to the people.
>
> —Victor Hugo, *Les Misérables*

"The war over the coal mines turned out like the war of independence," Kofirul said excitedly. "People joined in like Allah's *farishtas* [angels]." Kofirul was a chauffeur for a private company outside of Phulbari. He was also a part-time farmer with some land and a small-scale fruit orchard. He was not unique in drawing more than passing parallels between the liberation war and the mining protests. Many in Phulbari who were old enough to remember claimed that the last time they witnessed such violence, lived in such uncertainty, or experienced similar apprehension about the future was about four decades earlier during the nine months of civil war that led to Bangladesh's independence. Kofirul's statement added new meanings to these analogies. He lived in a cluster of villages in Birampur Upazila that some of the elders of his larger clan from the Rajshahi region in the northwest had occupied around 1968–69. Located on the banks of the river Padma, *nadibhangoner desh* (the country of river erosion) was how their ancestral home in Chapai Nawabganj was referenced, with which they maintained professional and affective ties.

What makes the case of Kofirul and others with similar itineraries relevant is the emplotment of their arrival story and the discriminations they faced since as a frontier narrative, the extent of which included being named dalal or *razakar* after the war.[7] During my fieldwork, it was the precariousness of their relationship with the land on which they lived and grew up, and the means of their livelihood, that had come under renewed scrutiny because of the impending plans for open-pit mining. For Kofirul and many others who had been squatters on government land for close to half a century, the topics of relocation and compensation and the related issue of land deeds elicited added anxiety. They were worried and at times simply scared to express their fears that in the absence of title deeds and other legal artifacts they would not be eligible for compensation. The stakes were admittedly high, and this was partly why they were eager participants in the movement protesting the coal mines. Activists from outside the area looked forward to wide participation from Kofirul's people in meetings and processions. That was also perhaps the reason why this village was one of the first I was encouraged to visit during my fieldwork.

Speaking with some of the elders who were among the first group of Chapayas (i.e., people of Chapai Nawabganj) who came to the Phulbari region decades ago, I gleaned a narrative of arrival framed in a language of bravery and innovation. It started with the man who headed the very first team and had since assumed a position of a village head. In their memories, bold men tamed a wild land and faced the animosity of locals, both Bengalis and *adibasi* (indigenous populations), often resulting in tense encounters. A man showed me the scar he had been carrying for years from an *adibasi*'s spear that had hit him in the chest. While some mentioned finding upon arrival thick forests rumored to contain wild animals (*bagh-bhalluk*—tigers and bears), others were more modest in their recollections and talked about a forest of *shal* trees already under attack by encroaching human habitation. By the time they found the forest, they only saw the stumps, which they removed to prop up new huts. The Padma, once one of the largest and fiercest rivers flowing through the eastern part of Bengal, was fast destroying acres of land and hundreds of villages along with it, including the ones where Kofirul and his family lived. From the banks of the Padma they came all the way to Phulbari, where land was in relative abundance. While the first group arrived in 1968, they kept in touch with home. Families and neighbors joined soon thereafter.

Things became difficult in 1971, as they did for the rest of the country. But the story of Kofirul's people was peculiar even by that standard. The whole village was named a collaborator, *razakar* in this case, soon after the war was over. The accusation forced them to go back to Rajshahi, though not to their own village but to a refugee camp where they sustained themselves for months on government relief. Some of them were sent to prison on "false" charges of murder and other antistate activities, such as hobnobbing with the Biharis. The Biharis (literally, those from the Bihar region in eastern India) were the large number of Urdu-speaking refugees in East Pakistan who were collectively branded collaborators, and later in independent Bangladesh, "non-citizens." They have been vilified, and for all intents and purposes "forgotten," for their alleged support of West Pakistan at the time of war (Siddiqi 2013). The people of Kofirul's larger clan were also accused of helping the Naxalites (Maoist radicals) who were the most active in the 1960s and 1970s in West Bengal, the northeast in India, and other parts of South Asia.

Reminiscences of this group of people highlighted a dialectic of accusation and assimilation regarding the collaborator—both historically and in the present. These people were caught in the mayhem of a recently ended war with identities in renewed flux. The lines between freedom fighters and criminals were often slippery, the distinction depending at times on whether or not the former had surrendered their arms to the allied Bangladesh-India forces. Their entire village, though much smaller in the early 1970s, was labeled a collaborator. The conditions under which they were implicated is aptly captured in a conversation between an elderly villager and myself:

> Villager: Then, after independence, we were called Naxals. But [the Naxals] just lived here, they ate. They came here like you did. They eat, come and live here. But the word of mouth [*prabad*] was that these people are cooperating with the Naxals.
>
> Author: So, they said that you people were helping the Naxals. Then how did the word "razakar" come in?
>
> Villager: Well, we are people of Rajshahi-Chapai. This was just a common saying [*janaprabad*], you see . . .
>
> Author: So, why did they arrest your people? What do you think?
>
> Villager: Well, apparently the Naxals were against them.
>
> Author: Against the muktis?
>
> Villages: [Nods] But there were many muktis also among them.
>
> Author: Among the Naxals?
>
> Villager: Yes. That they are Naxals we are not able to evaluate. A few of them came, said, "*Chacha* [Uncle], we will stay here at night. Give us some food." So, we gave food. That was how it was.
>
> Author: Did you people do *politics* [in English] at the time?
>
> Villager: No, we had no clue as to what *politics* was at the time. How can we ordinary people understand *politics*? We were just maintaining social ties [*othabosa, cholafera*] with them. We still maintain social ties with them. We have nothing for *rajneeti* [politics].

My interlocutor brought together—and confused—incidents that took place soon after the war ended the same way he used both past and present tenses to relate his memories. The first was the one in which four men of their village were arrested in charge of the murder of a well-known left activist with whom they claimed to have a good relationship. The second happened around the same time, within a couple of months of independence, when his whole village was torched and they were forced to leave for Rajshari. All this was facilitated by the accusation of collaboration by the muktis, the "freedom fighters" who were obviously running the show, having won a war. They were against the Naxals, that is, the Maoist radicals. This man and the others he represented were condemned for cooperating with the Naxals despite the lack of any express ideological affinity with them. The cooperation, as was repeatedly explained, was due to a sense of neighborly responsibility. When I asked him about why specifically *razakar*, a word that had particular connotations in this war that must be distinguishable from the Naxals who were also clearly enemies of the state, he said confidently that it was because they were Chapayas, that is, "outsiders" having come from so far away so recently. There was more to this accusation of collaboration, however, than simply being seen as foreign and, therefore, dangerous. Let me explain.

Sharif, another elderly gentleman, elaborated on some of the complexities of the events mentioned above. I quote this interaction at length:

> Author: Weren't you scared that the army might come, or . . . [during the war]
>
> Sharif: See, we had surveillance [*pahara*] in our village.
>
> Author: You had surveillance? So, who were guarding you, the Naxals?
>
> Sharif: No, at first there were no Naxals. When we first came here . . . there were these Biharis. . . .
>
> Author: There were Biharis here?
>
> Sharif: There were. There were a few Biharis here. When the Bengalis started being unfair to the Biharis, then we were the ones who helped in sending them to Phulbari. One person among them, . . . he was highly educated, a graduate. He worked for the military. One day he told me, . . . "I am one of the Khans [a Muslim surname which was also a popular shorthand for West Pakistanis], and the country is run by the Khans. The country belongs to the Khans and I am also a Khan. . . . You know everything. You people are pro-Pakistan." Well, we *were* all pro-Pakistan at the time. [The gentleman said] "I am telling you, join hands with these people [the Naxals]. Do you understand?"

Author: So, he had a sense that there might be some problem?

Sharif: Yes, because the country was still undecided [*desh takhono thik hoini*]. I was actually good friends with him. [He said], "The country is still not decided but I am telling you, you should very cautiously join hands with [the Naxals]." He was being so cautious as if he didn't even want Allah to know . . . like really carefully. So we were somewhat friendly with them. Mixed with them, that's all. . . . It was a Friday when the country gained independence. I went to the market on Saturday. I came back from the market and at that time there was this uproar [*damodol*], as if we wouldn't survive the day. I came back home. . . . We sent people to those with whom we were cooperating. They came in the evening to do the duty [of surveillance]. Those people did the duty. There were these other groups in the village in the south. They had started looting. Then these people here went and stopped them and they couldn't loot anymore. Since then, [the Naxals) stayed back. They camped here among us for a long time. We gave them rice and lentils, they ate. They cooked. They stayed. Then after staying for a while when they didn't surrender their arms, a rumor started that there are Naxals here. But by that time they were gone. They were not here anymore. After eight to ten days of their departure, our village was sieged. Having sieged the village, they threw us out. We were scared. They said, "You can stay if you want to or you can leave. We can't do anything about it. If there is any trouble, you'll be responsible for it." Then we left out of fear. . . . Nobody hurt us during the war. Nobody attacked us. But it was because we were socializing with [the Naxals]. . . . But if we hadn't done that already, maybe other parties would have caused problems. They would have vandalized. But nobody did that to us.

Sharif's detailed description of the events reflected the confusing times that he was remembering; indeed, "the country was not decided," as his West Pakistani acquaintance had told him in confidence. Sharif used "they" interchangeably to index the Naxals (Maoist radicals), the muktis (freedom fighters), and the Biharis (non-Bengali refugees). The relationship among these groups has a long and explosive history, which had become particularly violent around the time of the 1971 war. Bengali nationalism reached a crescendo toward the end of the 1960s, specifically with the People's Uprising (*Gono Obbhutthan*) against Ayub Khan's dictatorship (see the introduction). The relationship between Biharis and Bengalis grew tense. Ethnically tainted, their animosity became violent, since the Biharis, at least in some contexts, were known to sympathize with the cause of Pakistan. Radical Bengali nationalists had committed horrific acts against the Biharis in the aftermath of the war, collectively branding them as collaborators. In independent Bangladesh, the Biharis are still labeled "stranded Pakistanis," denied citizenship, and more or less written out of nationalist discourses and policies (Siddiqi 2013). It is a part of history that to date remains inadequately documented in dominant readings of the 1971 war (Schendel 2009). Naxals were long vilified by both the Pakistani and the new Bangladeshi state led by the Awami League, a mainstream party known to nurture deep antagonism against the radical left.

What stood out in this interaction was the ease with which Sharif admitted to his friendship with a Bihari gentleman. He not only revealed a collective sympathy for the Biharis, but also casually proclaimed to have been a supporter of Pakistan. At the time Sharif could have been easily labeled a collaborator for saying so. However, the reason behind the persecution of Sharif's community was the intimacy that it shared with the Naxals, as if it were the Naxals and not the West Pakistanis who were the enemies. Sharif and his people showed compassion for the Naxals without having much understood their politics; they shared food, and sought out their help when "other groups" (muktis or their allies) were looting and vandalizing in the heady days following freedom.

"FREEDOM FIGHTERS TURN COLLABORATORS"

The act of naming a collaborator, according to contemporary accounts of the resistance against the mines and as remembered by those labeled collaborators forty years ago, takes on the appearance of political strategy during moments of heightened social instability. It is tempting to read these accounts as the scapegoating of marginal social types (outsiders or

squatters) in turbulent times when identities among freedom fighters, radicals, criminals, or foreigners were in constant flux. But the actual events,
and more crucially their present narrations, belied such explanation. It is
true that these so-called collaborators helped Biharis escape the torture of
Bengalis. The latter were by then the master players having a new nation to
themselves. But it is also correct that the allegation of collaboration was
leveled against them not because they were Chapayias (meaning from the
Chapai Nawabganj region, and therefore, "foreigners") who were helping
the ethnic Others, but because of their reciprocal arrangement with the
Naxals, who were clearly—ethnically—one's own. There were even some
muktis among the Naxals, Sharif claimed, thus further breaking down
the very distinctions that were mobilized four decades ago to accuse
his people.

The distinctions were hardly tenable even forty years later as the head-
line of a news article in 2010 read, "Freedom Fighters Turn Collaborators."
In a written comment presented in parliament, the minister of law, Shafique
Ahmed, noted that forty-three members of the Awami League, the reigning political party, had been found involved with antiliberation activities
during the Independence War of 1971 (bdnews24.com 2010)—this despite
the monopoly of accusation and the political currency that the Awami
League seems to enjoy when naming a collaborator. The topic of punishing
the collaborators of 1971 has been debated—and deferred—in the decades
since independence. It was rejuvenated in 2009–10 as one of the post-
emergency government's main electoral promises. At least one prominent
collaborator who was also a leader of Jamaat-e-Islami was until quite recently a "foreigner"; Ghulam Azam, the late *amir*, had his Bangladeshi
citizenship revoked following accusations of collaboration and crimes
against humanity soon after independence. A "collaborator's tribunal" was
to be set up in January 1972, but the government of Bangladesh declared a
general amnesty the following year in exchange for Pakistan's recognition
of Bangladesh and the repatriation of thousands of Bengalis held in the
former West Pakistan (Schendel 2009: 172). Ghulam Azam got his Bangladeshi passport in the 1990s when the Bangladesh Nationalist Party, the
archrival of the Awami League, came to power and soon needed the support of Jamaat-e-Islami to form a coalition government.

Yet, collaboration as a social phenomenon, as I have situated it in Phulbari, exceeded the state or the international economy. Neither a foreigner nor necessarily a wealthy local, a collaborator did not bring any social resolution. In the cases of witchcraft, as studied by James Siegel in Indonesia, the category of the witch changed its form in the post-Suharto political climate, which in itself was marked by a crisis of recognition. In the case of the state's failure to recognize its citizens, and in times when established political patrimonial ties were in crisis, people accused others of witchcraft. These others were ordinary people like themselves—anybody could be a witch. The danger of being accused was pervasive, giving rise to violent deaths of those named witches.

The arrival of Asia Energy in Phulbari produced a political environment where day-to-day social and political ties became vulnerable in different, yet telling ways. Whereas most leaders of the mainstream political parties sided with the company and worked on its behalf, their followers across the villages felt that their land and livelihood were directly threatened, and became gradually alienated from a long-standing system of political patronage. The energy company played a crucial role in reconfiguring these relationships. As I was told rather bluntly, "Before it was the political parties that gave out money. Now it is the company who is doing it." The collaborator became the figuration of that which knew how to navigate the new political landscape.

Writing on Walter Benjamin's exposition on the intriguer, Samuel Weber adds, "The site and structure, the plot of the mourning play is thus neither unified, nor chaotic. It is the site of a conflict and of a divergence. It is neither that of the isolated individual (the tragic hero), nor of the liberated community prophesied by the death of that individual . . . It is the site of the plotter, a demonic but also comical figure" (Weber and Benjamin 2008: 155). Benjamin himself argues that the sovereign partakes of a creation in which ubiquitous guilt drives those who rule to become first tyrants, and then, often, martyrs. Unlike the Greek tragedies to which the *Trauspiele* have been unduly and mistakenly compared, in the latter there is an absence of any restitution of the "moral order of the universe" (Benjamin 2009). The pervasive suspicions, accusations, and deliberations around the dalal spelled out a world of destabilized authority to which members of a community—however fragmented—had attempted to ascribe some sense of morality, be it by burning money or by blaming others of collaboration. And yet, the acts themselves raised questions of moral authority, identity, and democratic struggle anew.

In post-emergency Bangladesh, the collaborator had stoked the most potent crowd politics. On the one hand, in the uprising of 2013 against the International Crimes Tribunal, urban Bangladesh saw a form of secular crowd that had challenged familiar forms of doing politics. The protesters' call for capital punishment simultaneously brought up anxieties of mob mentality and vigilantism that are long-standing liberal fears around collective sovereignty. On the other hand, the Islamist backlash against the uprising congealed disparate forces that have since become important stakeholders in national politics. Popular politics and the state were once again at odds with each other when it came to the familiar figure of the collaborator and the newly minted ones of the blogger and the militant (*jongi*). New attempts at recognition through digital technologies of enumeration and visualization have flourished in order to manage and harness the potentiality of these crowds. The next chapter continues with that story.

CHAPTER 5

THE BODY OF THE CROWD

DESPITE THE AWAMI LEAGUE'S campaign promises of justice for war crimes and advancements in the digital sector, little had changed since the army had stepped aside after the elections in 2009. A large number of citizens continue to be killed in "crossfires," an inaccurately named state-sanctioned strategy of killing without impunity that was rampant even before Sheikh Hasina won the national elections. Acting on a similar urgency with which the visual field was manipulated during the emergency—the photograph of the notorious kick in chapter 1 is a good example—the post-emergency government banned a 2010 exhibition named *Crossfire* that attempted to publicize the grim reality of extrajudicial executions by the police and their elite colleagues, the Rapid Action Battalion (Gonzalez 2010). The ban was lifted within a few days, as was the censorship of Facebook during that same year by the intervention of the high court. Still, Facebook and YouTube have been made inaccessible multiple times since. In November 2015, the government blocked the social networking site for three weeks, apparently in order to manage the spread of rumors, when the death penalties of convicted war criminals S. Q. Chowdhury and Ali Ahsan Mohammad Mujahid were upheld by the Supreme Court. These were two of the most high-profile sentences issued by the tribunal. In 2017, the cabinet division sought the opinion of the Bangladesh Telecommunication Regulatory Commission (BTRC) to take down Facebook for six hours every night because of the site's "detrimental effect on students" (Husain 2017). The potential move has already been parodied as "an analog approach to digital Bangladesh," a riff on the governmental tagline "Digital Bangladesh by 2021." The official decree to disrupt fast Internet connections to quell the student protests in August 2018, the Information and Communication Technology Act, and the persecution of activists and academics for spreading "rumors" are the most ironic abuses of power by a regime that prides itself on technological innovations.

An increasingly Internet-savvy populace has duly noticed the gap between the lofty ideals of a digital Bangladesh and the crude and clearly futile attempts at surveillance of the Internet. The cartoon in figure 9 is emblematic of the criticisms that such official measures generated during the weeklong censorship in 2010. Surfacing on Facebook, it grounds the irony of the ban in one of the highest sanctums of bureaucratic red tape, the office of the director general (DG) of BTRC. The figure shows two low-ranking government employees, or peons, as they are called, chatting before the closed door of the DG's office. Severed wires, a literal representation of the interruption in transmission, are scattered on the floor. The form of address (*tui* in Bangla) between the two characters suggests an egalitarian intimacy due to their comparable subordinate status in the pyramidal hierarchy of BTRC. The character on the left is curious to whom the man with the tray is bringing the alcohol—whisky and soda, read the labels on the bottles. The man with the drinks replies with a broad smile, "How can the DG be *taal* [a colloquial term for drunk] without alcohol? Only when *taal* can he dream of a Digi-taal Bangladesh."

"DG-taal," then, denotes the director general's drunkenness, which in Bangla with the adjective coming after the noun works perfectly insofar as grammar is concerned. The pun on "digital" of course succeeds due to the host of meanings associated with alcohol and the bureaucratic nightmare that is the regulatory commission. By imbibing alcohol whose purchase and consumption, bar some minor exceptions, is prohibited in a Muslim-majority country, the DG blatantly and predictably bypasses legal injunctions and gets to enjoy the good life. As the head of BTRC, however, he does not shy away from imposing draconian laws on the

FIGURE 9 A cartoon caricaturing the BTRC ban on social media. *Source*: Arifur Rahman, Cartoon Studio, https://cartoon1.wordpress.com/2009/03/10/dg-tal/.

citizens. Only under the influence of alcohol can the DG decide to censor Facebook, all the while paying lip service to the ongoing official campaign for technology-enhanced developmentalism.

This final chapter is located in post-emergency Bangladesh. Its primary sites are the physical and virtual spaces of politics and activism that are at once emergent and historically poignant. At one level, it explores a particular fascination with the body—of the collaborator, the blogger, and the militant—and its relationship to crowd politics in democratic Bangladesh. At another level, it sheds light on the proliferation of digital technologies that have enabled but also deeply impacted social and political communication. The ethnographic part of the chapter is based on my conversations with activists, bloggers, and political personalities directly involved in the protests against the International Crimes Tribunal in 2013 in Dhaka. I know many of them personally due to my ongoing research on environmental activism. The second part of the chapter engages primarily with visual texts, thereby offering striking parallels to the analysis of the visual culture of the emergency in chapter 1. I start at Shahbag, the physical site after which the 2013 uprising is named.

"Bloggers are not really street activists," Anik, an online activist, told me in March 2013.[1] This was weeks after a massive crowd of protesters had taken over a major junction in the capital city. Years after the uprising against coal mining in Phulbari and the end of the emergency period in late 2008, the protest at Shahbag was the most significant public political event in Bangladesh in the last decade. It was also one of a kind. A group of bloggers who had long been demanding justice for the war crimes of the 1971 war of independence sensed a conspiracy in the workings of the International Crimes Tribunal (ICT). Under the leadership of the Awami League, the government of Bangladesh had set up the ICT in 2010 to try the collaborators of the war of independence, and the ICT, in this case, had become the target of the spontaneous outburst. The bloggers occupied Shahbag, a busy crossroads in the middle of Dhaka, and rallied a crowd of thousands in a matter of days. In what quickly became known as the Shahbag movement, the seeming lenience in one of the tribunal's verdicts was being questioned. Because 2013 was an election year, the protesters suspected strategic negotiations between the government and

Jamaat-e-Islami, the largest Islamist opposition party. A number of Jamaat-e-Islami's high-ranking members were under trial, and it was believed the verdicts could very well be used in exchange for political concessions. In other words, long-held suspicions of foul play in the judicial process, the electoral system, the party in power, and the state in general had collectively stoked the anger of the relatively young organizers of the protests.

Anik was right in pointing out the curious role of online activists in Shahbag. It was not the streets but rather the virtual medium that was generally their playground and political field. And yet, through this movement, a part of the blogging community had transferred its grievances from the keyboard to a hectic but historically meaningful corner of one of the world's most crowded cities. Anik was one of the 135 protesters who formed a human chain on the afternoon of February 5. They were angry about the ICT's second ruling of life imprisonment and were demanding the death penalty for Abdul Kader Molla, a convicted war criminal and member of Jamaat-e-Islami. Theirs was generally a disembodied passion, Anik seemed to imply, but it was their transition from the screen to the street that gave the bloggers rare political recognition and unforeseen notoriety.

I met Anik while walking around Shahbag just a couple of days before. The area starting at the gate of the National Museum and stretching all the way to the Faculty of Fine Arts of the University of Dhaka was still cordoned off from traffic. Small groups of students, activists, bloggers, and political workers socialized as billboards with graphic appeals for justice and capital punishment hovered nearby (figure 10). Some of them were already peeling off. Peeking through them were familiar commercial exhortations of fairness products and mobile phone connectivity. Those who were gathering to start a torchlight protest to commemorate the forty-second year of national independence remembered the giant crowds of which they had been a part when the Shahbag movement was at its peak.

"You have no idea what it was like," a friend who had fought in the liberation war as a teenager told me as he guided me through the impromptu shrines that had cropped up on the street and the sidewalks

FIGURE 10 Billboards at Shahbag, March 2013. Photo by the author.

during the protest. They glorified and memorialized the war and were now in various stages of ruin. My friend said he visited Shahbag every day and found inspiration from the young soldiers fighting for justice. Even as our procession of hundreds started its journey from Shahbag, glowing under the flickering flames and circling the nearby University of Dhaka campus (figure 11), I could tell it was nothing compared to the crowds of early February 2013, images of which were beamed across the globe almost instantly thanks to the tech savvy urban protesters.

This rally in March 2013 took place a little over a month after the killing of Ahmed Haider Rajib. A self-proclaimed atheist blogger, Rajib was stabbed to death near his house in Dhaka for his antireligious Bangla blog (Hammer 2015). By May 2013, however, the equation had changed for good. The members of Hefazat-e-Islam took issues with Shahbag's secularist agenda. In response, they too occupied a congested roundabout only a few miles east of Shahbag, at Motijheel, the business district. Hefazat is a coalition of about a dozen religious associations based in more than 25,000 *qawmi madrasas*.[2] By 2013, with the support of the main opposition party and its allies, Hefazat was intervening in national politics with a confidence never seen before. Mirroring the very incitement that they were opposing, the Hefazat rally also demanded capital punishment for the bloggers. It took issue with the atheism expressed in the "blasphemous" writings of the Shahbag movement's organizers. The Hefazat activists demonstrated in the thousands, presented a thirteen-point manifesto to the government, which included harsh indictments of bloggers, and vandalized public property. The state violently repressed the uprising. The full extent of the nighttime operation is still unclear. To deflect accusations of harboring the atheists, the government arrested four bloggers under the Information and Communication Technology Act (Hossain 2013).

The self-consciously secular and religious crowds at Shahbag and Motijheel, respectively, revealed a competitive mimesis between the now powerful categories of atheist (*nastik*) and militant (*jongi*). While Shahbag was resolutely nonviolent, the Hefazat activists organized antigovernment showdowns that relied on well-known strategies of urban unrest. A negative intimacy between the secular and religious crowds

FIGURE 11 Torchlight procession at Shahbag, March 2013. Photo by the author.

mobilized in the Shahbag-Hefazat phenomenon also found analogous expression in the vigilantism across virtual and actual crowds, which is the focus of the second part of the chapter. In the shadow of the state killing of the Hefazat members and the arrest of Internet activists, the ritualized murders of bloggers, and the crowds that had set the events in motion, I offer here some final thoughts on crowdedness and popular politics in Bangladesh that pivoted on the question of the body. The "body-politics" that emerged in the wake of Shahbag and Hefazat are symptomatic—and not simply representative—of the ideological and social fissures that the protest movement of 2013 had cracked wide open. They played out partly in the streets of Dhaka, from Shahbag to Motijheel, and partly in the blogosphere. The traffic between physical space and cyberspace that these events so powerfully brought to public attention is now a part of their lasting legacies. No longer hidden behind usernames and moderated blog spaces and sheltered from print and satellite news media, bloggers and their words became fodder for the mill of contagious rumor that invited public scorn, governmental scrutiny, and at times, fatal violence. This chapter, then, is an ethnographic encounter with the unfolding relationships between an embodied politics such as street protests and the seemingly disembodied forms of digital political participation such as social media activism.

What I had heard in and around Shahbag in 2013 was neither reducible to unadulterated patriotism nor politically motivated denunciations of the movement. There was no shortage of either in print news or on television talk shows that were in a tizzy during the movement's heyday. Nor were my conversations limited to the human rights and feminist concerns with the death penalty, the procedural flaws of the tribunal, or the chauvinism in the movement's signs and slogans (K. A. Ahmed 2015; Bergman 2016; Amnesty International 2015). These were contested issues even when Shahbag was at its peak. In contrast, what stood out in the words and actions of my interlocutors was a general sense of despair. While various emotions, such as patriotism, pride, and disgust, ran high at Shahbag, I concentrate here on what I call political despair among these dedicated participants, which I came to realize has had a far wider reach. One of the main sources of this particular affect has been the opposition between the atheist-blogger (*nastik*) on the one side and the Islamist-extremist (*jongi*) on the other. The myriad ways in which this has impacted Bangladeshi politics is now one of Shahbag's unique, if unforeseen, legacies (Wasif 2015).

The despair around the ideological cleavage rested squarely on the body. An early provocation of this came from the controversy around the death of a blogger. The dead-body politics that followed assumed but also occasioned the atheist/believer divide and made way for more violence, including the murders of a number of religious activists and secular bloggers in the months and years to come. The other area where the body captured the political imagination was the presumed corporeal nature of nonsecular politics. The physicality, irrationality, and makeup of so-called religious affect seemingly distinguished the Shahbag protesters from their ideological opponents. This opposition echoes, as I will show, the analytical boundary between the people and the crowd in canonical writing on mass society, a point I explored in the introduction (Canetti 1984 [1962]; Dean 2016; Le Bon 2002 [1896]; Mazzarella 2010b; Jonsson 2013).

These two ways of foregrounding the body urge us to look beyond the protests' immediate context. They reflect some of the tensions around the carnal dimension of popular democracies, what Eric Santner has called "the flesh" (2011). That democratic societies cannot get rid of the problem of the bodily dimension of representation is made clear in the visual import of political assemblies; what matters is that "bodies" assemble (Butler 2015: 8). Acting in concert, Judith Butler argues, can be an embodied form of calling into question the inchoate and powerful dimensions of reigning notions of the political. Still, Butler dismisses collectivities that are not necessarily energized by the increased material vulnerabilities of everyday life. She is interested in finding "the people" in the demands that bolster a democratic ideal of equality and inclusivity. How, then, is one to situate Shahbag, from its bodily occupation of public space to its desire to seek justice through the management of the bodies of the collaborator, the blogger, or the Islamist militant? How do we go beyond a theme of arrested modernity, signaled by terms like "lynch mobs" or "fanatics" that have been used profusely to describe Shahbag and its detractors, respectively? And how do the antics and ambivalences surfacing in the wake of Shahbag expose some of the constitutive disappointments that riddle the project of modern democracy, surely in Bangladesh but elsewhere as well?

THE YOUNG PEOPLE HAD ENOUGH

Shahbag was at best a rumor of a revolution in a place where a sense of political malaise has long become business as usual. Armed with the seemingly unstoppable energy of youth, it was set to awaken the conscience of a middle-aged nation lost in historical amnesia. But if hope and despair make an antagonistic pair, then Shahbag had stirred up both with a rare intensity. It was an eruption that carried the echoes of the prodemocracy student uprising of the late 1980s and the antiauthoritarian agitations during the most recent state of emergency in 2007–8, though the comparisons stop there. The euphoria around Shahbag, however short-lived, was not just about envisioning a different democratic future, nor was it a demand for more transparency in the political process. Its core appeal lay in matters far more foundational to the existence of the nation. To redeem the past for the sake of the future was an idea that, though simmering in public political life for decades, found its loudest voice in Shahbag. It made both the desires and the disappointments far more palpable than any other collective protest in independent Bangladesh.

Shahbag also took place in a different world than most other youth-led movements to date. Keenly aware of recent democratic uprisings elsewhere, the digitally sophisticated generation connected with an international audience through blogs, tweets, Facebook updates, and images. Shahbag is by far one of Bangladesh's most photographed political events with an enormous digital footprint. Still, within months, the topic of Shahbag among its supporters, critics, and observers alike was tinged with profound disappointment. Its rather hasty fall from grace is perhaps not all that uncommon for spontaneous political events. From the Egyptian revolution and Greek anti-austerity showdowns to Occupy Wall Street and Black Lives Matter in the United States, a sense of disenchantment has prevailed over the dissipation of political energies (Dean 2016; Hamdy 2012; Shenker 2016). In the case of Shahbag, however, its afterlife demands our critical attention as much as the conditions of its rise, if not more.

This has to do with the unusual nature of the movement itself as well as a surge in counterrevolutionary forces since. For the same reason, it also compels us to consider despair as a significant political emotion.

The affective landscape of Shahbag has been commonly understood in terms of nationalist passion. My focus, as I said, is on a far more neglected though widespread affect, that of despair. As a political concept, despair is akin to distrust, cynicism, and crisis, each of which boasts considerable theoretical heft (Roitman 2013; Rosanvallon 2006; Sloterdijk 1988). My thinking about political despair looks beyond crisis. In this sense, it differs from how Sergei Oushakine and Lori Allen have observed the role of despair in postsocialist Russia and in Palestine during the second Intifada, respectively (Allen 2009; Oushakine 2009). In Russia, in the absence of a unifying cultural, political, and social framework, the trope of loss was the most effective symbolic device for those facing the new reality after communism. Allen offers a critique of the discourse of despair in relation to martyrdom in Palestine. The despair I observed during fieldwork, however, resonates more with Robyn Marasco's philosophical approaches, which see it as a *dialectical* passion that can never fully let go of hope, its familiar and estranged other. Despair, as Marasco points out, is not a pathology or paralysis but is rather in connection with the passions of critique and the energies of everyday life (Marasco 2015).

Shahbag's beginning was fueled by suspicions of foul play in the judicial process, the electoral system, and the state. Within weeks, it became a source of despair among some of its core participants and many others who watched it from outside. Instead of thinking of these moments of conflict as anomalous, I foreground them to understand the paradoxes and potentials of despair for democratic politics. Focusing on despair does not ignore Shahbag's continued relevance for Bangladeshi public life. It is quite the opposite. Shahbag has revealed ideological schisms that have gained exceptional affective density on questions of history, religion, justice, and democracy. The protests were followed by politico-religious backlash, ritualized murders of bloggers, violent state intervention against Islamist opposition, governmental repression of online activities, sporadic attacks on Hindu minorities, and an insidious discursive culture around the terms "atheist" and "blogger" that had just enough currency to change the very terms of national politics. This was a remarkable volte-face from the heady days of early February. How did a patriotic spectacle soon come to stand for its excesses, such as dogmatic secularism, untrammeled ethnic nationalism, or youthful impudence? What is it about Shahbag that rests on such oscillations of hope and despair, of intrigue and indifference, of identification but, more palpably, disappointment? And how does Shahbag shed light on the relationship between crowds and justice in the political history of Bangladesh?

Contrary to its title, the International Crimes Tribunal (ICT) was set up in 2010 as a domestic trial.[3] It realized the AL's electoral pledge to try the war criminals, a move deferred by all those in power, including the AL, in the four decades since independence. The party had convincingly won the national elections in 2008 with an enthusiastic endorsement from women and youth.[4] This post-1971 generation (*projonmo*) was the most vocal in demanding justice for war crimes and the trial of the collaborators (known variously as *dalal* or *razakar*, as discussed in chapter 4). The collaborators, on the other hand, were the source of debate as well as anger, confusion, and complicity at both political and personal levels, beginning with the war and continuing up to the present, with their political status shifting with each new regime—democratic or authoritarian (Mohaiemen 2011; Mookherjee 2015).

To some extent Shahbag carried forth the mission of the People's Court (*Gono Adalat*) led by Jahanara Imam decades earlier. Imam was the mother of a slain freedom fighter, the author of a famous book based on the diary she had kept during the war, and an ardent spokesperson for justice for war crimes.[5] Indeed, a giant portrait of Imam looked over the Shahbag crowd for weeks. The demand for a permanent statue of "the mother of the martyr" (*shahid janani*), however, had fallen on deaf ears. And yet, Shahbag's appeal surpassed that of *Gono Adalat* of the 1980s and early 1990s. The fact that this was a generation that had not been witness to the actual war added poignancy to its struggle for justice. Nine members of the largest religious party, the Jamaat-e-Islami (Jamaat), and two members of the largest opposition party, the Bangladesh Nationalist Party (BNP), were indicted in 2012 as suspects in war crimes. Shahbag's demand of death soon included the ban on religious politics of all kinds. The government responded by proposing amendments to the ICT law, allowing the prosecution to appeal the sentence, and decreasing the time for an appeal to be completed. This allowed the Supreme Court to convert Molla's verdict to the death penalty seven months after the protests began.

I might have arrived at Shahbag a few weeks too late, but its last whimper, as it were, stood out as a symptom of a political culture of which it was born and one that was emergent—for better or for worse—in its wake. For about twenty-two days, the Shahbag gathering seized a busy thoroughfare in a notoriously crowded city while keeping distance from direct party politics. It eschewed picketing, vandalism and arson, and violent strikes, all familiar strategies of street protest. At Shahbag, mostly but not exclusively middle-class students, activists, and intellectuals formed human chains, took oaths, sang songs, lit candles, collected signatures, and on one occasion, wrote public letters to the martyrs of the war in whose name they waged their current battle (Khatun 2013). They appeared restrained in their spontaneity, resolute in their arrogance, and responsible in their demand no matter the seeming disjuncture between its form and content—that of peaceful demonstration and the call for capital punishment.

Shahbag sits uncomfortably within a familiar framework of a political movement in yet another sense. Public protests across South Asia are scripted antagonistically to the state and/or as a collective struggle for rights. Shahbag may have started as the former but was later criticized for not accommodating more immediate yet long-standing social issues. Its awkwardness as a progressive formation was most powerfully captured in its core demand. Left-liberal sensibilities were offended by the practice of death penalty (Khan 2013; Mohaiemen 2013). The same sensibilities shape secular scholarly work and progressive politics broadly conceived. Popular agitation to influence the judiciary also raised concerns about the neutrality of the tribunal and disrespect for law and due process in the name of "the people." The human rights discourses that flourished parallel to Shahbag expressed reservations about its central slogan, *phansi chai*—we want the noose. It is important to note that the religiopolitical responses to Shahbag's purported atheism, however, did not question the practice of the death penalty, which remains the highest form of punishment in Bangladeshi law. Nor is Shahbag's singularity reducible to its class makeup, though surely socioeconomic factors heavily limited its physical and ideological reach.

People started gathering in front of the National Museum after the second verdict. Molla, found guilty on five out of six counts of crimes against humanity, was given a life sentence. The tribunal's first sentence, incidentally, was death. It was handed in absentia to Abul Kalam Azad, who had absconded a week before the court's ruling. Azad's disappearance and Molla's life sentence made those who were following the trial suspicious. A veteran activist shared her generational perspective in print: "The young people had enough of compromises and underhand dealings and wanted to state that though they were born after the liberation war, they were sick of major political parties playing politics of convenience with our own history" (Kabir 2013). The year 2013 was an election year. The stakes were high as were the speculations of a behind-closed-doors arrangement. The seeming leniency of Molla's sentence was a coded sign for a possible secret deal between the ruling party and Jamaat. The latter has a history of forming direct and indirect alliances with the two bourgeois parties that dictate national politics. Yet, Shahbag's allure and effects exceeded these electoral equations. The paradoxes of popular politics that it embodied overwhelmed standard critiques of political expediency, nationalism, human rights, and secularism, although their complex entanglement made it at once appealing and appalling for multiple communities of interest.

A DEATH FORETOLD

As the crowds started to disperse after about ten days of intense agitation, Rajib's murder changed the course of events, perhaps for good. I was talking to an activist intimate with the inner workings of the movement about this unfortunate turn of events. Rajib was killed a month or so earlier, on February 15, 2013. He was targeted for the antireligious thoughts that populated his Bangla blog, *Thaba Baba*. Neither the activist nor I at the time knew that this death would be the first of many more to come. Between February 2013 and April 2016, seven individuals were killed and many more threatened and/or critically injured for writing blogs, publishing books by these bloggers, or simply writing about the crimes. This excludes the killings of ethnic minorities, foreigners, and, in July 2016, the execution-style murders of more than twenty individuals in Dhaka, including both foreigners and Bangladeshis. Despite some arrests, and the verdict of capital punishment for two of Rajib's murderers, the ideology, affiliation, and physical whereabouts of the perpetrators remain a subject that has challenged state intelligence, spawned conspiracy theories, and encouraged political mudslinging (Barry 2015; Bergman 2015; Hammer 2015; Subramanian 2015).

Rajib's body was brought to Shahbag. Draped in a giant national flag, the coffin was at the center of a grand procession. It gained quasi-totemic significance as the crowds renewed their vows to guarantee punishment for the war criminals. Though the murder of the blogger galvanized the movement, it also turned "blogger" into a household name in a country of 160 million with only 15 million active Internet subscribers (Hammer 2015). The backlash against Shahbag rode on the alleged atheism of the bloggers. In May, the members of Hefazat-e-Islam occupied a major roundabout at Motijheel, the business hub of Dhaka. Hefazat was founded in 2010 to protest the government's secular education policy. In 2011, it had agitated against the women's rights policy that ensured equal inheritance for women and men. By 2013, its collaboration with the main opposition against Shahbag and its sheer bodily presence made it a force to reckon with. A Shahbag activist expressed his ambivalence about the specifics of Rajib's death as he recollected the day's events: "Around 9:30 at night the news came that a blogger named Rajib was stabbed to death. . . . Our plans of phasing out didn't take off. I realized right away, on that very evening, what's going on. *We* are trying to leave [Shahbag], but somebody wants us to stay. *They* want to push Shahbag towards terrorism; meaning, having shed blood they want to turn Shahbag towards fanaticism" (emphasis added).

He had texted Imran Sarkar upon hearing the news of the killing. Sarkar, a medical doctor by profession with a background in digital activism, has been the most visible spokesperson for Shahbag. The activist told him not to accept the dead body. "Just say this," he had reportedly told Sarkar, "that [Rajib] was an atheist, he donated his body to the medical science as a service to humanity. Don't take the body." But the plans to agitate around Rajib's death and thereby claim him as one of Shahbag's own were already under way. The activist continued with regret: "But thus, the Trojan horse named Rajib was inserted. We took him, and having done that, we got into trouble. We couldn't explain anything. . . . A defensive speech was offered. *We* went on the back foot. *They* took us to the field of religion" (emphasis added).

Rajib's family denied his authorship in some of the more controversial writing against Islam or the Prophet. Fellow bloggers posted photos of screenshots of Rajib's blog. They offered technical analysis of his virtual presence as evidence of hacking suspected to have taken place after his death. His last rites came under heavy scrutiny from all quarters. Some expressed sincere reservations about giving a religious burial to a self-proclaimed atheist. Others questioned the use of the national flag to honor the dead body and turning a young, insensitive blogger into a national hero.

Despite the repeated invocations of "we" and "they," the polarization is less certain than it appears at first blush. There are at least two sets of oppositions in the activist's recollections. These oppositions are fractally recursive, which is to say, the schism reproduces itself and results in further cleavages, which also involves the projection of an opposition onto another level (Irvine and Gal 2000). The resulting binaries provide the actors with discursive or cultural resources to claim and thereby create shifting ideas of communities, selves, and identities, within a cultural field (Irvine and Gal 2000: 38). For instance, the "we" is the collectivity of Shahbag, whose reputation could be jeopardized by either taking in or disowning Rajib's body. The "they," however, is not the Islamists, but the state and its disciplinary apparatus. The army intelligence branch, Directorate General of Forces' Intelligence (DGFI), was also sometimes mentioned as a possible player in similar speculations. The activist was worried that Rajib's death would help redraw this very distinction that could prove profitable for the powers that may be. With much prescience—and a pang of despair—he announced that the danger of fueling the opposition between Islamists and bloggers could spell doom for the movement.

A young woman not much older than Rajib spelled out the fear. She was at Shahbag on the first day and was still actively involved in the programs even when Shahbag's end as a movement was imminent. We spoke on the eve of Independence Day 2013 as she was gathering empty milk cans and bamboo sticks for the torch procession that was about to start. Her thoughts were clear on this:

> Shahbag couldn't avoid Rajib's death. The opponent targeted him because of two reasons. First, they needed somebody who was controversial. And second, he had to be indispensable for Shahbag. These two requirements were fulfilled by Rajib's death. You know, all kinds of people—Hindus, Muslims, Buddhists, Christians came here. Women, men, and *hijras* came. Believers came, nonbelievers came to Shahbag. They came with a specific agenda— the verdict of war criminals and the ban on Jamaat-Shibir.[6] At this moment, Jamaat-Shibir did the calculated killing to crush the spirit of Shahbag. They did more fieldwork than we did.

There was no doubt in her mind that the perpetrators were the Islamists, particularly Jamaat. This has been the most common view about this and the other deaths in the years since. And yet, she strayed from the standard version:

> Personally, I believe it was not necessary to bring Rajib's dead body here in Shahbag to show that he was a believer. We could have avoided adding more significance to Rajib for the Shahbag movement. His religious belief was not our headache, and it should have been kept separated from the movement. Yes, he joined us. I appreciate it. But it was unwise to try to prove that he was a believer. That was a wrong decision for the movement. Whoever said it for whatever reason, I don't care, but Rajib *was* an atheist.

Note the "we" in her proclamation. Rajib, retrospectively, became an outsider to the "we" of the movement despite his clear sympathies for its cause. In hindsight, his faith, or lack thereof, was a source of concern, an uncalled-for headache. No matter the raging debates around Rajib, for her, he *was* an atheist. Dealing with that fact could have proven far more beneficial for their cause than the politics around his corpse.

The preoccupation with Rajib's body drew paradoxical responses from the protesters. In wanting to deny the importance that Rajib gained posthumously, my friends reified the body as a mediator of political affect, as both means and meaning. Katherine Verdery, for example, writes about the properties of corpses that make them, in Lévi-Strauss's words, "good to think" as symbols (Verdery 1999). Death accounts for meanings, feelings, ideas of the sacred, and the nonrational that exceed the discourses of democratic procedure, electioneering, state institutions, and political parties (Hertz 2006; Klima 2002; Verdery 1999). Their corporeality is an important means to *localizing* a claim, the case of Rajib's corpse reminds us. As was apparent at the public funeral, religious reburial can nourish the dead person with religious associations (Verdery 1999).[7]

That Rajib's body was crucial to his resignification as a martyr is perhaps not all that surprising. The spectacles around corpses in sectarian strife, political demands, and nationalist struggles globally fortify claims to martyrdom and sacrifice that are powerful cultural tropes (Allen 2009; Chatterjee 2006; Hage 2003). On the significance of death and the Arab Spring, Ameera Mittermaier notes that the lens of death allows us to think about the uprisings beyond the framework of worldly politics (Mittermaier 2015: 588). In the Egyptian contexts, political demands were never far removed from supplications addressed to God or to the martyrs themselves. Rajib's case, curiously, highlights the same by showing how his lack of faith posed a hindrance to his becoming a proper martyr for the nation.

Nations are also thought of symbolically as bodies, at times feminine, as in *Bharat Mata* or Mother India, or tortured like the body of a persecuted minority (Axel 2000; Ramaswamy 2010). What is relevant for our purposes is Rajib's retrospective cooptation or exclusion based on a reading of his blogging activities as either patriotic/progressive or anti-Islamic, thus making his body the pivot around which the *astik/nastik* (believer/atheist) boundaries were being drawn and redrawn. By bringing the body to the physical and moral center of the Shahbag movement, the activists made themselves vulnerable to accusations of fostering atheism, or worse, being atheists. Rajib's atheism, inscribed on his dead body, was now an index for the atheism of the movement at large.

Clearly the "we" of Shahbag activism has been as volatile as the "they." A few regular participants described the division primarily as one between the *Moncho*, or the official platform, and the crowd that gathered around it for weeks on end. The *Moncho* is shorthand for the official name of the Shahbag platform, *Gonojagoron Moncho* (Platform for People's Uprising). This was another source of disenchantment among many intimately involved with the protests. Over time the *Moncho* changed its shape, or at least, its focus, suggesting overt allegiances to the ruling party's agenda. It signaled governmental cooptation of a part of the movement's leadership that, for many, spelled the beginning of Shahbag's end. That a huge public gathering such as at Shahbag was afforded security by metal detectors and closed-circuit cameras, and the fact (and in equal measure, rumor) of free food distributed among those who occupied the street corner, reeked of powerful support, at least for many Bangladeshis who were ideologically opposed to or suspicious of the movement's motives. Meanwhile the body of Rajib, of the collaborators, and of people who physically assembled at Shahbag or at Motijheel became the sites where struggles for legitimacy and accountability were being staged.

BODIES WITH BEARDS

The afterlife of Rajib's body clearly set the terms of the debates that have wracked the Bangladeshi public sphere since. The last thoughts of my activist friend on their political import are revealing for yet another reason. He was thinking of the long-term implications of the newly hyphenated identity, the atheist-blogger. He cited none other than the French theorist Alain Badiou to explain it to me: "I understand all this through Badiou. *Ours* is a historical riot and *theirs* is an immediate riot. They are not being able to turn immediate riot into historical riot. But we went there in the first leap. From there we have already gone to the 'event'" (emphasis added).

The schematic classification of riots, taken at face value, disturbs some of our ethnographic and historical sensibilities.[8] But its invocation by the Bangladeshi activist to comment on the war crimes protests and the Islamist backlash is more than a theoretical reference; it is, I would argue, a symptom. Here in this opposition lies an echo of the distinction between the crowd and the autonomous citizen/subject at the core of the liberal democratic imaginary (Mazzarella 2010a). To clarify what I mean, let me discuss a couple of crowd-related incidents from 2015 that are seemingly unrelated to either the Shahbag or Hefazat showdowns in 2013. The first happened on April 14, 2015, the first day of the Bengali New Year, when groups of men physically assaulted multiple women and children amid the celebrations near the University of Dhaka campus. A group of twenty to thirty young men attacked twenty women and one ten-year-old child near the Teachers Students Center on campus (Ahmed 2015). They were molested for hours at different locations, not far from each other. A bigger crowd of men stood by and watched. Many were seen with cell phones in hand taking photos or shooting videos. Witnesses claimed that police officers standing merely twenty yards away did not intervene. Except for one political activist, who happened to be at the spot and managed to rescue a victim from the melee, there was no immediate interference into the attacks. Most explanations ascribed this unfortunate fact to the density of the crowd. Incriminating CCTV footage, however, became public soon after. The surveillance camera feed made its way into newsroom exposés and was played on a loop on multiple cable television channels. The videos made the rounds on social networking sites and video-sharing websites.

The attacks were particularly shocking because the Bengali New Year, Pahela Baishakh, along with the primary site of its celebration on or near Dhaka University campus, is widely considered to be the last bastion of Bengali secularism (for more on secularism, see M. Huq 2008; S. Huq 2013). On New Year's Day when the festivities start at the crack of dawn and go on all day, one of the largest crowds gathers at Ramna Park and the university campus. A well-known cultural institution by the name of Chhayanat has been organizing the early morning celebrations with live musical performances at the public park for half a century. The nearby Faculty of Fine Art brings out a rally (*Mangal Shobhajatra*) that showcases local traditions with vibrant papier mâché installations every New Year. In 2016, the ornate procession made UNESCO's Intangible Heritage of Humanity list. The Pahela Baishakh fanfare is a national holiday and the country's biggest nonreligious festival. A particular brand of national, cultural secularism that these celebrations embody, one that the educated, secular-progressive bloc of Bangladesh holds dearly, has been seemingly under siege of late. In 2001, a New Year's Day bomb blast at the same spot killed ten people, including a suicide bomber. This was one of the early incidents of militant violence in the city. Harkat-ul-Jihad-al-Islami, a religious group that had been banned for extremism since 2005, took credit for the deaths.

Ekattor Television ran an exposé on the 2015 incidents of sexual violence at the festival. Ekattor TV (TV '71) is Bangladesh's fourth private satellite news channel, and its name is telling. By referencing the year of independence in its proper name, the TV channel directly sides with Bengali nationalism—a domain notoriously fetishized by the ruling Awami League to the extent that *muktijuddher chetona* or the spirit of the liberation war is now as much a powerful commodity as a political tagline. As the mainstream party, AL claims recognition for representing the voice of East Pakistan, now Bangladesh, during its fight for independence from the Western wing. Sheikh Mujibur Rahman, the nationalist leader and icon who steered the party in those heady days, is both the biological father of the current prime minister and the metaphorical father of the nation (*jatir pita*).

As already mentioned, the Awami League had a sweeping victory in the 2008 national elections. Two of its campaign promises caught the imagination of the youth, who came out to vote in large numbers; the first was establishing trials for war crimes (of which ICT was the logical conclusion), and the second was the promise of a digital Bangladesh as a part of Vision 2021, the electoral tagline that gestures toward the fiftieth anniversary of independence. "Digital" here denotes a rather nebulous future-looking agenda that would help the country cope with the challenges of the twenty-first century (Mursalin 2009; Rahman 2009). Despite the manifesto's key focus on technological advancements, the AL essentially drew from a glorified version of the nation's past. In 2009, Mustafa Jabbar, president of Bangladesh Computer Samity, stressed the connection in his book *Digital Bangladesh*: "As the citizens of Bangladesh had to fight against the armed forces of Pakistan to achieve independence, they have the right to live free, independent and developed lives. So it is important to

FIGURE 12 Screenshot 1. *Source*: Ekattor TV, "CCTV Analysis of Pohela Boishakh Sexual Harrassment on Women and Children," 2015. https://www .youtube.com/watch?v=5nltgVP4-mY.

implement the Digital Bangladesh program to fulfill the hopes and desires of the nation by using digital technologies" (cited in Shoesmith, Genilo, and Asiuzzaman 2014: 219). Through its name, Ekattor Television spells out its closeness to precisely this brand of nationalist political affect and by extension, its distance from religious politics, such as the one practiced by Jamaat-e-Islami and supported by Hefazat-e-Islam. The verdict against one of the Jamaat members had fueled the Shahbag movement, which went on to demand a moratorium on religious politics of any kind.

The channel aired a couple of videos of the harassment incident right after it happened in mid-April 2015.[9] On average two to three minutes long, the video reports were culled from hours of recording from the actual sites of the crime. They start by showing a festive crowd (figure 12). Women in their ethnic best are pushing through the crowd along with men in traditional attire. Street vendors are seen hawking foods and souvenirs while cycle rickshaws paddle through a throng of pedestrians. On Pahela Baishakh, the area near Ramna Park is off-limits to cars and other motor vehicles, as is the nearby University of Dhaka campus. The video story starts in color as the female voiceover reminds the viewer that

FIGURE 13 Screenshot 2. *Source*: Ekattor TV, "CCTV Analysis of Pohela Boishakh Sexual Harrassment on Women and Children," 2015. https://www .youtube.com/watch?v=5nltgVP4-mY.

the surveillance footage does not come with any sound. Farzana Rupa, a journalist well known for gritty and investigative reporting, edited one of the news reports. The video of two minutes, forty seconds, Rupa tells us, was edited down from sixty minutes of CCTV footage. It has since been made available on YouTube (Ekattor TV 2015).

In Rupa's report, the camera zooms in on a second screen shot of the CCTV footage, taken around 44 seconds into the video (figure 13). The video also turns black and white at this point, presumably to facilitate identification. Seen here is a bearded man in a white tunic standing in the middle of a crowd of men, women, and motorcycles. The viewer learns that during the few hours of the recorded footage, men far outnumbered women and almost no woman was seen without a male companion.[10] Within seconds, a red circle on the screen locates a specific spot in the crowd where a group of men surround a rickshaw carrying two women (figure 14). One of them is being forced to get off. Other color photographs of the same incident in print media have the faces of the women blurred out.

In the second installment of the video, the figure of the bearded man resurfaces. The superimposed circle separates this particular individual

FIGURE 14 Screenshot 3. *Source*: SaiF, "TSC Occurrence At Pahela Boishakh CCTV Footage (Ekattor TV)," 2015. https://www.youtube.com/watch?v=3Px RKtG5QJM.

from a sea of people. For the first time the physical description of the man in question holds a clue to the source of the gendered violence. He wore an embroidered *panjabi* (tunic) and sported a beard, a fact the journalist repeats at least twice in the short report. The man seems to have been hovering aimlessly for a while around this one spot, leading her to inquire after his motive.

A few seconds later in the report, the same man appears near a large group that was seen moving around together and allegedly participating in more than one episode of harassment (figure 15). Some of these men also sported beards, bandannas, and long tunics. A traditional piece of clothing, a *panjabi* is everyday attire for Bangladeshi men similar to the *kameez* for women. It is also a traditional equivalent of holiday formals for men regardless of religious affiliation, though devout Muslim men often wear simple long tunics when praying. The aimless wandering of this man with a beard, his proximity to the scene of crime, and his sartorial choices, according to the report, implicate him in the crimes. The report's focus on his outward appearance—which hints at his faith—is crucial. Long before the Shahbag movement found its distinct shape,

FIGURE 15   Screenshot 4. *Source*: Ekattor TV, "CCTV Analysis of Pohela
Boishakh Sexual Harrassment on Women and Children," 2015. https://www
.youtube.com/watch?v=5nltgVP4-mY.

numerous artistic and satirical representations of the collaborators of the
war highlighted and mocked the skullcaps and beards that are often read
as signs of (hyper) religiosity (Mohaiemen 2011; Mookherjee 2015). The
collaborators, some of them war criminals, were known to have betrayed
the ethnically Bengali East Pakistanis in their struggle for freedom, not
on the basis of Islam but on shared cultural heritage. In this particular
interpretation of the footage, the journalist draws from a well-worn language of culture wars—Bengali/secular versus Islamic—that were performed by the Shahbag and Hefazat crowds. The reporter concludes by
suggesting that an Islamist conspiracy is behind the attacks on Bangladesh's largest secular cultural institution.

There were multiple lines of reasoning running through the news coverage. From the chief of the local police station to the proctor of the University to the minister of education, various authoritative figures gave
public statements. A few of them completely denied that any harassment
ever took place. The police said they were unable to identify the faces in
the crowd despite the fact that avid users of social media were already
locating, accusing, and shaming the men caught on camera by going into

their Facebook accounts. Still others casually dismissed the public disrobing and molestation of women as boyish mischief. Until now, nobody has been punished for the crimes. Most people chalk this lack of prosecution up to the fact that many of the perpetrators were thought to be student cadres of the ruling party and therefore more or less unaccountable.

The televisual reporting of the New Year's Day events opens up several analytical possibilities about crowds and democratic politics. The figure of the crowd resists individuation and identification. The resulting confusion is more generally symptomatic of crowds; it is a form of confusion that challenges the "actuarial gaze" of the state and the media devoted to biopolitical policing (A. Feldman 2005). This kind of forensic visualization, Allen Feldman argues, helps identification and the management and mass marketing of risks. The reports on crowd violence on Pahela Baishakh used digital manipulation, such as slow motion, freeze-framing, and spatialization to disaggregate a collectivity. This was done to resurrect and then incriminate a figure of religious alterity: the radical Islamist. The sleeper body is the currency of the public safety apparatus, Feldman would say. A rise in surveillance technologies in public spaces in Bangladesh also points to increased efforts in controlling spaces and bodies more rigorously (banglanews24.com 2016). Ekattor TV tried to reinstate this controlling gaze through investigative reportage for its own purposes that need to be situated historically, since its roots remain firmly grounded in a specific brand of Bangladeshi nationalism. This secular, nationalist impulse gained renewed urgency in the post-Shahbag political climate of resurgent extremism, paranoia, and divisiveness.

Here one also needs to keep in mind the gender of the crowd. The South Asian crowd, as an empirical reality and a subject of intellectual enquiry, does not adhere to the gendered thinking that has informed classical European literature on the masses. In the writing on mass psychology and its fascination with the crowd, as I argued in the introduction, individuality has been understood as a masculine phenomenon and the masses a feminine one (Jonsson 2013). In the vast repertoire of South Asian studies, however, one finds a quintessentially masculine, if not male-dominated, crowd. Among the ethnic rioters across South Asia's cities (Tambiah 1997), the unruly peasants in colonial Uttar Pradesh (Amin

1988), or the mourning fans at the funeral of their favorite film star in Dhaka (Hoek 2012), we see crowds as men. They participate in protest or celebration the styles of which are culturally tied to young men. The *jouissance* of the urban masses ever-present in political rallies, communal showdowns, cinema halls, and religious functions is also culturally male (Hansen 2001; Prasad 2009; Verkaaik 2004). Trivializing sexual harassment as youthful dalliance is to be placed against this background. Men enjoy certain comfort in and control over public space that are not available to most women. For women in Bangladesh, from congested streets and markets to New Year's revelries and cricket victory celebrations, all carry explicit threats of bodily and verbal violence, a phenomenon that is widely recognized in South Asia by the unfortunate euphemism "eve-teasing" (Misri 2017).[11]

The video report also brings up what many may recognize as the familiar problem of "bad apples."[12] On the one hand, crowds are blamed as crowds for crimes such as the incidents of sexual molestation discussed above because, as Freud (1975 [1921]) famously pointed out, people are capable of certain excess, or madness, when they are in crowds. On the other hand, the crowd is exonerated as crowd by singling out the wrongdoers in it, the always-already criminal individuals who cynically try to do their business hiding in the crowd. Soon after the Bengali New Year incident, social media in Bangladesh went into overdrive. The uproar went hand in hand with online activism. A Facebook group called "Moja Loss?" started identifying the home pages of social media users seen in the CCTV footage. Moja Loss? has been known for spreading satirical memes about everyday social inconveniences and for trolling public figures, including political leaders and celebrities. The name of the group is equally significant. In Bangla, it is a colloquial and mildly accusatorial phrase that roughly translates as "Taking Fun?" The phrase has been popular among the youth and addresses (in the second person) the gazing spectator who is only interested in gratuitous viewing pleasures. The group itself has become more politically outspoken in recent years; in 2015, the moderator of Moja Loss? was taken into police custody in relation to an investigation into the group's apparently seditious and antigovernment posts (*Bangla Tribune* 2015).[13] In this case, theirs was a seemingly interventionist reaction to the idle responses of those in power. Neither the police nor the university officials attempted to or succeeded in incriminating anybody from the crowd. The ways in which Moja Loss? exposed the faces of the miscreants, by singling them out and sharing information about their personal lives drawn from their Facebook pages, forged a sense of *communitas* among the users of social media. In their quest for justice, they mimicked the very crowds that they held responsible, the same crowd capable of committing acts of public violence against women. After all, the Pahela Baishakh celebrations are legendary because of the kinds of crowds they attract, which are ideally educated, civic minded, and secular.

The stereotype of the religious crowd as filtered in the photos bears many of the significations attached to the crowd in canonical social theory (Canetti 1984 [1962]; Freud 1975 [1921]; Gould 2009; Jonsson 2013; Le Bon 2002 [1896]). The crowd represents a childish moment of savage indistinction; it is corporeal, affective, and irrational (Mazzarella 2015: 105). The opposition between the revelers at the secular (Bengali) cultural event and the bigoted Muslim predators with their tunics and beards reenacts the distinction between the crowd and the autonomous citizen/subject of liberal democratic thought (Mazzarella 2010a). Crowd-like behavior is often associated with face-to-face gatherings, embodied affect, and the dangers of new technologies (Cody 2015: 52). In this sense, the Hefazat-e-Islam uprising of 2013, or the Islamist crowd, more generally came to symbolize the quintessence of the crowd. The way mainstream media covered the Hefazat protests brings the point home. A vernacular news outlet wrote the following when covering one of the oppositional rallies organized by Hefazat:

> When asked the question, "Why did you come to the rally?" a couple of madrasa students (age 14) from Gazipur anonymously told banglanews24, "They [the bloggers] have insulted our prophet, they have insulted Islam, that's why we came to the procession." . . . When asked how they were insulted, they answered, "We don't know. Our *Boro Hujur* [senior teacher] knows. He told us to come, so we came."

The highlighted naïveté of the madrasa students contrasted sharply with the perceived power and perspicacity of the youth of Shahbag. Urban, middle-class children gathered here with their parents carrying placards that demanded death for the collaborators. Some even painted pro-hanging slogans on their bodies. The idea of children lending their voice to the demand for capital punishment has been lauded in die-hard patriotic circles as a sign of a nation coming of political age. The Hefazat activists, often quite young themselves, were bereft of such innocence or potential. They were alternatively criminalized and infantilized. Their gullibility resulted from their backwardness and their lack of (secular) education and proper political tutelage. Even when their protests were criminalized, the political insincerity of the madrasa student boiled down to ignorance, poverty, and distance from the mainstream of Bangladeshi society. The enlightened secular crowd, so to speak, was the constitutive other of the immoderate religious crowd.

The dismissal of or the rare sympathy shown to the clueless madrasa student was tinged with another affect, that of fear. Ostensibly, in 2013, the government had given Hefazat-e-Islam permission to hold the rally. Its implicit support for a nationwide transport strike, however, made it difficult for many madrasa students to travel to Dhaka. Manosh Chowdhury, a Bangladeshi anthropologist, writes about the actual obstacles that the Hefazat activists faced finding transportation to the capital to attend the protests and the urban bourgeois anxiety around the ghostly figure (*jujuburi*) of the Islamic militant: "The worried, educated TV audience of Dhaka, one that regularly gives its opinion on politics but is far less eager to act, saw a rally that was incomplete. However, its imagination was filled with the image of all those Hefazat activists who couldn't make it to Dhaka, whose arrival could have turned this into an enormous congregation. A cruel spectre [*jujuburi*] indeed" (Chowdhury 2013).

Or consider the autobiographical note in an English daily where an op-ed contributor who is educated in the madrasa system takes on the collective voice of seminary students: "You can't help it. You see us from afar—our messy beard, unkempt appearance, the distinct attire that sets us apart from others. With our straight-cut *panjabi* falling well below the knees, loose-fitting *paijama*, and a skullcap straight from history books, we remind you of the other side of progress" (Bay 2017).

The contradictory affects evoked by the crowd of madrasa students are comparable to a common understanding of nonsecular affect as being at once hyper- and hyporational, as a kind of disciplined indiscipline (Mazzarella 2013b). This is clearly a response to long-held assumptions about secularism as distinct from the physicality, or at the least, sentimentality of religious practices, which has urged many scholars to approach secularism in terms of the cultivation of distinct sensibilities, feelings, and embodied dispositions (Agrama 2012; Asad 2011; Hirschkind 2012; Mahmood 2009). Despite such representational politics in the Bangladeshi public sphere, the overlapping strategies of the so-called secular/atheist and Islamist activists were the most noticeable in the virtual medium, where in February and March of 2013, the websites of secular and religious organizations, institutions, and newspapers were getting hacked with relative regularity. Locating the actual identities of the bloggers from their screen names was another proof of digital literacy shared by the opposing camps. The common virtual platform that they all shared shows that the activists were mostly of the same age group and ultimately points toward a difficulty, if not impossibility, at social distinction. While, visually speaking, the figure of the poor madrasa student was the opposite of the Shahbag activist—modern, middle class, and the personification of a national-secular utopia—in reality, the boundaries were far messier.

The image-politics that emerged in the wake of Shahbag are symptomatic of the ideological and social differences that the protest movement of 2013 laid bare. Concepts such as insincerity, immediacy, or authenticity that are used to gauge popular political formations have been tagged on to the disparate crowds that have come about in and through these protests. A stereotypical portrayal of religious crowds, with their skullcaps, beards, and tunics, as irrational or expedient mobilized a highly potent ideological opposition. The iconography has fixed the coordinates of debate and discussion within Bangladesh and internationally. It is no surprise then that at one point the Wikipedia entry on "2013 Shahbag Protests" ended its section on "Counter-Demonstrations" with the following lines: "On 5 May, Hefazat-e-Islam protesters, aided by Bangladesh Jamaat-e-Islami and its youth wing *Chatra Shibir*, did violent protest activities in Dhaka that included arson, vandalism and burning of books.

The protesters from Hifazat-e-Islam [*sic*] fought with police. Later, the government indicated an official death toll of 11. *However, a grave digger said he had counted 14 bodies with beards"* ("2013 Shahbag Protest" 2015: emphasis added).

MOB 2.0

On the topic of vigilantism, I now come to a second example of crowd violence and its visual remediation. In July 2015, a thirteen-year-old boy, Samiul Alam Rajon, was killed by a group of men in Sylhet, a city in the northeast. Rajon, a poor boy who sold vegetables, was suspected of stealing a rickshaw van. He was tied to a pole and beaten by a rod. The twenty-eight-minute shaky cell phone video was shot on the spot and was uploaded to Facebook by someone who had found it on the Internet. Many people reasoned that the two or three men who were torturing the boy did not expect him to die and failed to contemplate the repercussions of sharing evidence on the Internet. Regardless, the voyeuristic pleasure of vigilante violence is not new to South or Southeast Asian public culture, where physically punishing thieves and pickpockets, or at times public lynching of petty criminals or witches, is neither novel nor the most shocking among other acts of public violence (Barker 1999; Siegel 2005). The recording and digital circulation of Rajon's murder, however, added a whole new element to an otherwise routine affair in a peripheral town. Facebook erupted over Rajon's death. The men tying him up, torturing him, taking photos, and laughing were identified from the camera footage. In late 2015, six people were given death sentences for the murder of Rajon and another young boy who fell victim to a mob attack soon after (BBC News 2015). The man who shot the video was given a life sentence. The verdicts that came out only four months after Rajon's murder were uncharacteristically fast for a system infamous for a corrupt and long-drawn-out judicial culture. One of Rajon's torturers was a migrant worker in Saudi Arabia who was recognized on Facebook. He had fled soon after the video got public attention and was brought back to Bangladesh with the help of his Bangladeshi coworkers and the Saudi authorities.

Rajon's death is not a one-off case of public cruelty against minors. Multiple stories of vigilante violence targeting poor and working-class children, often household help, have been in the news, mostly, it seems, because they end up on the Internet. #JusticeforRajon became a hash tag and a Facebook page almost immediately. Bloggers and regular Internet users voiced their outrage, frustration, and trauma. Some were more introspective and acknowledged their collective complicity in this culture of raw vengeance. Haunted by the sound of Rajon's cries in the video, the well-known blogger Arif Jebtik wrote, "I will probably not be able to sleep tonight. I will hear 'Somebody please save me' repeatedly. But I will probably sleep tomorrow. [M]aybe even the day after tomorrow." Another person expressed her fear in becoming the crowd on her Facebook post: "And those who are crying out in revenge that the perpetrators should be killed this way (eye for an eye), I am asking them what is the difference between those people and you?" (Sanyal 2015) "We all have blood on our hands," said Anushay Hossain in an article titled "Why Is My Country Numb to a Child's Murder?" (Hossain 2015).

One of the striking contrasts between the case of Rajon's death and the violence against women is the curiously contradictory responses of the state. The crowd of sexual molesters successfully evaded the actuarial gaze of the state, though not the gazes of digital media consumers, as the case may be. Rajon's murderers, on the other hand—many of whom were from working-class backgrounds themselves—were swiftly brought to trial. Some commentators have claimed that they would have never been caught without the help of social media. That may very well be the case. The issue, I believe, is not simply that everybody knew about Rajon because his death was filmed; what is of note is how the filming presupposed and harnessed crowd-affect. The kind of crowds that Rajon's death energized brings us again to the distinction between the so-called responsible citizens and criminal crowds. The tiresome tension between reason and affect that undergirds much thinking about crowds stops us from seeing how and when the differences are blurred, as middle-class users of social media respond to the supposed primitivism of the religious and/or the working-class crowd. This is a moment, in other words, when publics and crowds become one and the same (Cody 2015). Nested in this story is also a history of the arrival, proliferation, and application of technologies of sociality and surveillance such as the Internet, cell phones, and closed-circuit

cameras in an otherwise struggling economy with inadequate infrastructure (Quadir 2013). The contradictions of this technological unevenness
capture some of the fundamental ambivalences of mass democracy that
have taken a specific shape in Bangladesh but surely are not unique to it.

The global spread of flash mobs and the curiously Chinese phenomenon of "human flesh search" are two instances of the so-called dark un-
derbelly of cyberspace. The human flesh search started in China around
2001 and spread to other parts of East Asia where crowd-sourced virtual
detective work engages and rouses a large number of Internet users. Many
of them are online virtually at all times. These "netizens" (another coin-
age from East Asia) are powered by a combination of computer networking skills and human connection. They trace the original video links of
crimes and reveal the identities of the perpetrators.

Scholars of new media have been well aware that these sites, where
collaborative production of information and peer-to-peer, loose affiliations
take place, can also generate dangerous and destructive ideas and actions
(Tsou 2015). Idealized as a democratic space of exchange and an unregu-
lated playground, the Internet, in the Asian context and well beyond, is
in actuality neither (Shah, Sneha, and Chattapadhyay 2015; Shoesmith,
Genilo, and Asiuzzaman 2014). In their ability to form crowds and in-
dulge in affects associated with crowds, such as collective vengeance or
spontaneous outbursts, digital natives are able to stoke governmental and
ethical anxieties that travel between cyber and physical spaces. In India,
the state has banned the self-proclaimed apolitical flash mobs, even when
the meetings are planned to take place in upscale shopping malls just for
"fun" (Shah 2007). The human flesh search, for its part, tells a story that
resonates with the digital responses to mob violence in Bangladesh. The
cyberposse, as Tsou calls them, makes every possible detail of people's lives
known and has been responsible for their targets quitting or being fired
from jobs, changing their address, or even leaving town. The human flesh
search, according to Tsou,

> graphically depicts this kind of search that is conducted by human connec-
> tions rather than machine-based algorithms to locate the sources of infor-
> mation as well as calculate the relevance of the data for the sake of ferreting

out and hunting down the human target who has committed all sorts of wrongdoings, ranging from telling a lie, blocking the ambulance and flashing the middle finger, refusing to yield the seat to the elderly, abusing a cat, sexually harassing a girl, having an affair, hit-and-run to anything that is considered "immoral" or "improper" by the wide wired world which could virtually go wild in the name of justice and vengeance. (Tsou 2015)

The curious and far-reaching effects of the human flesh search, and its inchoate manifestations in the Internet culture in Bangladesh, bring us back to contagion. In the cases of molestation of women and torture of children, active social media users were responding to affective contagious encounters. As Tony Sampson argues in his eponymous book, virality is not simply an analogy; it is more than a representation of the hyperconnected nature of digital sociality (Sampson 2012). By unraveling the discursive and rhetorical references to viral disease, Sampson focuses on how discourse is intimately tied to a flow of contagious affect, feelings, and emotions. He believes human emotions spread universally like viruses across networks (Sampson 2012: 2–3). The anger, pity, and pain felt by the members of social media when watching and parsing the video footage of violence generates behavior that, true to crowd affect, has a mimetic quality. In revealing the criminals, some sheltered by the state and others not, the Internet users of Bangladesh became yet another crowd, or rather, Mob 2.0, as Tsou calls the participants in the human flesh search. In so doing, these "upright" citizens continually aim to secure the borders between themselves and the perpetrators and the stigma of mob violence. The latter are also users of social media and regular subscribers to cell phone technologies, thereby blurring the boundaries of social and economic distinction.

As of 2013, of the six billion cell phone subscribers worldwide, 77 percent lived in developing countries (Quadir 2013). Nearly 130 million of them were in Bangladesh at the end of February 2017.[14] The number soared since the early 1990s when mobile technology first arrived. Its use grew fast, which is not uncommon for poorer countries where rundown infrastructure and a labyrinthine bureaucracy make access to other means of communication, such as landlines, money exchange, or face-to-face interaction, far more cumbersome (cf. Rafael 2003). In a rather striking statistic, Dhaka has been recently ranked second among global cities in terms of the number of active Facebook users (Murad 2015). It outranked Jakarta and Mexico City. Most of these users access social media on their phones. The widespread popularity of cell phone technology in Bangladesh is duly noted in *Bangladesh's Changing Mediascape* (2014) in which the authors mention the two familiar figures of urban poverty— the rickshaw puller and the domestic worker:

> Initially a tool of rich urbanites the mobile phone has rapidly percolated down to the poorest sectors such as the rickshaw pullers and domestic servants . . . Phone costs are cheap by world standards: for example, a basic Nokia 1280 handset may be purchased for BTD 1650 (approximately US$25, and time credits purchased from street vendors for as little as US$1). . . . Mobile phones and the Internet, unlike the mass media per se, have been incorporated into Bengali culture as seemingly organic extensions of an essentially oral culture of the masses. (Shoesmith, Genilo, and Asiuzzaman 2014: 8)

The cell phone and the crowd enable each other in a process through which the "oral culture of the masses" comes into contact and remediates virtual space. In this rapidly growing site of ambivalent inclusion, rickshaw pullers and domestic workers seemingly brush virtual shoulders with the bourgeoisie. Here, identifying the so-called bad apples helps others in distancing themselves from the excessively cruel crowd, even when doing so demands indulging in comparable crowd affect. A competitive mimicry between the secular and religious crowds mobilized in the Shahbag-Hefazat phenomenon finds analogous expression in the vigilantism across virtual and actual crowds.

As the examples listed above show, secular and religious crowds, in their desires to be seen and heard by the powers that be, often end up mirroring each other. With an aim to mete out justice, individual online users of social media have acted in tandem, coming together and performing the excess and volatility associated with crowds. The mimetic quality of crowd behavior is noticeable at yet another level. The Shahbag crowd was mostly celebrated for avoiding familiar routes of antigovernmental protests and holding peaceful demonstrations that involved forming human chains, signing petitions, singing songs, lighting candles, and flying balloons. Its fundamental demand for the death penalty, however, made it a rather unique group of vigilantes. The relentless slogan "We want the noose" that defined Shahbag's core affect made many of its detractors and some sympathizers uncomfortable about the movement. Demanding capital punishment on the streets by bypassing due process would cast long shadows on the neutral functioning of the judiciary, many observers feared.

Still, reading Shahbag's demand as either spontaneous outburst or governmental ploy would be to simplify a social context in which people seek justice in ways that challenge and/or exist outside a liberal democratic framework. In the absence of a state owning up to its actions—the lack of accountability for public molesters or the death of Hefazat supporters are cases in point—people supposedly take matters into their own hands. To say this is not to absolve the cruelty or criminality of the acts, but instead to take note that whether physically violent or not, the call for adequate punishment demands a crowd for its execution. It also takes a crowd to protest the cruelty of collective violence against the disenfranchised or to make those in power answerable. The Bangladeshi state, in turn, has made its allegiances known in an opportunistic fashion, either by indulging or by repressing certain crowds over others. Since 2013, both Shahbag and Hefazat crowds have fallen in and out of favor with the ruling political elite for reasons that ultimately come down to political expediency. And yet, the story of the crowd, its remediation through increasingly cheaper technologies and its vexed relationship to institutions of power, is not reducible to the vagaries of the state. What happens when we start rethinking the public sphere, as I mentioned in the introduction, from an illiberal perspective? What happens, one might ask, when we start with the crowd—and the possibilities of politics that it opens up or forecloses—as constitutive of South Asian political modernity and not an aberration from it?

EPILOGUE

"#shahbag is nothing but a Twitter tag now" tweeted a young man in a Che Guevara bandanna a day before the Independence Day, in 2013. The lament was voiced only after six weeks of vibrant protests that took over a busy street corner at Shahbag. A few weeks later I was in Dhaka to see up close an event that had revealed and reified the fault lines in Bangladeshi politics in a manner unforeseen. A historian colleague based in the United States rolled his eyes when he heard about my intellectual interest in Shahbag. I was startled by the reaction because only recently, as I recalled, many in the diaspora like him were glued to their news feeds to follow Shahbag's unfolding. They—we—avidly consumed the visual updates, often of great artistic merit, being beamed from thousands of miles away. The disenchantment expressed in the diasporic academic's gesture, I realized, had a wider reach. In Shahbag I was welcomed by fading street art and peeling billboards with glaring images of the gallows. But for a group of regulars milling around in the evenings and on the weekends, I saw a drastically thin crowd.

This chapter began by locating the political potential of the widespread affect of despair in a post-Shahbag political climate in Bangladesh. It showed the ways in which some of the most devoted fighters of Shahbag's cause articulated their despair in the face of what continues to be a murky political present. The aftermath of the uprising with its calculated killings and a careful management of fear has turned out to be the exact opposite of what many activists and their sympathizers envisioned for the movement and the nation at large. The body—that of the collaborator, the blogger, or the religious radical—took center stage in multiple articulations of justice.

The paradoxes that this brings up, such as the liberal strategies of protest for an illiberal cause, or the counterrevolutionary effects of a progressive assembly, are not simply contradictions that define what is now known as the Shahbag movement. In their despair the Shahbag activists brought to surface a much deeper sense of disappointment that haunts the project of mass democracy. But it is equally important to remember, as Robyn Marasco suggests, that consciousness in despair is not only morose or unhappy; it is "a restless and energetic passion" (Marasco 2015). And, as the activists in Dhaka made abundantly clear, the restless and energetic passion of despair is also the passion for critique. Perhaps for this reason, despair, rather than lacking political value, is in fact an efficacious affect to confront some of the challenges of popular democracies, as much in Bangladesh as elsewhere.

THROUGHOUT MY FIELDWORK in Phulbari, signs against mining, the mining company, or their collaborators were everywhere. They were plastered on mud huts, the walls of *paka* office buildings, and the backs of vibrantly decorated rickshaws. One such slogan, small and barely legible, caught my eye as I came out of a house in a village more than a year after three people were killed in a paramilitary shooting. The message was handwritten, smudged, and on the verge of being covered up by newer inscriptions. It was clearly missing the aesthetic conventions of political graffiti, and reiterated a sentiment echoed in abundance all over Phulbari: "We don't want coal mines; we don't want coal mines destroying agricultural land" (*koyla khoni chaina/krishijami dhwangsa kore koyla khoni chaina*) (figure 16).

This version of the protest's core demand stood out because of its expression in the local dialect of the Dinajpur region; it had never made it to the official script of the movement. *Khoni*, the Bangla word for "mine," became *khuni*, "murderer" or "killer." The double entendre, neatly folded into a mere spelling mistake, rang strangely true. The mine's giant craters would force thousands of villagers out of their homes and take away precious cultivable land. The scramble for resources got particularly violent when many of them stood up against the state that was protecting the company's interest, only to be beaten up or shot at. The writing on the wall, like the Asia Energy logo on the T-shirt mentioned in the introduction,

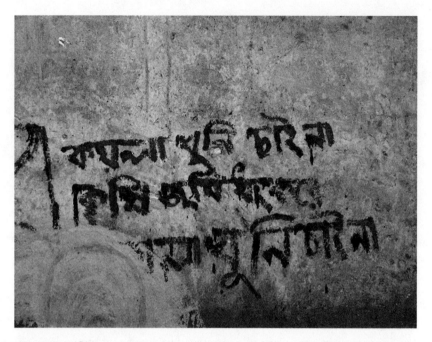

FIGURE 16 Slogan against coal mining on a mud hut in Phulbari. Photo by the author.

was much more than a powerful pun. It stood for multiple voices of the political that jostled for authority and legitimacy in Bangladesh during my fieldwork.

A decade down the road, the project still hovers over the people in Phulbari as they cautiously go about their everyday business not knowing what is in store. The government of Bangladesh has publicly acknowledged the dangers of surface mining in the region, but the company, now called GCM, has been actively plotting a return (Faruque 2017). Despite the protests that put Phulbari on the map, the sign on the wall and the multiple sovereignties represented in the pronouncement remain as marginalia to official narratives of democratic achievement in Bangladesh. In the past decade, Bangladeshi politics has made quite a few international headlines on the surge in political and religiously motivated violence. Its politics has been directly linked, in certain quarters, to the "excesses" of Shahbag, be it ardent secularism, youthful arrogance, or extraconstitutional demands. The relative success of Phulbari gave traction to ecological awareness, which then generated concerted opposition to potentially hazardous power plants—both nuclear and coal-fired. At the same time, the secretive and execution-style murders of minorities, "atheist" writers, and foreigners have emerged as unexpected avenues for articulating and enacting sovereignty. Despite the power of public assemblies that created the condition of the events discussed in this book, the isolated figures of the blogger, the militant (*jongi*), and the collaborator (*dalal* or *razakar*) have surfaced as actors and scapegoats in a complex reconfiguration of authority, politics, and justice. The Bangladeshi state has come down hard on all three. While alleged terrorists, criminals, and drug dealers are regularly killed in organized state violence euphemized as "crossfires," secular bloggers are arrested or threatened for hurting religious sentiments of the Muslim majority. Many of them are now in exile. The collaborator had already become a national obsession, though, as I show in chapter 5, perhaps most spectacularly with the founding of the International Crimes Tribunal.

These events are, in effect, nodes in a long chain of negotiations, some more routine than others, between basic governance policies, state repression, and political violence that characterize a vast portion of the postcolonial world. Bangladesh's double postcoloniality—first in relation to British rule and later to West Pakistani hegemony—bears on the present in a manner that is somewhat unique within the larger South Asian political landscape. The kind of politics that has emerged from the debris of 1971 and the everyday dealings with the functions and activities of modern governmental systems, what Partha Chatterjee has called popular politics, is what has partly interested me in this book (Chatterjee 2006). What I observed more frequently, however, was that the spectacular protests were often made up of imperceptible politics that is the modus operandi of the crowd. The unfolding trajectory of Bangladesh's democracy is best understood by historically and anthropologically locating the role and the ruse of collective political agency, one that I have dubbed as *janata*.

Politics here takes place in crowded places and needs a crowd to have any relevance. In May 2017, for instance, a monument on the premises of the Supreme Court in Dhaka became a new, though perhaps not all that unlikely symbol of a political discord that gathered remarkable affective force since at least 2013. The stainless-steel sculpture of a blindfolded woman in a sari holding a sword and scales iconographically hearkened back to the conventional representation of Themis, the Greek goddess of justice. It was installed in front of the court in December 2016. Bangladeshi artist Mrinal Haque, whose artwork dots an otherwise haphazardly ornate metropolitan city, had designed the statue.

Arguing on the grounds that the anthropomorphic sculpture was an example of idol worship and therefore forbidden in Islam, Hefazat-e-Islam staged angry protests. The authorities gave in to the pressure from Hefazat, who has been in the limelight since the Shahbag-Motijheel showdown of 2013. But groups of secular activists also took position outside the court's gates in counterprotest. Cordoned off from the premises where workmen dismantled the statue in the dark of night, they saw in the government's concession to the religiously framed demands a new political move looking ahead to the 2018 general elections. Toward dawn, the secular protesters tried to break through the Supreme Court's gates to halt the removal, but "police officers were deployed to repel the crowd with tear gas and water cannons, and the sculpture was placed on a truck and driven away" (Manik and Barry 2017).

The government's decision was a major victory for Hefazat, who issued a general call within hours to destroy or remove all human iconography from public view, barring the confines of Hindu temples. The story of this particular sculpture, however, did not end here. Following a court order, it was hastily relocated in a couple of days to a less prominent spot inside the court compounds and hidden from the main road. The artist maintained that the statue was not a reproduction of the Greek goddess, while the prime minister, in a public meeting with Hefazat leadership, sounded rather irked. She pointed out that the "Greeks had a certain type of costume, but here a statue has been built and is wearing a sari," a seeming discrepancy that made her question why the statue of Greek Themis would be erected in Bangladesh at all. A deliberately flippant comment bypassed the controversy around the heated topic of representational art in a Muslim-majority society and in effect made way for its swift removal.

The protests of May at the court premises, as it turned out, were just the beginning. Inside the highest sanctum of Bangladeshi judiciary, another fight was brewing up with much more significant and long-term ramifications for the fate of Bangladeshi democracy. In early August, the Appellate Division of the Supreme Court released the full text of a rather long verdict that scrapped the sixteenth amendment to the constitution. A majority in the Parliament had passed the amendment in 2014, which gave itself the power to remove Supreme Court judges for misconduct or incapacity. Chief Justice Surendra Kumar Sinha came to face the wrath of the prime minister, incumbent politicians, and party loyalists after the document was made public. Pro–Awami League lawyers demonstrated at bar associations across the country, a few former justices doubted Sinha's ability to draft the long manuscript in less than a month, and political bigwigs from the ruling party questioned the chief justice's integrity, maturity, and at times sanity. Incidentally, Sinha was the first minority judge to hold the country's highest judicial post and was appointed by a partisan president with the blessings of the Awami League regime.

The official vendetta against the chief justice, his face-off with the attorney general during deliberations, and the physical occupation of the court premises are new to the Bangladeshi public sphere—this despite a vibrant culture of public protest that I have outlined in the book. Admittedly, this was not the first time that the law became a contentious public issue to be resolved in street confrontations. Shahbag is a glaring example. Yet, this was probably the first time that a verdict regarding a constitutional amendment attracted this level of public attention. Party activists did what they did best—taking to the street and making demands on the basis of crowd power. Once more, the Hefazat uproar against the sculpture of "Lady Justice" and the protests against the verdict bore uncanny resemblances to each other. What interests me the most as I conclude my ethnographic account of popular protest in Bangladesh, however, is the content of the document, its language, which was the source of governmental consternation. Indeed, it has raised anew the paradoxes of popular sovereignty and political representation in Bangladesh. The judgment that the seven members of the Supreme Court Appellate Division produced brings us back to questions of crowds and postcolonial democracy with which I started this book.

"No nation, no country is made of or by one person," Sinha wrote in a judgment that partly aimed at salvaging the spirit of a collectivity that played a formative role in the march toward national independence. This single line had been excerpted and became an empty signifier where disparate meanings were tagged onto the chief justice's words in order to cast him as disloyal. The sentence was deemed incendiary since it was a snub, apparently, to the political role of Sheikh Mujibur Rahman, the "father of the nation," in Bangladesh's quest for freedom. Sinha went on to emphasize that people from all walks of life, "except few religiously fanatic ideologues and their evil companions," had participated in the struggle for independence (Supreme Court of Bangladesh 2017: 61). Sinha cautioned the media against misquoting him, but when it came to the established political culture, the chief justice hardly minced his words: "In our country a disease has infected us and the name of that disease is 'myopic politicization,'" he wrote (Supreme Court of Bangladesh 2017: 54). The proposed amendment would seriously threaten the independence of the judiciary, a sine qua non of modern democracy, he added, since it would give politically motivated lawmakers control over the tenure of the judges at the Supreme Court.

It was to "collective political wisdom" that Sinha turned, reminding his audience that the country was, after all, called the People's Republic of Bangladesh. The judge was also the moral custodian of the constitution, which emerged from the collective political wisdom of the people. This "We-ness" was the key to nation building. Comparing the constitutions of the United States and Bangladesh, both born of violence and sacrifice, he distinguished between the connotative and denotative powers of the "We." In a Derridean vein, and echoing J. L. Austin, Sinha stressed that the constitution and the amendments to them were not just words, but deeds-flesh-and-blood (cf. Austin 1975; Derrida 1986). On the "We, the People" in the American constitution, he wrote, "These words did more than promise popular self-governance. They also embodied and enacted it—like the phrase 'I do' in an exchange of wedding vows and 'I accept' in a contract—the Preamble's words actually performed the very thing they described." (Supreme Court of Bangladesh 2017: 33). The first word of the first sentence of the preamble of the Bangladesh constitution is

"We." For this reason, people "are the true achiever of the sovereignty and hence the constitution" (Supreme Court of Bangladesh 2017: 51).

This was precisely the national "We" that had run its course, at least in certain influential political quarters, during the emergency. The preference for the singular over the plural and the second person over the first in the letters that Dr. Yunus had addressed to the nation attempted to mark a distinct break from the past. It was an attempt at interpellating an individual citizen, who was not a member of the crowd the way Kasu Mia, for example, had turned out to be. Years later, in democratic Bangladesh, a similar disdain for the national "We" became articulated in the vicious criticisms that the sixteenth amendment verdict and, by extension, the chief justice elicited among the ruling party and its allies. Ironically, Justice Sinha's proclamation in the judgment that the constitution will live only if it is alive in the hearts and minds of the people of the country turned out to be precisely the case. By the end of 2017, Sinha went on leave, left the country, and in a few weeks, submitted his resignation from abroad.[1]

On the question of "populism," Jason Frank has noted that the nature of language and its relation to politics becomes particularly urgent in periods of crisis (Frank 2018). Populism is a good example. Despite its emergence from a commitment to popular sovereignty, it gets bad press because, seemingly, it is only some of the people who are really "the people" and the populist leader acts only on their behalf. Then what to make of the case in hand where a constitutional amendment, even when proposed in the name of the people, manages to rattle the seat of power? The sovereign "people" is imperious, Sinha wrote in the verdict, because all power must flow from it, but it is vague because it is anonymous (Rosanvallon 2006); "the people" does not exist except through approximate successive representations of itself. It is simultaneously all-powerful and impossible to find. In his effort to resurrect a perhaps purer sense of "populism," I argue, Sinha ended up affronting an increasingly rabid cult of personality and an emergent authoritarianism, which are also often considered concomitant with populist affect. For those in power, the people, rather than being imperious as in Sinha's reading, should have instead been represented as the crowd of nineteenth-century political theory, following the leader en masse and basking in reflected glory.

But the crowd is much more—and often much less—than these official expectations. The fact that Sinha's relatively straightforward commitment to some of the normative assumptions of liberal democracy was enough to cost him his job reveals a heightened role of paranoia in Bangladeshi politics. From constitutional amendments to "anti-nationalist rumors," a fear of collective self-representation haunts the project of democracy in Bangladesh. *Janata*, I submit, is an apt name for it. This book has captured many such moments in which the people—as crowds, mobs, or masses—has made its presence felt in assertions of democracy that may not look like so to those who stand behind more normative models of the concept, or seek them out in voting behavior surveys and nationalist histories. The crowd and not the coffee shop is more and more the locus in which publicness is performed and communicated (Morris 2013). These collectivities are mass mediated but not always connected in the sense in which serialized digital connection often stands for communication, as it did for Yunus when he implored the individual citizen to send him text messages.

The crowd, it is also often said, cannot speak; it screams (Jonsson 2013: 23).[2] A need for mediation, therefore, has surfaced in well-known writings on mass politics, from Marx's *Eighteenth Brumaire of Louis Bonaparte* to Shahid Amin's archive from colonial South Asia, for example. The passions of the peasants needed to be channeled into political speech and action by revolutionary vanguards or nationalist leaders. The *sadharan janta* or ordinary folks in colonial north India showed characteristically unhealthy nervous excitement, Shahid Amin found in a *Pioneer* report from 1921. It compared Indian crowd affect to the general habitus of the European peasants of the Middle Ages (Amin 1988). Examples of deep devotion and childlike manifestations of affection for the Mahatma (the widely used title for Gandhi) populated contemporary press coverage and political propaganda. The simple, guileless *kisans* (peasants) showed a mule-like obstinacy when demanding the right to *darshan* (audience) or when using the Mahatma's name in violent protests or looting. It appeared as though the task of the *janta* was "to congregate in large numbers, 'feast their eyes on the Mahatma,' count themselves lucky, and after such brief taste of bliss return to their inert and oppressed existence."

"Please refrain from being noisy," Gandhi implored the crowds in a giant gathering in Gorakhpur (Amin 1988).

In *Jiban Amar Bon*, the novel by Mahmudul Huq, Khoka hears a grumble, which soon becomes a roar. Still, political enactments of rallies, *michhil*, and public assemblies include but also exceed spoken and written utterances (Butler 2015). The coming together of the crowd is an expressive function prior to any particular claim or utterance it may make. For Judith Butler, "showing up, standing, breathing, moving, standing still, speech, and silence are all aspects of a sudden assembly, an unforeseen form of political performativity that puts livable life at the forefront of politics. And this seems to be happening before any group lays out its demands or begins to explain itself in proper political speech" (Butler 2015: 18).

The essence of the contemporary crowds of democracy movements, antiglobalization rallies, or religious groups, as in Tunis, Zagreb, New York City, or Dhaka, for that matter, is visibility. The assemblies that are cropping up and taking over public spaces from South Asia to Southern Europe today are more seen than heard. This specularization is an effect of the mass mediated environment within which populism now thrives. The political value of having a voice or being heard is transferred to "being seen to speak" (Morris 2013), which in turn is being fundamentally reshaped by digital technologies and new tools of security and surveillance, or infrastructures of representation (Gürsel 2012). Satellite television channels, automatic cameras, cell phones, video surveillance systems, virtual social networks, and blogs aid in the formation and dispersion of crowds.

Crowds are visible, technomediated, sometimes hard to hear though always drawn to hearsay. They may be accidental but also physically locatable. A crowd also frequently eludes enumeration and naming, and escapes like vagabonds, uprising peasants, and wandering poor (Papadopoulos, Stephenson, and Tsianos 2008). They leave traces in the form of thousands of used pairs of sandals on the streets of Manila the day after a march for democracy (Rafael 2003), or as slogans hastily written on mud walls soon to be plastered over by newer messages.

INTRODUCTION

1. Sheikh Hasina was barred from returning to Bangladesh after her father, Sheikh Mujibur Rahman, and the rest of his family were killed in a military coup in 1975. She was allowed back in 1979. Later, Khaleda Zia, as the widow of another slain president and the leader of Bangladesh Nationalist Party was under house arrest a few times when H. M. Ershad was in power in the 1980s. Yet, those episodes hardly compare to the dramaturgical effect of their imprisonment in 2007. This was partly due to the lack of publicity that such political drama received because of the repressive nature of Ershad's authoritarianism and the absence of (mostly privately owned) satellite television channels that have thrived in the decade after Ershad's rule. More important than the question of public visibility, I believe, is the ideological grounding of this governmental move. It was obvious that Zia, as opposed to Hasina, was being incarcerated because of her decision not to participate in the national elections that would give legitimacy to a military dictator's dubious attempt at performing democracy. Zia's noncooperation at the time had earned her the widely used epithet *aposhheen netri*, or "uncompromising leader," among supporters and followers. This time around, both leaders were imprisoned on charges of massive corruption. Ten years later, Zia was imprisoned again on corruption charges, a move widely understood as politically motivated as her nemesis Hasina has been the prime minister for almost a decade. Zia was still waiting for her bail hearing during the writing of this book.

2. http://bdlaws.minlaw.gov.bd/pdf_part.php?id=367.

3. Kajri Jain (2016) writes about the remediations of religious images and spaces in India, in which she tracks the emergence of a specific form of public to the late colonial moment. The word for this particular form of publicness is the Sanskrit *sarvajanik* (*sarva* means "all" and *jan* stands for "people"). The root, *jan*, is found in everyday Bangla words such as *janata* and *janagan*. Unlike the *janata* or the public, *sarvajanik* is neither an affect-laden rallying point nor a name for a collective political actor. It is more or less an occasional heuristic for a normative sociospatial configuration, writes Jain.

4. As documentary heritage, the speech is now inscribed at UNESCO's Memory of the World Register.

5. *Jiban Amar Bon* was first published in 1976 after being serialized in the weekly magazine *Bichitra*.

6. In the censor's discourse, the public space of the movie theater is imagined as a place where women and men can enact spectator-citizenship on equally autonomous terms (Mazzarella 2013a). This, I believe, is apt for South Asian public spaces, more broadly, a topic I discuss again in chapter 5.

7. The members of the National Committee were largely, ideologically left and included the participants of Baam Ganotantrik Front (Left Democratic Front) and a consortium of eleven smaller and more radical left parties (Shahidullah n.d.). It has been a relatively diverse organization since with active involvement of intellectuals, feminist leaders, and student activists, among others. Its Phulbari chapter was formed in 2005 and has since aided in organizing and publicizing events around the coal project and sustaining the protest culture.

8. This description of the events is based on my collection of eyewitness accounts of the day, both oral and published. It is the most skeletal version culled from many impassioned and (by necessity) fragmented recollections of people who happened to be there physically. I offer the outline with those qualifications in mind. For a more detailed order of the events, see Luthfa (2011) and Faruque (2017).

9. A divisional headquarters and a major urban center relatively close to Phulbari.

CHAPTER 1

1. The Bangla caption of the film poster includes the credits for story line, "special attraction," casting, production, acknowledgements, and foreign marketing. "Special thanks" are also offered to the Bangladesh military, which is a snide reference to the power and sway that the army has on the two parties. It could be also read as a quiet concession to the crucial role that the military played during the Emergency and 2009 national elections.

2. A recent exception to this is the open letter that twenty-three Nobel laureates and global leaders, including Dr. Yunus, had sent to the United Nations Security Council on behalf of the plight of the persecuted Rohingya population of Myanmar in late 2016.

3. For former U.S. president Bill Clinton, Muhammad Yunus is a man who should have long ago won the Nobel Prize. Cited in Ahmed, "Bangladesh's Face to the World" (2010).

4. If *cleansing* was the operative theme of the emergency, then from the highest echelons of Bangladeshi political elite to the dirty kitchens of the restaurants that fed the masses, the spectacle was unavoidable. Assistant commissioner of the police Rokonuddoula took it upon himself to reveal adulterations in the food industry. He became a figure of horror for restaurateurs and a hero to the middle classes, and was hailed for his courage and charisma for making a nation finally see what it was eating. Even the quintessentially hot pink cotton candy sold by sidewalk vendors, for the first time in my memory, lost its colorful appeal and faded, literally, into white.

5. Vicious and substantive critiques of the Grameen Bank that circulate in Bangladesh are predominantly in Bangla. One of the most notable of these is Badruddin Umar's *Yunuser Daridro Banijyo* (2011), the first edition of which came out soon after the Nobel Prize was announced. However, given the left-leaning political affiliations of their authors, and their relatively marginal status, they do not carry the same weight or perform the same task as, for example, a statement issued by Sheikh Hasina.

6. I do not mean to suggest that a clearer picture would solve the problem of recognition. While I proceed to show how the ID card in question raises theoretical concerns about state initiatives in identification, the argument about the distorted photos, includ-

ing the reactions to them, indicates that the middle-class citizen writing in the newspaper is particularly frustrated by the inability of the photograph to properly identify him. I believe that the "irritation" that he experiences needs to be taken seriously in order to understand the emotional investments certain kinds of citizens have in various state projects of identification.

7. In *The Utopia of Rules*, David Graeber (2015: 57) considers the emptiness and circularity of bureaucracy as idiocy. "It is not so much that bureaucratic procedures are inherently stupid," Graeber writes, "or even that they tend to produce behavior that they themselves define as stupid—though they do do that—but rather, that they are invariably ways of managing social situations that are already stupid because they are founded on structural violence." His argument about the stupidity of bureaucracy supports mine as I argue how Kasu Mia, while embodying the stupidity that presumably lies beyond the political in turn reveals the stupidity and violence of social and political structures.

8. For a discussion of the state as the sublime, see Thomas Hansen's *Wages of Violence: Naming and Identity in Postcolonial Bombay* (Hansen 2001).

9. The Bangladesh army's proclamation is uncannily resonant with Jawaharlal Nehru's speeches on politics and development in newly independent India. Theorizing the uniqueness of South Asian postcolonial sovereignty, Dipesh Chakrabarty (2007: 3293–94) reminds us that Nehru was not against students taking an interest in political matters. Such interest was part of the process that would make them into citizens. However, he adds, "[The students'] actions were reminiscent of the anti-British nationalist movement of the pre-independence period. . . . It was somehow acceptable when students of a country under foreign rule resorted to them. But they were 'not the sign of a free nation.'" This view on the appropriateness of student agitations is echoed in Bangladesh as well where a possible ban on student politics keeps resurfacing as a topic of deliberation every now and then in the face of political disorder. And yet, similar to the argument about the efficacy of breaking laws under colonial rule in Nehru's vision, the role of violent student politics in some of the landmark events in Bangladesh's history, such as the language movement of 1952 or the 1971 war of independence, is justified and in fact celebrated in popular culture and nationalist histories.

10. As Jalal Alamgir has noted, the nameless warrants against thousands were in effect "Go to Jail" cards to be used with indiscretion by the Joint Forces in arresting political activists from university campuses. For a longer discussion, see "Bangladesh's Fresh Start" by Jalal Alamgir (2009).

11. There is a parallel here between the writings about crowds and multitudes that William Mazzarella has labeled as their "negative intimacy," by which he means that a theory of multitudes needs the figure of the crowd as its abject other.

CHAPTER 2

1. The social life of Islam's paintings was different from the circulation of other objects of art. They weren't "high art" in the sense that they were only exhibited on gallery walls. Islam was well known in Phulbari as much for his profession as a signboard artist

as for his paintings memorializing the movement; the latter were available at his house for guests to see. In 2009, some Dhaka-based activists organized an exhibition of his art at a prominent gallery, which also generated some press coverage.

2. Electronic mail sent to Phulbari_Resistance listserv in April 2008.

3. For instance, the Phulbari treaty signed between the people of Phulbari and the government in 2006 was described in some media as "eyewash." Among other things, the treaty demanded the expulsion of Asia Energy, a ban on the export of coal and the involvement of foreign companies, and compensation for the dead and wounded. The emergency government questioned the authenticity of the document. "The promise to void the contract signed with Asia Energy made by the BNP [Bangladesh Nationalist Party] and Jamaat [e Islami] alliance government was an eyewash; the promise was made to divert the attention of the protesting people," claimed an article published in August 2007, precisely a year after the signing of the treaty (*Financial Express* 2007).

4. *Taka* is the national currency of Bangladesh. In 2008, one dollar equaled Tk. 77–78.

5. The circulation of dirty, torn money was not exclusive to Phulbari, of course. In 2006, it had become a national concern. A Bengali daily reported that almost 100 percent of Tk. 2 bills in the country are dirty and/or torn. Depending on the quality of the paper, a paper bill has an average lifespan of a year to a year and a half. The circulation period is now stretched up to five years. The longevity of a bill depends on its physical use. A fish seller, for instance, tends to touch his money with wet hands. Likewise, a rickshaw puller's money, generally folded into his *lungi* at the waist, gets wet when he pulls his rickshaw in the rain, thus cutting short the physical life of the paper bills (*Prothom Alo*, August 14, 2006).

6. I hesitate to give an exact date because of the confusion around the issue of acquiring licensing for mining. Starting with BHP, an Australian company that transferred its license to Asia Energy which soon became a subsidiary of Global Coal Management and even later, GCM, Plc., the story of signing the contract between the government of Bangladesh and the corporation is highly contested. Over the years, both (in their various avatars) have retracted or revised earlier versions of how and when the coal project was given an official nod, if at all, and under what conditions.

7. Asia Energy press release, Dhaka, June 21, 2006.

8. Despite this statement, as Christine Haigh of *Global Justice Now* notes, NCP's report did not take into account the possible human rights violations should the mining actually take place. Also, the note in the report that GCM has failed to "foster confidence and trust in the society in which it operates" is a gross understatement given the number of deaths, injuries, and other forms of violence that had already happened in Phulbari (Haigh 2015).

9. Although the first of its kind in Bangladesh, the form and content of the Phubari movement shares many similarities with the events in Nandigram in neighboring West Bengal (India). A few months after the violence in Phulbari, in March 2007, farmers in Nandigram challenged the state acquisition of land for a chemical hub that resulted in at least fourteen deaths. (For more details on the political and social context of Nandigram, see Cross 2014; Dhara 2008).

10. The quote is excerpted from a report by Commons Hansard compiled from the verbatim accounts of U.K. parliamentary proceedings, as cited in an electronic mail sent to the listserv Phulbari_Action on May 2, 2008.

11. This contrasts with Delwar Hussain's description of another Bangladeshi township at the heart of a routine coal trade with India. About the daily life of this raffish border town in the northeast, Hussain says:

> It is teeming with thousands of dark-skinned, gaunt labourers, a fretwork of bones protruding out of their sweaty, taut muscles, their backs and hamstrings tight in desperate efforts. I jump out of their way as they push, lug, heave and pull carts laden with bulky sacks of coal towards the river. Soot has ground itself into their skin and it clouds the paths they walk on. . . . Every so often heavy trucks lumber into Bangladeshi Boropani with coal on their backs. (Hussain 2013: 3)

12. The gifts distributed among the villagers over time became suspect because of the notorious corruption of Asia Energy. Despite some early meetings in 2005 when the company tried to create awareness of the project, their activities were nothing compared to the elaborate CSR activities noted, for example, by Marine Welker in Indonesia (Welker 2009). The lack of information available in Bangla and the misrepresentation of the villagers' presence at these meetings as their "approval" for the project were deeply resented by the residents.

13. This happened despite a 99 percent bill payment record of the 56,000 clients in the Kansat area as confirmed by the general manager of a rural electricity management company called *Polli Bidyut* that buys power from state-owned Power Development Board for nationwide distribution (Muhammad 2007).

14. Homi Bhabha's "mimic man" comes to mind (Bhabha 1997).

15. My aim here is not to reiterate or undermine the significance of land in the agricultural imagination, a fact well documented in the literature on peasant politics in Bengal. Reaffirming the importance of land is not to suggest that money is or has not been vital in the reproduction of peasant life. Andrew Sartori has shown how Muslim peasants of East Bengal were already dependent on credit despite the fact that property (as land) was formative of both peasant and Muslim identities (Sartori 2014).

16. In saying this I do not mean to suggest a diminished importance of the material basis of production. Shapan Adnan and Andrew Sartori have both highlighted the ongoing significance of land as a means of production by looking at land grabbing under neoliberalism, within and outside Bangladesh (Adnan 2013; Sartori 2014). My point here is to highlight the seeming importance of consumption in the everyday functioning of late capitalism.

17. Originally in English, the newspaper that ran this story could hardly claim any local readership and consequently much impact in her everyday life.

18. Heonik Kwon observes money-burning within Vietnamese ritual settings where a wide circulation of votive currency in the form of U.S. dollars has been recently noted. He has situated this trend against the backdrop of the trauma of Vietnam's war with the United States as well as propitiatory and other rituals in practice across Southeast Asia (Kwon 2007). Julie Chu has found American currency as the favored form of

offering in cosmic exchanges in a rural Chinese village. Migration to the United States and resulting remittances now play a distinct role in its religious and social life. The paper bills used to decorate the bride's hair in Papuan weddings, for example, reveal what had to be in plain view—that is, its fetish character—though in this case more as what Arjun Appadurai in a different context has called a "literal fetish" (Appadurai 1986; Rutherford 2001).

CHAPTER 3

1. Bangladesh Rifles. Since a violent mutiny in 2011, the paramilitary is now called Border Guards Bangladesh.

2. Section 144 is a section of the Bangladeshi (and Indian/Pakistani) Code of Criminal Procedure, which prohibits "unlawful assembly," defined by the congregation of five or more persons, organizing public meetings, and carrying of firearms. It can be invoked for up to two months.

3. On August 30, 2006, the Phulbari treaty was signed between the member-secretary of the National Committee to Protect Oil, Gas, Mineral Resources, Power and Ports on behalf of the "people of Phulbari" and the government, represented by the mayor of Rajshahi Division, the regional administrative center. The six-point treaty demanded, among other things, the expulsion of Asia Energy, a ban on the export of coal and the involvement of foreign companies, and compensation for the dead and wounded.

4. Both Natore and Jaipurhat are districts in the Rajshahi Division, the largest administrative unit, which also includes Phulbari. They are about seventy and eighty-five miles, respectively, from Majeda's house.

5. By "adult" here I mean the socially acceptable age for marriage and not necessarily the legal minimum age, which is eighteen for women and twenty-one for men. Most women in rural Bangladesh are married off much earlier, and Majeda admitted to being married when she was quite young. The fact that in her mid- to late forties she already had a grandchild corroborates this familiar pattern.

6. About U.S. $45.

7. *Vangari* (a hybrid of English "van" and Bangla *"gari,"* meaning any wheeled vehicle) is the most common and affordable mode of transportation in rural Bangladesh. Although their forms vary from region to region, around Phulbari they are cycle-rickshaws with a wood plank placed crosswise on top that seats about six adults at a time.

8. Unocal (Union Oil Company of California) has since merged with Chevron Corporation and became its subsidiary in 2005 (www.chevron.com). For more on the incident, see "Dhaka Seeks $650m for Gas Losses" (BBC News 2005) and "Bangladesh Faces Energy Dilemma" (Chowdhury 2006), both published by the BBC.

9. Carlo Ginzberg, in a wonderful reading of Freud's conclusions of the Wolfman case, points out the lack in Freud's knowledge of Slavic folklore and fairytales that must have impacted the Russian patient's infantile dreams. Ginzberg's critique, though not a dismissal of Freud's approach through the unconscious and his privileging of the primal scene, brings up the historical contexts that the latter failed to consider in this case despite his attention to them in the more familiar cultural background of his Viennese patients,

for instance. Hearing Dipu's son's description of the witch and how much it was embedded in folkloric and commercial cultural representations reminded me of Ginzberg's writing. Rosalind Morris also observes a comparable phenomenon with ghosts in Southeast Asia. For more on this topic, see Ginzberg's essay, "Freud, the Wolf-Man and the Werewolves," in *Clues, Myths, and the Historical Method* (Ginzburg 1992) and Morris's essay "Giving Up Ghosts: Notes on Trauma and the Possibility of the Political from Southeast Asia" (Morris 2008a).

CHAPTER 4

1. English subtitles of mainstream action movies often featured on the posters constitute a curious paradox in Bangladesh film publicity. Despite being a regular part of the posters, the English epithets are peculiarly foreign to those who walk by or sit at roadside joints and catch a glimpse of these multicolor snapshots of a film's storyline. Many targeted viewers of Bengali mainstream movies are unable to read English. The status of English in this postcolony is imbued with a familiar aura of the foreign, which is at once a source of seduction and suspicion, and consistently, of legitimation. As Lotte Hoek has convincingly argued, the walls that are adorned by film posters are the sites of the production of a cinematic public that does not necessarily overlap with the audience of the films. For a detailed discussion of movie posters and public space in Bangladesh, see Hoek (2016).

2. The article *ora* (they) is not uncommon as a part of a film title. Another movie contemporary to *Ora Dalal* was *Ora Gaddar*, *gaddar* being a synonym for traitor. This, in turn, is part of a larger trend in naming a series of films using the same formula as an original successful hit, such as *Hero No. 1*, *Goonda No. 1*, and so forth. The source of this current trend in naming of Bangladeshi films is partly influenced by a series of recent Hindi blockbusters that used a similar formula.

3. Foreigners, in the strict sense of people of different nationality, were not a novel sight in this area. In fact, the Korean officers in the nearby granite factory and the Chinese contractors of the Barapukuria coal mines about ten miles from Phulbari frequently visited the markets here. It was not at all uncommon to find Chinese men sitting on a *vangari* like regular villagers. Locals made casual comments comparing the Koreans with the Chinese, though the foreigners' presence did not seem to create much stir. It would seem the arrival of Asia Energy has inaugurated a discourse about foreignness that exceeded the boundaries of national identity.

4. One of my host families, locatable somewhere in the middle of the local middle class, did not have telephone connections until 2008 when I left Phulbari. They had one mobile set that functioned as a quasi-landline because the older couple almost never took it out of the house. It was safely kept on a table in their bedroom, also a convenient place to charge it for future use. They acquired a landline in 2009 when the former member of parliament from the area and a close family friend was reelected and facilitated a successful transaction with the telecommunications bureaucracy to ensure a landline for my host family. Their domestic worker, Salma, did not have one yet, though she frequently went to one of the many neighborhood mobile booths to make calls. She sported a phone

during my follow-up trip in 2009. One Valentine's Day that I spent in Phulbari, my research assistant bought SIM cards for his girlfriend (and himself) as a gift to make use of the special deals offered by network providers that promised cheaper and longer conversations. Most men and many women that I knew in the township had more than one SIM card in their possession at any given moment. They changed the cards regularly and often in the middle of a single conversation depending on the hour of the day of their use. Despite all this, most people did not have long conversations over phones and instead relied heavily on the phenomenon of "missed calls." "Give me a 'miss call'" (*amake ekta "miss call" dio*) was by this time an acceptable refrain across Bangladesh. People connected via calls with the tacit understanding that their calls would be deliberately ignored so as not to incur any cost to the caller. Relatively poorer or younger users were almost never expected to call *and* talk except during discount hours. Still, all kinds of people regardless of social standing sent and received "miss calls" as messages; the trace of a call not received functioned as a code for various kinds of messages whose meanings were agreed upon by the parties in contact.

5. Grameenphone's policies changed around 2006–7, when the telecommunication giant (the majority of whose shares belonged to Telenor, a Norwegian multinational company) made it mandatory for every subscriber to register their already-existing SIM cards, and thus hiked up the number of required documents for applying for a new SIM.

6. Jokes and pointed commentaries on the activist leaders' actions were mostly dictated by their respective party affiliations and other aspects of social relations, such as kinship ties. It soon became easy to predict who would pick on whom in public and who would refrain from doing so. This, however, does not negate the fact that a high number of humorous allegations were leveled against the leaders over and beyond such alliances and enmities.

7. *Razakar* (also written and pronounced *rajakar*) is the other disparaging though more specific descriptor for the collaborators of 1971. Razakars (original in Persian meaning "volunteer") were members of a group composed of mostly pro-Pakistani Bengalis and Urdu-speaking migrants living in East Pakistan. Through the East Pakistan Razakar Ordinance (promulgated by General Tikka Khan on June 1, 1971) and a Ministry of Defense ordinance (promulgated September 7, 1971), *razakars* were recognized as members of the Pakistan army. They were allegedly associated with many atrocities committed against Bengali civilians by the Pakistan army during the 1971 war.

CHAPTER 5

1. Anik is a pseudonym.

2. *Qawmi madrasas* are outside the purview of Bangladesh Madrasa Education Board. They are charitable organizations that run on private donations.

3. The two tribunals have so far convicted more than twenty-five individuals of crimes against humanity since their founding in 2010. Eleven individuals have been sentenced to death, which, though mostly popular within Bangladesh, have garnered criticism by international human rights organizations.

4. The same cannot be said of the January 2014 general elections, when the current party in power went ahead with the elections in the absence of its largest opposition, the Bangladesh Nationalist Party (BNP). The latter demanded a reelection under a caretaker government, which has not been heeded by the government despite the controversial election results.

5. Under the leadership of Jahanara Imam, protests were held against the appointment of Ghulam Azam as the chief of the Jamaat-e-Islami. Azam was still a Pakistani citizen. The agitations later resulted in *Gono Adalat*, the People's Court, where Azam was given a death sentence. The BNP government charged twenty-four organizers of the court, including Jahanara Imam, for sedition.

6. *Shibir* or *Islami Chhatro Shibir* is the student wing of Jamaat-e-Islami. They are often mentioned together, such as in this instance.

7. Perhaps the most striking, and literal, example of this comes from the scientific preservation of Lenin's body during and after the Soviet era. Commenting on the curious case of "Lenin's two bodies," Alexei Yurchak makes a connection between the sovereign and his body in line with Santner's discussion of the flesh (Yurchak 2015). Both are influenced by Kantorowicz's famous argument about "the king's two bodies." Yurchak looks at the relationship between the form and the biological content of Lenin's body. He concludes that the rigorous means through which the authenticity of Lenin's bodily appearance is being maintained has less to do with the corpse than with what Leninism meant for the Soviet Union from the 1920s to the early 1990s. It is that figure of sovereign Leninism, he argues, that the Moscow lab has been maintaining and improving for the last ninety years (Yurchak 2015).

8. To be fair to Badiou, his argument is not particularly about Islamist crowds. Rather, the book theorizes the uprisings in the Middle East and Europe. Written in 2008, with the translation coming out in 2012, Badiou is also responding to the contemporary political and racial tensions raging across France.

9. Another video published by the same user who had also uploaded the Ekattor TV report shows the women being attacked in the crowd much more clearly. It includes interviews with the person who tried to help a victim, the vice chancellor of the University of Dhaka, and other eyewitnesses. This installment, however, does not offer the analysis found in the video I analyze in the chapter. The video is no longer available on YouTube.

10. https://www.youtube.com/watch?v=5nltgVP4-mY.

11. According to a report by ActionAid Bangladesh, 50 percent of Bangladeshi women are subjected to unwanted touching in market places and 30 percent have been victims to "eve-teasing" (*Daily Star* 2017).

12. I thank William Mazzarella for alerting me to this aspect of the crowd.

13. The vigilante impetus of Moja Loss? preceded the New Year's Day events. In 2014, the group had publicized a video on Facebook in which a man was seen slapping a woman riding a rickshaw on her own. Moja Loss? asked for help in catching the perpetrator from the footage, which eventually led to his identification (*Bangla Tribune* 2015).

14. See the website of the Bangladesh Telecommunication Regulatory Commission, www.btrc.gov.bd.

CONCLUSION

1. In a tell-all book digitally published in 2018, Sinha describes his forced exile:

Following the decision on September 13, the parliament passed a resolution calling for legal steps to nullify the verdict. The prime minister and other members of her party and ministers blasted me for going against the Parliament. Cabinet members including Prime Minister begun smearing me alleging misconduct and corruption. While I remained confined at my official residence, and lawyers and judges were prevented to visit me, media were told that I am unwell and have sought medical leave. Various ministers said I will go abroad on medical leave. On October 14, as I was compelled to leave the country, I tried to clear the air in a public statement that I am neither unwell nor am I leaving the country for good. I was hoping that my physical absence combined with court's regular vacation will allow the situation to calm down and good sense will prevail, the government will understand the essence of the verdict—upholding the independence of judiciary—is beneficial to the nation and the State. Finally, in the face of intimidation and threats to my family by the country's military intelligence agency called the Directorate General of Forces Intelligence, I submitted resignation from abroad. (Introduction to *A Broken Dream: Status of Rule of Law, Human Rights, and Democracy* by Justice Surendra Kumar Sinha)

2. The physical gathering signifies more than what is being said. Vicente Rafael noticed something similar when the protesters of People Power II in the Philippines went out in the streets to overthrow President Joseph Estrada in early 2001. After the first group of middle-class agitators with cell phones and cameras left the streets, the poor masses that wanted Estrada back in power marched to the president's house. They were seen as savage and disorderly in both speech and appearance. In the bourgeois imagination, their visibility was uncanny because the poor, though ubiquitous, were habitually rendered voiceless and invisible. In this instance, they made an attempt at communication that could neither be summed up nor fully accounted for by those who heard them. Unprepared to hear the crowd's demand, the middle classes could only regard it as monstrous (Rafael 2003).

WORKS CITED

Adnan, Shapan. 2013. "Land Grabs and Primitive Accumulation in Deltaic Bangladesh: Interactions between Neoliberal Globalization, State Interventions, Power Relations and Peasant Resistance." *Journal of Peasant Studies* 40(1): 87–128.

Agrama, Hussein Ali. 2012. "Reflections on Secularism, Democracy, and Politics in Egypt." *American Ethnologist* 39(1): 26–31.

Ahmed, Arif. 2015. "Boishakh Celebration: Women Harassed Near TSC." *Dhaka Tribune*, April 15. https://www.dhakatribune.com/uncategorized/2015/04/15/boishakh -celebration-women-harassed-near-tsc.

Ahmed, Fakhruddin. 2010. "Bangladesh's Face to the World." *Daily Star*, April 5. https:// www.thedailystar.net/news-detail-132956.

Ahmed, K. Anis. 2015. "Things We Don't Write: K Anis Ahmed on the Murdered Writers of Bangladesh." *Guardian*, December 9. http://www.theguardian.com/books/the -writing-life-around-the-world-by-electric-literature/2015/dec/09/things-we-dont -write-k-anis-ahmed-on-the-murdered-writers-of-bangladesh.

Ahmed, Moeen U. 2009. *Shantir Shopney: Somoyer Smriticharon*. Dhaka, Bangladesh: Asia Publications.

Ahmed, Rahnuma. 2008a. "A Beginner's Guide to Democracy." *Meghbarta*, March 8.

———. 2008b. *Bisrinkhol Drissho: Pourush, Public Sriti O Censorship*. Dhaka, Bangladesh: Yogayog and Drik.

Ahmed, Rahnuma, and Shahidul Alam. 2008. "Against Surveillance: More on the National ID Card." *New Age*, October 13.

Ahmed, Tanim. 2008. "People Power at Phulbari." *New Age*, August 26.

Alamgir, Jalal. 2008. "State(ments) of Emergency: Anti-Democratic Narratives in Bangladesh." In *Anti-Democratic Thought*, edited by Erich Kofmel, 141–65. Exeter, UK: Imprint Academic.

———. 2009. "Bangladesh's Fresh Start." *Journal of Democracy* 20(3): 41–55.

Allen, Lori A. 2006. "The Polyvalent Politics of Martyr Commemorations in the Palestinian Intifada." *History and Memory* 18(2): 107–38.

———. 2009. "Martyr Bodies in the Media: Human Rights, Aesthetics, and the Politics of Immediation in the Palestinian Intifada." *American Ethnologist* 36(1): 161–80.

Althusser, Louis. 2001. *Lenin and Philosophy, and Other Essays*. New York: Monthly Review Press.

Amin, Shahid. 1988. "Gandhi as Mahatma: Gorakhpur, Eastern UP, 1921–2." In *Selected Subaltern Studies*, edited by Ranajit Guha and Gayatri Chakravorty Spivak, 288–348. New York: Oxford University Press.

————. 1995. *Event, Metaphor, Memory: Chauri Chaura, 1922–1992*. Berkeley: University of California Press.

Amnesty International. 2015. "Bangladesh: Two Opposition Leaders Face Imminent Execution after Serious Flaws in Their Trials and Appeals." Amnesty International, October 27. https://www.amnesty.org/en/latest/news/2015/10/bangladesh-imminent -executions/.

Anderson, Benedict. 1991. *Imagined Communities: Reflections on the Origin and Spread of Nationalism*. Rev. and extended ed. London: Verso.

Appadurai, Arjun. 1986. *The Social Life of Things: Commodities in Cultural Perspective*. Cambridge: Cambridge University Press.

Apter, Andrew H. 2005. *The Pan-African Nation: Oil and the Spectacle of Culture in Nigeria*. Chicago: University of Chicago Press.

Aretxaga, Begoña. 1997. *Shattering Silence: Women, Nationalism, and Political Subjectivity in Northern Ireland*. Princeton, NJ: Princeton University Press.

Asad, Talal. 2011. "Thinking about the Secular Body, Pain, and Liberal Politics." *Cultural Anthropology* 26(4): 657–75.

Asia Energy Corporation. 2006. *Bangladesh: Phulbari Coal Project. Summary Environmental Impact Assessment.* Prepared by Asia Energy Corporation (Bangladesh) Pty Ltd for the Asian Development Bank.

Asian Development Bank. 2011. "Speech by Paul Heytens, Country Director, Asian Development Bank in Dhaka at the ICC Conference on Energy and Growth." Mandaluyong, Metro Manila, Philippines: Asian Development Bank.

Austin, J. L. 1975. *How to Do Things with Words*. Edited by J. O. Urmson and Marina Sbisà. 2nd ed. Cambridge, MA: Harvard University Press.

Axel, Brian Keith. 2000. *The Nation's Tortured Body: Violence, Representation, and the Formation of a Sikh "Diaspora."* Durham, NC: Duke University Press.

Azad, Humayun. 2003. আমরা কি এই বাংলাদেশ চেয়েছিলাম? [Is this the Bangladesh we had wanted?]. http://www.amarboi.com/2014/01/amra-ki-ei-bangladesh-cheyechilam -humayun-azad.html.

Azoulay, Ariella. 2008. *The Civil Contract of Photography*. New York: Zone Books.

Bablu, Aminul Islam. 2006. "Raktojhora 26 August" [Blood-stained August 26]. *Naya Duniya*, December.

Baer, Ulrich. 2002. *Spectral Evidence: The Photography of Trauma*. Cambridge, MA: MIT Press.

Banerjee, Prathama. 2006. *Politics of Time: "Primitives" and History-Writing in a Colonial Society*. New Delhi: Oxford University Press.

banglanews24.com. 2016. "CCTV in Govt Buildings Soon." banglanews24.com, July 28. http://www.banglanews24.com/english/national/article/54229/CCTV-in-govt -buildings-soon.

Bangla Tribune. 2015. "'মজা লস' নিয়ে যত কথা: অ্যাডমিন দুই দিনের রিমান্ডে" [All about "Moja Loss?" Admin on Two-Day Remand.]. *Bangla Tribune*, December 11. http://www.bangla tribune.com/country/news/59563.

Barker, Joshua. 1999. "Surveillance and Territoriality in Bandung." In *Figures of Criminality in Indonesia, the Philippines, and Colonial Vietnam*, edited by Vicente L. Rafael, 95–127. Ithaca, NY: Cornell University Press.

Barry, Ellen. 2015. "Bangladesh Pushes Back as Warnings of ISIS Expansion Gather Steam." *New York Times*, October 30. http://www.nytimes.com/2015/10/31/world/asia/bangladesh-isis-terrorism-warnings.html.

Barthes, Roland. 1981. *Camera Lucida: Reflections on Photography*. New York: Hill and Wang.

Bataille, Georges. 1985. *Visions of Excess: Selected Writings, 1927–1939*. Minneapolis: University of Minnesota Press.

Bay, Badiuzzaman. 2017. "Confessions of a Madrasah Student." *Daily Star*, July 17. http://www.thedailystar.net:8080/opinion/society/confessions-madrasah-student-1434082.

BBC News. 2005. "Dhaka Seeks $650m from Gas Losses." BBC News, February 16. http://news.bbc.co.uk/2/hi/south_asia/4271551.stm.

———. 2007. "Professors Jailed in Bangladesh." BBC News, December 4. http://news.bbc.co.uk/2/hi/south_asia/7126849.stm.

———. 2015. "Bangladesh Boy Killings: Six Sentenced to Death," BBC News, November 8. http://www.bbc.com/news/world-asia-34761620.

bdnews24.com. 2007. "Tk 300 Crore Army Offer to Produce National ID Cards." bdnews24.com, February 17. https://bdnews24.com/bangladesh/2007/02/17/tk-300-crore-army-offer-to-produce-national-id-cards.

———. 2010. "Freedom Fighters Turn Collaborators." bdnews24.com, September 22. https://bdnews24.com/bangladesh/2010/09/22/freedom-fighters-turn-collaborators.

Bedi, Heather Plumridge. 2015. "Right to Food, Right to Mine? Competing Human Rights Claims in Bangladesh." *Geoforum* 59 (February): 248–57.

Benjamin, Walter. 1977. *Illuminations*. New York: Schocken Books.

———. 1978. *Reflections: Essays, Aphorisms, Autobiographical Writings*. New York: Harcourt Brace Jovanovich.

———. 2009. *The Origin of German Tragic Drama*. London: Verso.

Benveniste, Émile. 1971. *Problems in General Linguistics*. Coral Gables, FL: University of Miami Press.

Bergman, David. 2015. "Bangladesh Politico: Twelve Things You Need to Know about the Recent Killings in Bangladesh." *Bangladesh Politico* (blog), November 3. http://bangladeshpolitico.blogspot.com/2015/11/eleven-things-you-need-to-know-about.html.

———. 2016. "The Politics of Bangladesh's Genocide Debate." *New York Times*, April 5. http://www.nytimes.com/2016/04/06/opinion/the-politics-of-bangladeshs-genocide-debate.html.

Berlant, Lauren. 1997. *The Queen of America Goes to Washington City: Essays on Sex and Citizenship*. Durham, NC: Duke University Press.

———. 2008. *The Female Complaint: The Unfinished Business of Sentimentality in American Culture*. Durham, NC: Duke University Press.

Bern Declaration and BankTrack. 2007. "Credit Suisse Involvement in Phulbari Coal Project, Bangladesh," December. Letter to Chairman, Credit Suisse Group.

Bhabha, Homi. 1997. "Of Mimicry and Man." In *Tensions of Empire: Colonial Cultures in a Bourgeois World*, edited by Ann Laura Stoler and Frederick Cooper, 152–60. Berkeley: University of California Press.

Butler, Judith. 2015. *Notes toward a Performative Theory of Assembly*. Cambridge, MA: Harvard University Press.

Callan, Alyson. 2008. "Female Saints and the Practice of Islam in Sylhet, Bangladesh." *American Ethnologist* 35(3): 396–412.

Canetti, Elias. 1984 [1962]. *Crowds and Power*. Translated by Carol Stewart. New York: Farrar Straus Giroux.

Caruth, Cathy. 1996. *Unclaimed Experience: Trauma, Narrative, and History*. Baltimore: Johns Hopkins University Press.

Chaity, Afrose Jahan. 2018. "What Makes Dhaka the Second Worst City to Live In?" *Dhaka Tribune*, August 17. https://www.dhakatribune.com/bangladesh/dhaka/2018/08/17/what-makes-dhaka-the-second-worst-city-to-live-in.

Chakrabarty, Dipesh. 2000. *Provincializing Europe: Postcolonial Thought and Historical Difference*. Princeton, NJ: Princeton University Press.

———. 2007. "'In the Name of Politics': Democracy and the Power of the Multitude in India." *Public Culture* 19(1): 35–57.

———. 2011. " রাজনীতির রাস্তা " [The streets of politics]. In ইতিহাসের জনজীবন ও অন্যান্য প্রবন্ধ [The social life of history and other essays]. Kolkata: Ananda Publishers.

Chatterjee, Partha. 1993. *The Nation and Its Fragments: Colonial and Postcolonial Histories*. Princeton, NJ: Princeton University Press.

———. 2006. *The Politics of the Governed: Reflections on Popular Politics in Most of the World*. Leonard Hastings Schoff Lectures edition. New York: Columbia University Press.

Chowdhury, Afsan. 2006. "Bangladesh Faces Energy Dilemma." BBC News, September 19. http://news.bbc.co.uk/2/hi/south_asia/5357458.stm.

Chowdhury, Manosh. 2013. "Hefazat & Casual Middle Class's Politics-Desire." *Alal O Dulal* (blog), April 13. http://alalodulal.org/2013/04/13/middle-class/.

Chu, Julie Y. 2010. *Cosmologies of Credit: Transnational Mobility and the Politics of Destination in China*. Durham, NC: Duke University Press.

Cody, Francis. 2009. "Inscribing Subjects to Citizenship: Petitions, Literacy Activism, and the Performativity of Signature in Rural Tamil India." *Cultural Anthropology* 24(3): 347–80.

———. 2015. "Populist Publics: Print Capitalism and Crowd Violence beyond Liberal Frameworks." *Comparative Studies of South Asia, Africa and the Middle East* 35(1): 50–65.

Cohen, Lawrence. 2016. "Duplicate, Leak, Deity." *Limn*, March. http://limn.it/duplicate-leak-deity/.

Cohn, Bernard S. 1996. *Colonialism and Its Forms of Knowledge*. Princeton, NJ: Princeton University Press.

Comaroff, Jean, and John Comaroff. 2002. "Alien-Nation: Zombies, Immigrants, and Millennial Capitalism." *South Atlantic Quarterly* 101(4): 779–805.

Comaroff, Jean, and John L. Comaroff, eds. 1993. *Modernity and Its Malcontents: Ritual and Power in Postcolonial Africa*. Chicago: University of Chicago Press.

———. 2006. *Law and Disorder in the Postcolony*. Chicago: University of Chicago Press.

Coronil, Fernando. 1997. *The Magical State: Nature, Money, and Modernity in Venezuela*. Chicago: University of Chicago Press.

———. 2011. "Oilpacity: Secrets of History in the Coup against Hugo Chávez." *Anthropology News* 52(5): https://doi.org/10.1111/j.1556-3502.2011.52506.x.

Cross, Jamie. 2014. *Dream Zones: Anticipating Capitalism and Development in India*. London: Pluto Press.

Daily Star. 2008. "National ID." *Daily Star*, April 30. https://www.thedailystar.net/news-detail-34364.

———. 2017. "'50% Women Face Unwanted Touching at Markets.'" *Daily Star*, July 16. http://www.thedailystar.net:8080/country/50-percent-bangladesh-women-face-unwanted-touching-at-markets-shopping-says-actionaid-study-1434028.

Das, Veena. 1995. *Critical Events, an Anthropological Perspective on Contemporary India*. New Delhi: Oxford University Press.

———. 2004. "The Signature of the State: The Paradox of Illegibility." In *Anthropology in the Margins of the State*, edited by Veena Das and Deborah Poole, 225–52. Santa Fe, NM: School of American Research Press.

Das, Veena, and Deborah Poole, eds. 2004. *Anthropology in the Margins of the State*. Santa Fe, NM: School of American Research Press.

D'Costa, Bina. 2015. "Of Impunity, Scandals and Contempt: Chronicles of the Justice Conundrum." *International Journal of Transitional Justice* 9(3): 357–66.

Dean, Jodi. 2002. *Publicity's Secret: How Technoculture Capitalizes on Democracy*. Ithaca, NY: Cornell University Press.

———. 2016. *Crowds and Party*. Brooklyn, NY: Verso.

Derrida, Jacques. 1986. "Declarations of Independence." *New Political Sciences* 15 (Summer): 7–15.

Dhaka Tribune. 2013. "No Open Space in Dhaka for Political Programmes." *Dhaka Tribune*, May 5. https://www.dhakatribune.com/uncategorized/2013/05/05/no-open-space-in-dhaka-for-political-programmes.

Dhara, Tushar. 2008. "Nandigram Revisited: The Scars of Battle." *Infochange*, April. http://infochangeindia.org/agenda/battles-over-land/nandigram-revisited-the-scars-of-battle.html.

Doward, Jamie, and Mahtab Haider. 2006. "The Mystery Death, a Town in Uproar and a $1bn UK Mines Deal." *Guardian*, September 3. http://www.guardian.co.uk/world/2006/sep/03/bangladesh.

Economist. 2007. "The Minus-Two Solution." *Economist*, September 6. https://www.economist.com/asia/2007/09/06/the-minus-two-solution.

Ekattor TV. 2015. "CCTV Analysis of Pohela Boishakh Sexual Harrassment on Women and Children." Ekattor TV, April 18. https://www.youtube.com/watch?v=5nltgVP4-mY.

Ethirajan, Anbarasan. 2010. "Bangladesh to Shut Gas Stations." BBC News, August 12. http://www.bbc.co.uk/news/world-south-asia-10960337.

Evans-Pritchard, E. E. 1976. *Witchcraft, Oracles, and Magic among the Azande*. Abridged with an introduction by Eva Gillies. Oxford: Clarendon Press.

Farquhar, Judith. 2009. "The Park Pass: Peopling and Civilizing a New Old Beijing." *Public Culture* 21(3): 551–76.

Faruque, M. Omar. 2017. "Mining and Subaltern Politics: Political Struggle against Neoliberal Development in Bangladesh." *Asian Journal of Political Science* 26(1): 65–86.

FE Investegate. 2007. "Asia Energy PLC Announcements | Asia Energy PLC: Change of Name." Investegate.Co.Uk, January 17. http://www.investegate.co.uk/article.aspx?id=200701111034383583P.

Feldman, Allen. 1991. *Formations of Violence: The Narrative of the Body and Political Terror in Northern Ireland*. Chicago: University of Chicago Press.

———. 2005. "On the Actuarial Gaze." *Cultural Studies* 19(2): 203–26.

Feldman, Ofer, and Christ'l de Landtsheer, eds. 1998. *Politically Speaking: A Worldwide Examination of Language Used in the Public Sphere*. Westport, CT: Praeger.

Ferdous, Abdullah A. 2007. "The ID Conundrum." *New Age*, January 28.

Ferguson, James. 1994. *The Anti-Politics Machine: "Development," Depoliticization, and Bureaucratic Power in Lesotho*. Minneapolis: University of Minnesota Press.

Financial Express. 2007. "Minu's Deal on Phulbari Coal Mine Illegal: Law Ministry." *Financial Express*, August 30.

Foster, Robert. 1998. "Your Money, Our Money, the Government's Money: Finance and Fetishism in Melanesia." In *Border Fetishisms: Material Objects in Unstable Spaces*, edited by Patricia Spyer, 60–90. New York: Routledge.

Frank, Jason. 2015. "The Living Image of the People." *Theory & Event* 18(1). https://muse.jhu.edu/article/566086.

Freud, Sigmund. 1950 [1920]. *Beyond the Pleasure Principle: A New Translation*. Translated by James Strachey. New York: Liveright.

———. 1975 [1921]. *Group Psychology and the Analysis of the Ego*. Translated and edited by James Strachey. New York: Norton.

———. 2003 [1905]. *The Joke and Its Relation to the Unconscious*. Translated by Joyce Crick. New York: Penguin.

Gamburd, Michele Ruth. 2004. "Money That Burns like Oil: A Sri Lankan Cultural Logic of Morality and Agency." *Ethnology* 43(2): 167–84.

Gardner, Katy. 2012. *Discordant Development: Global Capitalism and the Struggle for Connection in Bangladesh*. London: Pluto Press.

Ghosh, Golokendu. 1987. *Samsad Student's Bengali-English Dictionary*. Calcutta: Sahitya Samsad.

Ginzburg, Carlo. 1992. *Clues, Myths, and the Historical Method*. Baltimore, MD: Johns Hopkins University Press.

Gonzalez, David. 2010. "Where Death Squads Struck in Bangladesh." *Lens* (blog), March 16. https://lens.blogs.nytimes.com/2010/03/16/showcase-137/.

Gordillo, Gaston. 2006. "The Crucible of Citizenship: ID-Paper Fetishism in the Argentinean Chaco." *American Ethnologist* 33(2): 162–76.

Gordon, Avery. 1997. *Ghostly Matters: Haunting and the Sociological Imagination*. Minneapolis: University of Minnesota Press.

Gould, Deborah. 2009. *Moving Politics: Emotion and ACT UP's Fight against AIDS*. Chicago: University of Chicago Press.

Graeber, David. 2001. *Toward an Anthropological Theory of Value: The False Coin of Our Own Dreams*. New York: Palgrave.

———. 2015. *The Utopia of Rules: On Technology, Stupidity and the Secret Joys of Bureaucracy*. Brooklyn, NY: Melville House.

Guha, Ranajit. 1983. *Elementary Aspects of Peasant Insurgency in Colonial India*. New Delhi: Oxford University Press.

Gulati, Mohinder, and M. Y. Rao. 2007. "Corruption in the Electricity Sector: A Pervasive Scourge." In *The Many Faces of Corruption: Tracking Vulnerabilities at the Sector Level*, edited by J. Edgardo Campos and Sanjay Pradhan, 115–58. Washington, DC: World Bank.

Gunter, Bernhard G. 2010. "The Impact of Development on CO_2 Emissions: A Case Study of Bangladesh until 2050." Bangladesh Development Research Center (BDRC). http://www.bangladeshstudies.org/files/WPS_no10.pdf.

Gupta, Akhil. 2015. "An Anthropology of Electricity from the Global South." *Cultural Anthropology* 30(4): 555–68.

Gürsel, Zeynep Devrim. 2012. "The Politics of Wire Service Photography: Infrastructures of Representation in a Digital Newsroom." *American Ethnologist* 39(1): 71–89.

———. 2017. "Visualizing Publics: Digital Crowd Shots and the 2015 Unity Rally in Paris." *Current Anthropology* 58(S15): S135–48.

Hage, Ghassan. 2003. "'Comes a Time We Are All Enthusiasm': Understanding Palestinian Suicide Bombers in Times of Exighophobia." *Public Culture* 15(1): 65–89.

Haigh, Christine. 2015. "The Global System for Holding Corporations to Account Is in Need of Serious Reform." *Guardian*, February 10. http://www.theguardian.com/global-development-professionals-network/2015/feb/10/the-global-system-for-holding-corporations-to-account-is-in-need-of-serious-reform.

Hamdy, Sherine F. 2012. "Strength and Vulnerability after Egypt's Arab Spring Uprisings." *American Ethnologist* 39(1): 43–48.

Hammer, Joshua. 2015. "The Imperiled Bloggers of Bangladesh." *New York Times*, December 29. http://www.nytimes.com/2016/01/03/magazine/the-price-of-secularism-in-bangladesh.html.

Hansen, Thomas Blom. 2001. *Wages of Violence: Naming and Identity in Postcolonial Bombay*. Princeton, NJ: Princeton University Press.

Hardt, Michael. 1999. "Affective Labor." *boundary 2* 26(2): 89–100.

Hardt, Michael, and Antonio Negri. 2005. *Multitude: War and Democracy in the Age of Empire*. New York: Penguin.

Hashmi, Taj. 2007. "Feedback." *New Age*, January 22.

———. 2017. "Corruption in Bangladesh: Perceptions vs. Reality." *Daily Star*, February 4. http://www.thedailystar.net/op-ed/corruption-bangladesh-perceptions-vs-reality-1355818.

Hashmi, Taj ul-Islam. 1992. *Pakistan as a Peasant Utopia: The Communalization of Class Politics in East Bengal, 1920–1947*. Boulder, CO: Westview Press.

Hegel, G. W. F. 1998 [1807]. "Phenomenology of Spirit: Preface," trans. A. V. Miller. In *The Hegel Reader*, ed. Stephen Houlgate, 50–69. Oxford: Blackwell.

Hertz, Robert. 2006. *Death and the Right Hand*. London: Routledge.

Hetherington, Kregg. 2012. "Agency, Scale, and the Ethnography of Transparency." *PoLAR: Political and Legal Anthropology Review* 35(2): 242–47.

High, Mette M. 2013. "Polluted Money, Polluted Wealth: Emerging Regimes of Value in the Mongolian Gold Rush." *American Ethnologist* 40(4): 676–88.

Hirschkind, Charles. 2012. "Beyond Secular and Religious: An Intellectual Genealogy of Tahrir Square." *American Ethnologist* 39(1): 49–53.

Hobbes, Michael. 2014. "Welcome to the Traffic Capital of the World." *New Republic*, July 2. https://newrepublic.com/article/118416/what-dhaka-bangladesh-traffic-capital-world-can-teach-us.

Hobbes, Thomas. 1982 [1651]. *Leviathan*. London: Penguin Classics.

Hoek, Lotte. 2012. "*Mofussil* Metropolis: Civil Sites, Uncivil Cinema and Provinciality in Dhaka City." *Ethnography* 13(1): 28–42.

———. 2013. *Cut-Pieces: Celluloid Obscenity and Popular Cinema in Bangladesh*. New York: Columbia University Press.

———. 2016. "Urban Wallpaper: Film Posters, City Walls and the Cinematic Public in South Asia." *South Asia: Journal of South Asian Studies* 39(1): 73–92.

Honig, Bonnie. 2017. *Public Things: Democracy in Disrepair*. New York: Fordham University Press.

Horkheimer, Max, and Theodor W. Adorno. 1972. *Dialectic of Enlightenment*. New York: Seabury Press.

Hossain, A. 2015. "Why Is My Country Numb to a Child's Murder?" *Daily Beast*, August 17. http://www.thedailybeast.com/why-is-my-country-numb-to-a-childs-murder.

Hossain, Emran. 2013. "Bangladesh Arrests 'Atheist Bloggers,' Cracking Down on Critics." *Huffington Post*, April 3. http://www.huffingtonpost.com/2013/04/03/bangladesh-bloggers_n_3009137.html.

Houlgate, Stephen, ed. 1998. *The Hegel Reader*. Malden, MA: Blackwell.

Huberman, Jenny. 2010. "The Dangers of Dalali, the Dangers of Dan." *South Asia: Journal of South Asian Studies* 33(3): 399–420.

Hull, Matthew S. 2008. "Ruled by Records: The Expropriation of Land and the Misappropriation of Lists in Islamabad." *American Ethnologist* 35(4): 501–18.

———. 2012. "Documents and Bureaucracy." *Annual Review of Anthropology* 41(1): 251–67.

Huq, Mahmudul. 1976. *Jībana āmāra bona* [Life is my sister]. Ḍhākā: Jātīya Sāhitya Prakāśanī.

Huq, Maimuna. 2008. "Reading the Qur'an in Bangladesh: The Politics of 'Belief' Among Islamist Women." *Modern Asian Studies* 42 (Special Double Issue 2–3): 457–88.

Huq, Samia. 2013. "Defining Self and Other." *Economic and Political Weekly* 48(50).

Husain, Ishtiaque. 2017. "Facebook Ban: Analog Approach to Digital Bangladesh?" *Dhaka Tribune*, April 3. http://www.dhakatribune.com/feature/tech/2017/04/03/facebook-ban-digital-bangladesh/.

Hussain, Delwar. 2013. *Boundaries Undermined: The Ruins of Progress on the Bangladesh/India Border.* London: Hurst.

India-Forums.com. 2007. "Sheikh Hasina Sneers at Nobel Winner Yunus's Bid to Enter Politics." India-Forums.com, February 18. https://www.india-forums.com/news/bangladesh/20255-sheikh-hasina-sneers-at-nobel-winner-yunus-bid-to-enter-politics.htm.

Irvine, Judith T., and Susan Gal. 2000. "Language Ideology and Linguistic Differentiation." In *Regimes of Language: Ideologies, Polities, and Identities*, edited by Paul V. Kroskrity, 35–84. Santa Fe, NM: School of American Research Press.

Jain, Kajri. 2016. "Gods in the Time of Automobility." *Current Anthropology* 58(S15): S13–26.

Jonsson, Stefan. 2013. *Crowds and Democracy: The Idea and Image of the Masses from Revolution to Fascism.* New York: Columbia University Press.

Kabir, Khushi. 2013. "How Our Generation Sees Shahbag." *Alal O Dulal* (blog), March 6. http://alalodulal.org/2013/03/06/shahbag-khushi-kabir/.

Kalafut, Jennifer, and Roger Moody. 2008. *Phulbari Coal Project: Studies on Displacement, Resettlement, Environmental and Social Impact.* Dhaka, Bangladesh: Samhati Publications.

Kale, Sunila. 2014. *Electrifying India: Regional Political Economies of Development.* Stanford, CA: Stanford University Press.

Kantorowicz, Ernst. 2016. *The King's Two Bodies: A Study in Medieval Political Theology.* Princeton, NJ: Princeton University Press.

Karim, Fariha. 2010. "WikiLeaks Cables: US Pushed for Reopening of Bangladesh Coal Mine." *Guardian*, December 21. http://www.guardian.co.uk/world/2010/dec/21/wikileaks-cables-us-bangladesh-coal-mine.

Karim, Lamia. 2011. *Microfinance and Its Discontents: Women in Debt in Bangladesh.* Minneapolis: University of Minnesota Press.

Karim, Piash. 2006. "I Never Knew Nasreen." *Daily Star*, June 9. http://archive.thedailystar.net/2006/06/09/d60609150492.htm.

Kaviraj, Sudipta. 1997. "Filth and the Public Sphere: Concepts and Practices about Space in Calcutta." *Public Culture* 10(1): 83–113.

Khan, Mubin S. 2008. "The Price of Being Bangladeshi." *New Age*, extra edition, July 27.

Khan, Naveeda. 2006. "Of Children and Jinn: An Inquiry into an Unexpected Friendship during Uncertain Times." *Cultural Anthropology* 21(2): 234–64.

Khan, Tanzimuddin Muhammad. 2006. "Mineral Resources, Phulbari Movement and Lessons from Nigeria." *Daily Star*, September 17. http://archive.thedailystar.net/2006/09/12/d6091215011122.htm.

Khan, Zeeshan. 2013. "Critics Denounce Bangladesh Death Sentence." *Al Jazeera*, September 19. http://www.aljazeera.com/indepth/features/2013/09/20139191236579783.html.

Khatun, Samia. 2013. "Bring Up the Bodies." *Caravan*, April 1. http://www.caravanmagazine.in/perspectives/bring-bodies.

Klein, Naomi. 2007. *The Shock Doctrine: The Rise of Disaster Capitalism.* New York: Henry Holt.

Klima, Alan. 2002. *The Funeral Casino: Meditation, Massacre, and Exchange with the Dead in Thailand*. Princeton, NJ: Princeton University Press.

Kunreuther, Laura. 2018. "Sounds of Democracy: Performance, Protest, and Political Subjectivity." *Cultural Anthropology* 33(1): 1–31.

Kwon, Heonik. 2007. "The Dollarization of Vietnamese Ghost Money." *Journal of the Royal Anthropological Institute* 13(1): 73–90.

Laclau, Ernesto. 2007. *On Populist Reason*. London: Verso.

Lakier, Genevieve. 2007. "Illiberal Democracy and the Problem of Law: Street Protest and Democratizatio in Multiparty Nepal." In *Contentious Politics and Democratization in Nepal*, edited by Mahendra Lawoti, 252–72. Los Angeles: Sage.

Larkin, Brian. 2013. "The Politics and Poetics of Infrastructure." *Annual Review of Anthropology* 42(1): 327–43.

Le Bon, Gustave. 2002 [1896]. *The Crowd: A Study of the Popular Mind*. Mineola, NY: Dover Publications.

Lee, Benjamin. 1997. *Talking Heads: Language, Metalanguage, and the Semiotics of Subjectivity*. Durham, NC: Duke University Press.

Lee, Benjamin, and Edward LiPuma. 2002. "Cultures of Circulation: The Imaginations of Modernity." *Public Culture* 14(1): 191–213.

Lewis, David. 2011. *Bangladesh: Politics, Economy and Civil Society*. Cambridge: Cambridge University Press.

Ludden, David. 2011. "The Politics of Independence in Bangladesh." *Economic and Political Weekly* 46(35).

Luthfa, Samina. 2011. "Everything Changed after the 26th: Repression and Resilience against the Phulbari Coal Mine Bangladesh." Working Paper 193. Queen Elizabeth House Working Paper Series, University of Oxford. https://www.academia.edu/1013131/Everything_Changed_after_the_26th_Repression_and_Resilience_against_the_Phulbari_Coal_Mine_Bangladesh.

MacLean, Ken. 2014. "Counter-Accounting with Invisible Data: The Struggle for Transparency in Myanmar's Energy Sector." *PoLAR: Political and Legal Anthropology Review* 37(1): 10–28.

Mahmood, Saba. 2009. "Religious Reason and Secular Affect: An Incommensurable Divide?" *Critical Inquiry* 35(4): 836–62.

Mahmud, Wahiduddin. 2017. "Pathways to Human Development: Explaining the Bangladesh Surprise." VoxDev, August 16. http://voxdev.org/topic/health-education/pathways-human-development-explaining-bangladesh-surprise.

Manik, Julfikar Ali, and Ellen Barry. 2017. "Statue of Woman Removed from Bangladesh's Supreme Court." *New York Times*, May 26. https://www.nytimes.com/2017/05/26/world/asia/bangladesh-statue-justice-supreme-court-islam.html.

Marasco, Robyn. 2015. *The Highway of Despair: Critical Theory After Hegel*. New York: Columbia University Press.

Masco, Joseph. 2014. *The Theater of Operations: National Security Affect from the Cold War to the War on Terror*. Durham, NC: Duke University Press.

Massumi, Brian. 1998. "Event Horizon." In *The Art of the Accident*. Rotterdam, The Netherlands: V2, Lab for the Unstable Media. http://www.v2.nl/archive/articles/event-horizon.

Maurer, Bill. 2006. "The Anthropology of Money." *Annual Review of Anthropology* 35(1): 15–36.

———. 2015. *How Would You Like to Pay? How Technology Is Changing the Future of Money*. Durham, NC: Duke University Press.

Mazzarella, William. 2006. "Internet X-Ray: E-Governance, Transparency, and the Politics of Immediation in India." *Public Culture* 18(3): 473–505.

———. 2009. "Affect: What Is It Good For?" In *Enchantments of Modernity: Empire, Nation, Globalization*, edited by Saurabh Dube, 291–309. New Delhi: Routledge India.

———. 2010a. "Beautiful Balloon: The Digital Divide and the Charisma of New Media in India." *American Ethnologist* 37(4): 783–804.

———. 2010b. "The Myth of the Multitude, or, Who's Afraid of the Crowd?" *Critical Inquiry* 36(4): 697–727.

———. 2013a. *Censorium: Cinema and the Open Edge of Mass Publicity*. Durham, NC: Duke University Press.

———. 2013b. "Mind the Gap! Or What Does Secularism Feel Like?" In *The Sahmat Collective: Art and Activism in India since 1989*. Chicago: Smart Museum of Art. https://smartmuseum.uchicago.edu/exhibitions/the-sahmat-collective-art-and-activism-in-india-since-1989/.

———. 2015. "Totalitarian Tears: Does the Crowd Really Mean It?" *Cultural Anthropology* 30(1): 91–112.

Misri, Deepti. 2017. "Eve-Teasing." *South Asia: Journal of South Asian Studies* 40(2): 305–7.

Mitchell, Lisa. 2018. "Civility and Collective Action: Soft Speech, Loud Roars, and the Politics of Recognition." *Anthropological Theory* 18(2–3): 217–47.

Mitchell, Timothy. 2009. "Carbon Democracy." *Economy & Society* 38(3): 399–432.

Mittermaier, Amira. 2015. "Death and Martyrdom in the Arab Uprisings: An Introduction." *Ethnos* 80(5): 583–604.

Mohaiemen, Naeem. 2008. "Yes, I Voted." *Daily Star*, December 30. https://www.thedailystar.net/news-detail-69228.

———. 2011. "Flying Blind: Waiting for a Real Reckoning on 1971." *Economic and Political Weekly* 46(36): 40–52.

———. 2013. "Shahbagh: The Forest of Symbols." Alalodulal. https://alalodulal.org/2013/02/22/shahbagh-symbols/.

Mookherjee, Nayanika. 2015. *The Spectral Wound: Sexual Violence, Public Memories, and the Bangladesh War of 1971*. Durham, NC: Duke University Press.

Morgan, Edmund S. 1989. *Inventing the People: The Rise of Popular Sovereignty in England and America*. New York: Norton.

Morris, Rosalind C. 2004. "Intimacy and Corruption in Thailand's Age of Transparency." In *Off Stage/On Display: Intimacy and Ethnography in the Age of Public Culture*, edited by Andrew Shryock, 225–43. Stanford, CA: Stanford University Press.

———. 2006. "The Mute and the Unspeakable : Political Subjectivity, Violent Crime, and 'the Sexual Thing' in a South African Mining Community." In *Law and Disorder in the Postcolony*, edited by Jean Comaroff and John Comaroff, 57–101. Chicago: University of Chicago Press.

———. 2008a. "Giving Up Ghosts: Notes on Trauma and the Possibility of the Political from Southeast Asia." *Positions: East Asia Cultures Critique* 16(1): 229–58.

———. 2008b. "The Miner's Ear." *Transition* 98: 96–114.

———, ed. 2009. *Photographies East: The Camera and Its Histories in East and Southeast Asia*. Durham, NC: Duke University Press.

———. 2013. "Theses on the New Öffentlichkeit." *Grey Room* (April): 94–111. https://doi.org/10.1162/GREY_a_00108.

Mrázek, Rudolf. 2002. *Engineers of Happy Land: Technology and Nationalism in a Colony*. Princeton, NJ: Princeton University Press.

Muhammad, Anu. 2007. *Phulbari, Kansat, Garments 2006*. Dhaka, Bangladesh: Srabon Prokashoni.

———. 2009. "Grameen and Microcredit: A Tale of Corporate Success." *Economic and Political Weekly* 44(35).

———. 2011. "Gas Raptanir Chukti! An Interview with Anu Muhammad." *Shaptahik*, June 9. http://www.shaptahik.com/v2/?DetailsId=5376.

———. 2014a. "বিদ্যুৎও চাই, অযথা বেশি দামও নয়" [More power, but less price hike]. *Prothom Alo*, http://www.prothom-alo.com/opinion/article/167037/বিদ্যুৎও_চাই_অযথা_বেশি_দামও_নয়.

———. 2014b. "Natural Resources and Energy Security: Challenging the 'Resource-Curse' Model in Bangladesh." *Economic and Political Weekly* 49(4).

———. 2015. "Bangladesh—A Model of Neoliberalism." *Monthly Review*, March. http://monthlyreview.org/2015/03/01/bangladesh-a-model-of-neoliberalism/.

Muir, Sarah, and Akhil Gupta. 2018. "Rethinking the Anthropology of Corruption: An Introduction to Supplement 18." *Current Anthropology* 59(S18): S4–15.

Muller, Mark, and Roger Moody. 2009. "Bangladesh's Untapped Coal Potential." *Daily Star*, June 2. https://www.thedailystar.net/news-detail-90796.

Murad, M. 2017. "Dhaka Ranked Second in Number of Active Facebook Users." bdnews24.com, April 15. http://bdnews24.com/bangladesh/2017/04/15/dhaka-ranked-second-in-number-of-active-facebook-users.

Mursalin, Tamnun E. 2009. "Towards Vision2021 of a Digital Bangladesh." *Financial Express*, February 8.

Nash, June. 1993. *We Eat the Mines and the Mines Eat Us: Dependency and Exploitation in Bolivian Tin Mines*. New York: Columbia University Press.

Navaro-Yashin, Yael. 2007. "Make-Believe Papers, Legal Forms and the Counterfeit: Affective Interactions between Documents and People in Britain and Cyprus." *Anthropological Theory* 7(1): 79–98.

———. 2013. "Breaking Memory, Spoiling Memorization: The Taksim Protests in Istanbul." *Cultural Anthropology*, October 31. https://culanth.org/fieldsights/411-editorial-breaking-memory-spoiling-memorization-the-taksim-protests-in-istanbul.

Nostromo Research. 2008. "Phulbari Coal: A Parlous Project." Prepared by Roger Moody, Nostromo Research for Bank Information Center, Washington, DC.

Ortega y Gasset, José. 1932. *The Revolt of the Masses: Authorized Translation from the Spanish.* New York: Norton.

Oushakine, Serguei Alex. 2009. *The Patriotism of Despair: Nation, War, and Loss in Russia.* Ithaca, NY: Cornell University Press.

Papadopoulos, Dimitris, Niamh Stephenson, and Vassilis Tsianos. 2008. *Escape Routes: Control and Subversion in the Twenty-First Century.* London: Pluto Press.

Parry, Jonathan P., and Maurice Bloch. 1989. *Money and the Morality of Exchange.* Cambridge: Cambridge University Press.

Peebles, Gustav. 2012. "Filth and Lucre: The Dirty Money Complex as a Taxation Regime." *Anthropological Quarterly* 85(4): 1229–55.

Pelkmans, Mathijs. 2018. "Doubt, Suspicion, Mistrust . . . Semantic Approximations." In *Mistrust: Ethnographic Approximations*, edited by Florian Mühlfried, 171–80. London: Transcript.

Pemberton, John. 2009. "Ghost in the Machine." In *Photographies East: The Camera and Its Histories in East and Southeast Asia*, edited by Rosalind C. Morris, 29–56. Durham, NC: Duke University Press.

Phadke, Shilpa, and Sameera Khan & Shilpa Ranade. 2011. *Why Loiter? Women and Risk on Mumbai Streets.* New Delhi: Penguin Books.

Pinney, Christopher. 2011. *Photography and Anthropology.* London: Reaktion Books.

Prasad, M. Madhava. 2009. "Fan Bhakti and Subaltern Sovereignty: Enthusiasm as a Political Factor." *Economic and Political Weekly* 44(29): 68–76.

Quadir, Iqbal Z. 2013. "Adam Smith, Economic Development, and the Global Spread of Cell Phones." *Proceedings of the American Philosophical Society* 157(1): 67–91.

Rafael, Vicente L. 1997. "'Your Grief Is Our Gossip': Overseas Filipinos and Other Spectral Presences." *Public Culture* 9(2): 267–91.

———. 2003. "The Cell Phone and the Crowd: Messianic Politics in the Contemporary Philippines." *Public Culture* 15(3): 399–425.

Rahman, Ferdousour. 2009. "Towards a Digital Bangladesh." *Financial Express*, January 10.

Ramaswamy, Sumathi. 2010. *The Goddess and the Nation: Mapping Mother India.* Durham, NC: Duke University Press.

Riaz, Ali. 2016. *Bangladesh: A Political History since Independence.* London: I. B. Tauris.

Riles, Annelise, ed. 2006. *Documents: Artifacts of Modern Knowledge.* Ann Arbor: University of Michigan Press.

Roitman, Janet. 2013. *Anti-Crisis.* Durham, NC: Duke University Press.

Ronell, Avital. 2002. *Stupidity.* Urbana: University of Illinois Press.

Rosanvallon, Pierre. 2006. *Democracy Past and Future.* Translated by Samuel Moyn. New York: Columbia University Press.

Rose, Jacqueline. 2004. "Introduction." In *Sigmund Freud: Mass Psychology and Other Writings*, vii–xlii. London: Penguin UK.

Rosen, Jody. 2016. "The Bangladeshi Traffic Jam That Never Ends." *New York Times*, September 23. https://www.nytimes.com/2016/09/23/t-magazine/travel/dhaka-bangladesh-traffic.html.

Rutherford, Danilyn. 2001. "Intimacy and Alienation: Money and the Foreign in Biak." *Public Culture* 13(2): 299–324.

———. 2008. "Why Papua Wants Freedom: The Third Person in Contemporary Nationalism." *Public Culture* 20(2): 345–73.

Ruud, Arild Engelsen, and Mohammad Mozahidul Islam. 2016. "Political Dynasty Formation in Bangladesh." *South Asia: Journal of South Asian Studies* 39(2): 401–14.

Sadique, Mahfuz. 2015. "Closure from 1971 Bangladesh War Comes at a High Cost." BBC News, April 18. http://www.bbc.com/news/world-asia-32349922.

Saleque, Engr. Khondkar A. 2011. "Bangladesh' Energy Crisis: Anatomy of Failure." *Energy Bangla*, May 9.

Samaddar, Ranabir. 2002. *Paradoxes of the Nationalist Time: Political Essays on Bangladesh*. Dhaka, Bangladesh: University Press Limited.

Sampson, Tony D. 2012. *Virality: Contagion Theory in the Age of Networks*. Minneapolis: University of Minnesota Press.

Santner, Eric L. 2011. *The Royal Remains: The People's Two Bodies and the Endgames of Sovereignty*. Chicago: University of Chicago Press.

Sanyal, P. R. 2015. "A 13-Year-Old Boy's Horrific Death Becomes Viral Facebook Video in Bangladesh," Public Radio International, July 17. https://www.pri.org/stories/2015-07-17/13-year-old-boys-horrific-death-becomes-viral-facebook-video-bangladesh.

Sartori, Andrew Stephen. 2014. *Liberalism in Empire*. Berkeley: University of California Press.

Scarry, Elaine. 1985. *The Body in Pain: The Making and Unmaking of the World*. New York: Oxford University Press.

Schendel, Willem van. 2009. *A History of Bangladesh*. Cambridge: Cambridge University Press.

Schmitt, Carl, Tracy B. Strong, and Leo Strauss. 2007. *The Concept of the Political: Expanded Edition*. Translated by George Schwab. Chicago: University of Chicago Press.

Schnitzler, Antina von. 2016. *Democracy's Infrastructure: Techno-Politics and Protest after Apartheid*. Princeton, NJ: Princeton University Press.

Scott, David. 2004. *Conscripts of Modernity: The Tragedy of Colonial Enlightenment*. Durham, NC: Duke University Press.

Scott, James C. 1998. *Seeing Like a State: How Certain Schemes to Improve the Human Condition Have Failed*. New Haven, CT: Yale University Press.

Scott, James C., John Tehranian, and Jeremy Mathias. 2002. "The Production of Legal Identities Proper to States: The Case of the Permanent Family Surname." *Comparative Studies in Society and History* 44(1): 4–44.

Sen, Amartya. 2013. "What's Happening in Bangladesh?" *The Lancet* 382(9909): 1966–68.

Senders, Stefan John, and Allison Truitt, eds. 2007. *Money: Ethnographic Encounters*. Oxford: Berg.

Shah, Nishant. 2007. "The Curious Incident of the People at the Mall: Flashmobs and Politics of Technologised Interaction in India." Paper presented at the Association of Internet Researchers conference 8.0 titled *Let's Play*. Vancouver, BC, Canada, October 17–20.

Shah, Nishant, Puthiya Purayil Sneha, and Sumandro Chattapadhyay, eds. 2015. *Digital Activism in Asia Reader*. Lüneburg, Germany: meson press eG.

Shahidullah, Prokousholi Sheikh Muhammad. n.d. "বাংলাদেশের তেল-গ্যাস-খনিজসম্পদ ও জাতীয় স্বার্থ রক্ষার আন্দোলনের সংক্ষিপ্ত ইতিবৃত্ত" [A short history of the struggles to protect oil, gas, mineral resources and national interests of Bangladesh]. Dhaka, Bangladesh.

Shenker, Jack. 2016. "The Future of the Egyptian Revolution." *Guardian*, January 16. http://www.theguardian.com/books/2016/jan/16/future-egypt-revolution-tahrir -square-jack-shenker.

Shoesmith, Brian, Jude William Genilo, and Md Asiuzzaman, eds. 2014. *Bangladesh's Changing Mediascape: From State Control to Market Forces*. Bristol, UK: Intellect.

Siddiqi, Dina. 2013. "Left Behind by the Nation: 'Stranded Pakistanis' in Bangladesh." *Sites* 10(2): 150–83.

Siegel, James T. 1997. *Fetish, Recognition, Revolution*. Princeton, NJ: Princeton University Press.

———. 2005. *Naming the Witch*. Stanford, CA: Stanford University Press.

Silverstein, Michael. 1976. "Shifters, Linguistic Categories, and Cultural Description." In *Meaning in Anthropology*, edited by Keith H. Basso and Henry A. Selby, 11–55. Albuquerque: University of New Mexico Press.

Simmel, Georg. 1978. *The Philosophy of Money*. London: Routledge & Kegan Paul.

Sinha, Justice Surendra Kumar. 2018. *A Broken Dream: Rule of Law, Human Rights, and Democracy*. N.p.: Lalitmohan-Dhanabati Memorial Foundation.

Sloterdijk, Peter. 1988. *Critique of Cynical Reason*. Minneapolis: University of Minnesota Press.

Smith, James H. 2015. "'May It Never End': Price Wars, Networks, and Temporality in the '3 Ts' Mining Trade of the Eastern DR Congo." *HAU: Journal of Ethnographic Theory* 5(1): 1–34.

Sobhan, Rehman, ed. 2005. *Privatization in Bangladesh: An Agenda in Search of a Policy*. Dhaka, Bangladesh: Center for Policy Dialogue, University Press Limited.

Sofa, Ahmed. 2006. *Nirbachito Probondho*. Dhaka, Bangladesh: Mowla Brothers.

———. 2007. *Omkar*. 4th ed. Dhaka, Bangladesh: Mohammad Liaquatullah of Student Ways.

Stewart, Kathleen. 1996. *A Space on the Side of the Road*. Princeton, NJ: Princeton University Press.

———. 2007. *Ordinary Affects*. Durham, NC: Duke University Press.

Stoekl, Allan. 2007. *Bataille's Peak: Energy, Religion, and Postsustainability*. Minneapolis: University of Minnesota Press.

Strassler, Karen. 2010. *Refracted Visions: Popular Photography and National Modernity in Java*. Durham, NC: Duke University Press.

Subramanian, Samanth. 2015. "The Hit List." *New Yorker*, December 21. http://www.newyorker.com/magazine/2015/12/21/the-hit-list.

Sudworth, John. 2007. "Photo the Bangladesh Army Cannot Stand." BBC News. August 28. http://news.bbc.co.uk/2/hi/south_asia/6966467.stm.

Sultan, Nazmul. 2015. "Anonymous People and the Insidious Logic of Petrol Bomb Terror." *Daily Star*, February 10. http://www.thedailystar.net/op-ed/anonymous-people-and-the-insidious-logic-petrol-bomb-terror-1606.

———. 2016. "জনতা নামের কর্তা: 'জীবন আমার বোন' এবং মুক্তিযুদ্ধের ঘটনাচরিত্র" [The actor called "Janata": *Jiban Amar Bon* and the liberation war as an event]. bdnews24.com, January 18. http://arts.bdnews24.com/?p=6333.

Suykens, Bert. 2017. "The Bangladesh Party-State: A Diachronic Comparative Analysis of Party-Political Regimes." *Commonwealth & Comparative Politics* 55(2): 187–213.

Suykens, Bert, and Aynul Islam. 2013. "Hartal as a Complex Political Performance: General Strikes and the Organisation of (Local) Power in Bangladesh." *Contributions to Indian Sociology* 47(1): 61–83.

Supreme Court of Bangladesh. 2017. "Civil Appeal No. 6 of 2017."

Tambiah, Stanley J. 1997. *Leveling Crowds: Ethnonationalist Conflicts and Collective Violence in South Asia*. Berkeley: University of California Press.

Tarde, Gabriel. 2014 [1903]. *The Laws of Imitation*. Translated by Elsie Clews Parsons. New York: Henry Holt.

Tarlo, Emma. 2003. *Unsettling Memories: Narratives of the Emergency in Delhi*. Berkeley: University of California Press.

Taussig, Michael. 1977. "The Genesis of Capitalism Amongst a South American Peasantry: Devil's Labor and the Baptism of Money." *Comparative Studies in Society and History* 19(2): 130–55.

———. 1999. *Defacement: Public Secrecy and the Labor of the Negative*. Stanford, CA: Stanford University Press.

Thiranagama, Sharika, and Tobias Kelly, eds. 2010. *Traitors: Suspicion, Intimacy, and the Ethics of State-Building*. Philadelphia: University of Pennsylvania Press.

Tsing, Anna Lowenhaupt. 2000. "Inside the Economy of Appearances." *Public Culture* 12(1): 115–44.

Tsou, YiPing (Zona). 2015. "Digital Natives in the Name of a Cause: From 'Flash Mob' to 'Human Flesh Search.'" In *Digital Activism in Asia Reader*, edited by Nishant Shah, Puthiya Purayil Sneha, and Sumandro Chattapadhyay, 179–96. Lüneburg, Germany: meson press eG.

"2013 Shahbag Protests." 2015. Wikipedia. https://en.wikipedia.org/w/index.php?title=2013_Shahbag_protests&oldid=696080507. (*Note*: The article has been archived because of multiple issues.)

Umar, Badruddin. 2004. *The Emergence of Bangladesh: Class Struggles in East Pakistan*. Karachi: Oxford University Press.

Urban, Greg. 2001. *Metaculture: How Culture Moves Through the World*. Minneapolis: University of Minnesota Press.

Uz Zaman, Nasir. 2018. "Freedom of Movement: Take Back the Night." *New Age*, November 4. http://www.newagebd.net/article/54957/freedom-of-movement-take-back-the-night.

Verdery, Katherine. 1999. *The Political Lives of Dead Bodies: Reburial and Postsocialist Change*. New York: Columbia University Press.

Verkaaik, Oskar. 2004. *Migrants and Militants: Fun and Urban Violence in Pakistan*. Princeton, NJ: Princeton University Press.

Virilio, Paul. 2007. *The Original Accident*. Cambridge: Polity Press.

Walsh, Andrew. 2004. "In the Wake of Things: Speculating in and about Sapphires in Northern Madagascar." *American Anthropologist* 106(2): 225–37.

Warner, Michael. 1990. *The Letters of the Republic: Publication and the Public Sphere in Eighteenth-Century America*. Cambridge, MA: Harvard University Press.

———. 2002. "Publics and Counterpublics." *Public Culture* 14(1): 49.

Wasif, Faruk. 2009. জরুরী অবস্থার আমলনামা: বাংলাদেশের সিভিক-মিলিটারি-কর্পোরেট গণতন্ত্র [Tales of the emergency: The civic-military-corporate democracy of Bangladesh]. Dhaka, Bangladesh: Shuddhashar.

———. 2015. "#SOSBangladesh: Who Is Behind Deep Politics?" *Alal O Dulal* (blog), December 5. http://alalodulal.org/2015/12/05/deep-politics-4/.

Webb, Martin. 2012. "Activating Citizens, Remaking Brokerage: Transparency Activism, Ethical Scenes, and the Urban Poor in Delhi." *PoLAR: Political and Legal Anthropology Review* 35(2): 206–22.

Weber, Samuel. 2001. "The Sideshow, or: Remarks on a Canny Moment." In *Deconstruction: A Reader*, edited by Martin McQuillan, 351–60. New York: Routledge.

Weber, Samuel, and Walter Benjamin. 2008. *Benjamin's Abilities*. Cambridge, MA: Harvard University Press.

Welker, Marina A. 2009. "'Corporate Security Begins in the Community': Mining, the Corporate Social Responsibility Industry, and Environmental Advocacy in Indonesia." *Cultural Anthropology* 24(1): 142–79.

West, Harry G., and Todd Sanders, eds. 2003. *Transparency and Conspiracy: Ethnographies of Suspicion in the New World Order*. Durham, NC: Duke University Press.

Wilce, James M. 2003. *Eloquence in Trouble: The Poetics and Politics of Complaint in Rural Bangladesh*. New York: Oxford University Press.

Wolin, Sheldon S. 1981. "The People's Two Bodies." *Democracy* 1(1): 9–24.

World Bank. 2011. "Speech by Ellen Goldstein, Country Director, The World Bank in Dhaka at the ICC Conference on Energy and Growth." http://www.worldbank.org/en/news/speech/2010/04/13/speech-by-ellen-goldstein-country-director-the-world-bank-dhaka-at-the-icc-conference-on-energy-and-growth.

Yeh, Rihan. 2017. *Passing: Two Publics in a Mexican Border City*. Chicago: University of Chicago Press.

Yunus, Muhammad. 2007. *Creating a World without Poverty: Social Business and the Future of Capitalism*. New York: PublicAffairs.

Yurchak, Alexei. 2015. "Bodies of Lenin: The Hidden Science of Communist Sovereignty." *Representations* 129(1): 116–57.

Zelizer, Viviana A. 1994. *The Social Meaning of Money*. New York: Basic Books.

Žižek, Slavoj, Eric L. Santner, and Kenneth Reinhard. 2005. *The Neighbor: Three Inquiries in Political Theology*. Chicago: University of Chicago Press.

INDEX